WE ARE
EVERYWHERE

WE ARE EVERYWHERE

EDITED BY HARRIET ALPERT

THE CROSSING PRESS / FREEDOM, CALIFORNIA 95019

LIBRARY OF CONGRESS
Library of Congress Cataloging-in-Publication Data

We are everywhere: writings by and about lesbian parents / edited by
Harriet Alpert.
    p.   cm.
    ISBN 0-89594-309-3:   ISBN 0-89594-261-5 (pbk.):
    1. Lesbians' writings, American. 2. Lesbianism—Literary collec-
tions. 3. Lesbian mothers—Literary collections. 4. Parent and child—Literary collections. 5. American literature—20th century.
I. Alpert, Harriet.
PS509.L47W4 1988
810'.8'09287—dc19   87-38092
                                                          CIP

ACKNOWLEDGEMENTS

Having learned to read at age five, and having never left the house without my book since, I have had occasion to read many acknowledgements. It is thrilling to have the opportunity to thank those who have contributed to the making of *We Are Everywhere*:

To the main mothers in my life, Mariellen Langworthy, Camille Tischler, Lisa Wichman and Anne Pelavin, I want to express my appreciation for including me in so many ways in your childrearing over the past two decades, and for valuing my advice and experience in working through difficult times with your children. And I want to express my appreciation to my mother, Anne Alpert, for her love and support during this project and for the legacy of chutzpah she has passed on to me.

Thanks to Cheryl Kennedy for her perspective on the history of lesbian parenting; to Elly Bulkin for raising my consciousness around terminology; to Aimee Sands for making her wonderful documentary, *We Are Family*, available to me; to Sea Gnomes Women's Guest House for providing refuge; to Irene Zahava for her warmth and interest; to Connie Lorman for listening; and to Kate Dunn, my editor at Crossing, for the contribution she has made to Women's publishing and for finding a way to include me in that.

Special thanks to Cary Joseph who was there with enthusiasm for the opening of Smedley's Bookshop and has been here with encouragement for this book. For twelve years he has accompanied me along a path, sometimes rocky, often flowered, and even stayed to nudge me around the corner.

Lastly, I want to thank Susan Eschbach, my partner. Although she has refused the title of co-editor, I want to acknowledge the hours and hours she spent working on editing this book. Her respect for each manuscript that was submitted and her skill in helping to clarify each piece were invaluable in shaping this collection. Her pride in herself, in me, and in the mothers who were waiting for this book has guided me throughout this project.

For my mother, Anne Alpert.
And for Susan.

CONTENTS

PREFACE

The seeds for this project began germinating in 1976, shortly after Kate Dunn, Camille Tischler and I opened Smedley's Bookshop. We had come together in the second wave of feminism to begin what we hoped would be not only a small business, but a center for women's art and ideas. Women used the store to find out what was going on in our upstate New York town, what was happening in the larger feminist community, and to find each other. Those years were filled with tears and laughter as we discovered the commonalities among us.

Support groups and study groups packed our evenings at Smedley's. Soon after we opened, we were asked to sponsor a group for lesbian mothers coming together to share concerns and support with each other. The woman making this request was a lesbian mother of two school-age children, who, due to an impending custody battle and job concerns, could not publicize the group herself. Our role in helping to form this group deepened my awareness and sense of appreciation for the risks taken by lesbian mothers. Years later, and from my current perspective as a social worker and therapist, I still feel a surge of energy in my own and my clients' lives as we continue to struggle toward self-love and empowerment for all. The story of a portion of that struggle is told by the women in *We Are Everywhere*.

This book has been a joy for me. My contacts with those whose works are included here have dotted my life with experiences that I value for their warmth and for the pride they make me feel. From the babies that I held, while mothers grabbed a few hours to write, to sitting with teenage daughters as they shared tales of "life with moms," to discussions with adoptive parents about their outrage at the repressive Massachusetts Foster Care Policy, this book has taken me to many places that I treasure and now joyfully share with readers.

Letters of thanks, of anticipation and of enthusiasm arrived from lesbian moms in Mississippi, Hawaii, Kansas and Maine. With gratitude to the women who shared their stories and to those who were not able to be included, I take pride in affirming that We Are Everywhere.

Mariellen Langworthy

I am a forty-four year old feminist therapist and school psychologist who has, surprisingly, rooted herself in New England. Mothering continues to be a major part of my life even though my children are adolescents and adults. My mothering and our family making has happened in many contexts including a traditional nuclear family, communal living with four adults and eight children, living with a lover and my children, and living alone with my children. We have transitioned dissolutions as well as reconciliations. The greatest joy currently is watching my children each move into adulthood and make their own choices.

INTRODUCTION

Mariellen Langworthy

We Are Everywhere spoke to me in many ways, on many levels. As I read, the stories echoed a decade of conversations, delight and tears shared with Harriet about mothering, about being lesbian and about being women. I loved reading about women from all over this nation. The stories by my sisters of color added to and challenged my personal knowing of the world. I recognized moments from over two decades of daily life with my two daughters, son and step-daughter. Some of the words of the daughters soothed my innermost fears while others pushed at my ever present mother-guilt. I resonated with the special struggles and rewards of raising a son. Being a stepmother without official title, I was fascinated with the relationships of the children with their "others." As a woman and a lesbian, I was moved in my own places of pain and joy grown from more than four decades of living in a world that often tries to fragment, distort and diminish my experiences by holding up pictures of who I must be in order to be seen. I felt the courage of all the women whose pieces are included in this book in their insistence to expand, rather than diminish, the notion of who is family.

Clearly, *We Are Everywhere*, is about challenging, confronting and changing the disparate and frozen stereotypical images that keep all of us prisoners, whether we are lesbians, or mothers, or neither. This book is about hope and about being free.

Patriarchal culture embraces and extolls motherhood as the primary identity for women while condemning lesbianism as unnatural, despicable and unspeakable. Being lesbian will, in most courts of our nation, disqualify a woman of her motherhood credentials more surely than child abuse, neglect, or abandonment. Some women in this book have lost their children, others have fought and won; still others have chosen the devastation of anonymity or invisibility to protect themselves and their children. Even in the lesbian culture, until very recently, motherhood and lesbianism have been held as antithetical. Both realities could not be true. The images of being a lesbian could not tolerate the role of mother.

But the truth is that for as long as there have been women, there have been lesbian mothers—women with children, loving, cherishing and somehow making their lives with women. It is well past the time to break the silence and shed the invisibility. It is time for us to listen and to be instructed by these lives and images.

We Are Everywhere gives voice to the stories, feelings, ideas and experiences of women and children. This telling of the truth of these lives breaks the stranglehold of stereotypes and shatters cultural images of motherhood and of lesbianism. The telling of the truth through the sharing of these mundane and richly varied daily experiences reaches profoundly to the core of our collective soul. For those of us who are lesbian mothers or parenting figures and can find some piece of our own reflection, these shared images strengthen us and give us courage to build our lives— and the lives of our children—in ways that are congruent, reflective and sustaining. For those whose life experiences seem different from the women and children in this book, these stories offer the gift of witnessing another's reality and the opportunity of letting the old perceptions and beliefs be shifted. In these ways, this is a book about the hope and possibility of change.

We Are Everywhere is a celebration of both the comforting similarity and the rich diversity of women creating their own lives. Together, these myriad combinations of people naming themselves as family is like a picture album. Each piece is a photograph giving us new images and new possibilities to use in defining ourselves. *We Are Everywhere* makes me remember my daughter telling me, "Sometimes your choices made me mad; but because you struggle to be true to yourself, you let me see that I can examine my own life and have the courage to be whoever I am."

Julia Perez

I am a Puerto Rican woman living in Cambridge, Massachusetts. As mothers of three, with one on the way, my lover Cheryl and I have enjoyed parenting—we find it hard at times but the rewards are many. This is particularly true as our children enter adolescence. I am also a veteran of the U.S. Army. I am currently working on an anthology about women veterans and have produced a video called, Invisible Force, Women in the Military.

PRIDE

Julia Perez

This has been a hard year for me as a mother. The girls are truly into their teens. Shelley is fifteen, Margo is fourteen, and Maria, who is eleven, has what appears to be a case of the creeping teens. This year I have had to take a hard look at my "liberal attitudes" on childrearing and at issues of control. Cheryl and I have had long conversations on what's out there for our kids—and on where we should pick our battles. Is it important for them to be in bed by 10:00 p.m.—or is it important that they are not out there drugging and being sexual? Do we fight over the dishes or do we remember that they still let us know where they are and bring their friends over, including their boyfriends—an issue which is not so simple for children of lesbians. That way, they leave themselves vulnerable to the boys who, if they do not get their way sexually, can say, "It's because you are just like your mother."

This year Gay Pride was very special to us. This year the older girls made a conscious decision to march with us. For three years they have not wanted to go; they did not want their friends and other people to think that they, too, were lesbians. They are supportive of us and our friends, but as members of a sometimes cruel subgroup—teens—they do not want to be seen as different. So when they said they would go with us to the march, I had to sit down and let it sink in.

When we got to City Hall Plaza, the girls asked what the green balloons meant. We explained that they represented people who had died of AIDS. They asked if they could get balloons to carry in the parade. We said yes. After getting three balloons, they went around saying hello to people who had known them since they were small. It was a good feeling to watch them, to know what it meant for them to have made that leap from being nervous and afraid of being seen at Gay Pride to carrying green balloons and marching.

As I marched, my mind drifted to the conversations with other teenage children of lesbians about what it means to have mothers who are out. When I ask, "How has your mother being a lesbian impacted on you?" the answer has generally been the same. At one point, they did not want their friends to know because they did not want to be made fun of, to be seen as different, and there are still some people they do not let know. The daughter of a friend said, "When I was little, I didn't want my friends to know, so I didn't invite them over to my house. But as I grew older, I cared less, and once I reached high school it just didn't matter. If they couldn't accept me, it was their problem, not mine."

Being around her and some other teenage children of my lesbian friends proves to me that we are doing well as parents. Our daughters are not really vulnerable to adolescent male harassment. When they bring their boyfriends over, they command respect. This is because they respect us and therefore themselves, a feeling that comes from our own self-respect and our demand that all differences be valued. It was this respect, I think, that brought them to Gay Pride.

My mind comes back to the march. Friends say, "Hi, I just saw your girls. Boy, they sure have grown. How did you convince them to come?"

"We didn't. They came on their own," we say proudly.

We have many issues to deal with, issues that come because our children are growing and becoming adults. They test us to the point of absolute insanity. They push till we are almost one with the wall. We get the nasty answers, the rolling of the eyes that say we don't know what we are talking about. They don't like our books, want our lesbian posters off the wall, say we take everything too seriously— and yet here they are marching with us.

Is it worth it? Must be—Cheryl's baby is due in November.

MARGO

The new question in our household is "What are you trying to say?" It starts out by me being what I think is perfectly clear with my thirteen-year-old daughter (who, in another life, was probably an excellent lawyer). In any event, here I am being what seems to me to be a reasonable person. So I stand there and say, "Okay, here's the game plan: no phone calls until all the homework is done." "No, you can not stay until eleven. I don't care what other mothers do." "Yes, I realize I don't know where it's at, but you can not go to the video arcade," and so on. Of course, during all of these interactions I have on my most serious "I-am-your-mother" look.

She, on the other hand, looks at her nails, then stands with one foot slightly forward, her hip thrown to the side, chin up, and waits patiently for me to finish. Then she says, languidly, "What do you mean by that?"

At which point many things go zipping through my mind. For example: "What the hell do you think I am trying to say?" Or, I might see myself jumping up and down, screaming like a fool, frothing at the mouth. But I neither say nor do the things in my mind. "You know what I mean," I say.

She looks me straight in the eye, something I was brought up in my Puertorican household never to do. "Okay, just checking," she says, and she goes out of the room to finish her homework or get back to whatever she was doing before we got into it.

If I smoked, this would be a perfect time to light up a cigarette. I go back to my book.

"Mom."

I look up at this sweet child with the pleading look on

her face.

"Mom, I know my homework isn't done but I just have to make one very important phone call."

"What is it?"

"I have to call W-I-L-D LOVE LINE. I told (she names one of her girlfriends) that I would call for her because her mother doesn't let her use the phone. She's really counting on me to do this. Please, Mom."

"No!" and I look down at my book.

"Okay, but I don't know why you're getting so upset. It's only one phone call. I mean, what's the big deal?"

Should I answer that? No. Of course not.

She stamps out of the room. I remember the chubby-cheeked, brown baby with fuzzy hair stamping her feet at two years old. "No" was her favorite word. Such a cutie-pie. Such little feet. They didn't stamp very hard. I wonder if living with teens is the same as living with "the terrible two's"—wonderful, sweet little creatures one moment and monsters the next. I recall one of Cheryl's friends saying that living with teens was a unique experience—"one day you put your sweet baby to bed and the next day there would be a raving gorilla in its place. So you dig a trench, stock up on bananas and throw the children a few every once in a while when they get hungry. One thing is for sure: you have to have a sense of humor."

I think she was right.

TO BEVERLY

Back in 1971, when my ex-lover and I decided to have a child, we didn't know any other lesbians with children or any who were contemplating having children. We had been living together for sixteen years and felt that, although we were having problems with our relationship, we could overcome them and provide a good home for a child. In retrospect, I know we should have looked more closely at our problems, but we just didn't think in those terms. In any event, I agreed that I would be the one to have the child, and I started charting.

In 1972, with the help of a friend, I got pregnant. He was someone I worked with at that time. The pregnancy was uneventful and Beverly and I excitedly waited for the birth of the baby. Of course our very straight neighbors and family didn't know what to make of what appeared to be a pregnancy out of nowhere. They had gotten accustomed to seeing us without any males coming into our house, besides my brothers. They were very curious as to who the father of the baby was, but were afraid to ask the question. We provided no answers, letting them come to their own conclusions.

Planning for the baby was exciting and we talked about all the things we could do with this new little person coming into our household. We went to Lamaze classes, shopped for baby clothes and prepared for the big moment. In April of 1973 Margo was born. Beverly loved Margo from the very beginning. Margo was her baby as much as she was mine.

It was a joy having a baby, although for me it was also extremely tiring. We were not prepared for the emotional and physical exhaustion that comes from lack of sleep at the beginning. Nevertheless, for Beverly and I, having

Margo was wonderful.

Having a baby created stress and made the problems in our faltering relationship more obvious. We had not been in touch with how much the relationship was in trouble. By the time the baby was two Beverly and I separated.

At that time I didn't give much thought to how Beverly was dealing with the loss of her child. For a time I let Margo spend a day each weekend with her, but Beverly's new lover made it clear that she didn't appreciate having the baby around so I stopped the visits. It didn't occur to me that Beverly would be in any kind of pain or that she wouldn't get over not having a child anymore.

It is now, when so many lesbians are having babies and I see the extent to which their lovers are involved with the process, and how much they feel that this is their child, that I think of Beverly.

I see their sadness and I remember the sadness in Beverly's eyes when she said to me the day we parted, "What about the baby?" I answered, "It's my baby" with little thought to her feelings or what she was saying.

That was so long ago, twelve years to be exact, and now I have begun to understand her sadness because my lover is pregnant and I feel so much that this is my child, too. I would be sad if I could not be around for this baby's life. I wanted to write this so Beverly would know I understand. Even though Margo remembers Beverly, she now has another parent besides myself who, because of the years we've had together, is her family. And, I respect that in a way that I would not have in 1972.

Sandy Boucher

I am a fifty-one year old former midwesterner who has lived in the San Francisco Bay Area for the last 25 years. My piece in this book is drawn from experience in a women's liberation collective household in the early seventies, where the communal care of children was seen as important political work.

I have done a Buddhist meditation practice for the last seven years, and have just finished a book called Turning the Wheel: American Women Creating the New Buddhism (Harper and Row, March 1988). I spent the summer of 1987 in South East Asia, most of that time as an "Anagarika" (eight-precept Buddhist nun) in a nunnery in Sri Lanka.

My previous books include Heartwomen (Harper & Row, 1982), The Notebooks of Leni Clare (Crossing Press, 1982), and Assaults and Rituals (Mama's Press, 1975). I earn my living teaching, writing, and consulting in the Bay Area.

ROSALIE

Sandy Boucher

[Two sections of a novel in progress]

I

How will he accept her being in bed with Jan, now, if he wakes up afraid or cold and comes from the children's room to crawl in bed with her? Her body remembers Aaron's small form curved inside hers, his feet tucked between her knees to warm them. Rosalie looks at her son in the airplane seat next to her. Her parents have dressed him like a little man, in a sports jacket that twists around his chest, now, as he slumps against the window. One end of his bowtie sticks up against his throat. Five years old: he seems so tall to her now.

Half-asleep, with a puckered sullen mouth, he holds against his chest the plastic replica of the plane they are flying in. Bought for him by Grampa at the airport in New Mexico.

In the back bedroom at Ortega Street, as they lay holding each other, Jan had asked her about him: what sort of person was he, this child? How would he respond to all of them in this new life they had planned for him? Rosalie didn't know. She hoped it would be all right, wandered off into her thoughts about him, and said finally, "I have been so lenient with him out of guilt."

She has let her parents shape him, out of guilt. Her father who himself had only girls treats this boy like a son, dotes on him, favors him over her sisters' children, who are only girls. Pete Mikolsky becomes a great lumbering child himself when Aaron is there. They share an intimacy that no one else can enter. And yet in the family they dun into Aaron a reverence for his mother, as if there were some mystical connection between them.

He came from her unwilling body. The quinine she drank, the deliberate falls she took: nothing could dislodge the bit of flesh taking shape in her. And when it was too late for these measures, there was the unwed mothers home where after the labor she could sign the papers to give him up for adoption. Until her parents discovered she was pregnant and convinced her to keep him. She was twenty-one.

Rosalie looks down at her hands in her lap. Broad hands, the fingers splayed. Hands that can hammer, draw, paint, model in clay, dig in the dirt, hold a chisel, measure, and yet are soft and flexible, never somehow hardened or calloused by the work she does. Looking at these hands that are slowmoving, precise, she thinks about her life with Aaron.

It has been lived in tiny apartments—the child dragged out of bed and fed and dressed and taken across town each morning on a bus to the babysitter's house where five children squalled and fought, left there while Rosalie went to work, picked up again at twilight, and then the long exhausted bus ride home, the other passengers irritated if he whined or cried, turning to fix her with disapproving stares. One evening on the crowded bus he had been making small rhythmic noises— a *little* child then. He was happy that day and amused himself with a plop-plop-plopping of his lips and tongue. She was holding him on her lap so that someone else could have the seat beside her, was paying little attention, soothed actually by the sounds, tired from work, just glad he wasn't dragging at her or asking her for things. When a man in the seat in front of them turned around, his face tight with exasperation, and snapped, "Can't you keep that kid quiet!" Rosalie shrank from him, and could not reply, as Aaron's body went rigid, pulling back against her chest. Guilty, both of them. (There is no place for this child. He has no right to exist.)

Then a voice erupted from the seat behind Rosalie— a woman's voice coming taut and angry and so loud the whole bus heard, "Why *should* she! Is he *hurting* anyone? Is he *hurting you!?*"

Rosalie bent her head, so filled with gratitude that she could not turn to meet the woman's eyes. But she carried the voice with her all evening like a gift, feeling for those few hours that there was someone with her in her life.

In their apartment they were always alone together. Rosalie was new to the city, and anyway, she was too busy to make friends, did not know how to, really. She would try to get him to go to sleep early so that she could read or study, trying to prepare for the time when she could—somehow—go back to school. (But *how*, when the babysitter and the bus fare, their rent and food, took all she earned? She studied anyway, stubbornly working against the hopelessness.) Her greatest joy in him was watching as he played with the wooden blocks and pegs she bought him. (To buy them meant sitting at her desk at noon eating a sandwich while the others from the office went cheerfully out to lunch together. It meant turning away from the show window where she stood looking longingly at the sketch pads and tubes of paint, the inks and pencils and canvasses that would have let her realize those insistent visions that appeared in her dreams at night.) She sat with him on the floor and watched him handle the shapes, ponder them — a quiet, contained child—she watched him discover combinations. Sometimes when he was frustrated she would move a block for him, slide it into the position for which he was searching. Instead of buying a new coat that winter she turned her worn cloth coat fuzzy-side-out and sewed ribbon at the cuffs and neck. And with the money she bought an elaborate set of blocks, finger paints and paper, for him—the kind of toys his grandparents did not give him.

He was slow to speak, and shy (like her), and later when they lived in a neighborhood of many children, he let the others play with the fancy toys his grampa sent him, so they would like him. And those children, unused to the opulence of miniature plastic Coke machines, Old West Forts, and soldier dolls with extra uniforms, unused to the lenience of Rosalie, went crazy in his room, smashing the toys, stealing them, while he stood helplessly by or, sometimes, fought them in screaming impotence. Rosalie had grown up solitary, wandering in whatever fields or woods or hills happened to be near the latest house her parents rented, only her dog for company. She had been happy that way, and she did not understand this city frenzy and brutality.

Sometimes it all grew too heavy in her, in that time after the hour in the crowded bus, after the long day at work, he whining with fatigue, refusing to eat his dinner (she knew that meant she was not a good mother), the rooms so poor and cluttered around her. Sitting with him at the table, seeing his face obstinately set, lips held tight together, refusing this hundredth time the vegetables and meat she had cooked for him, she was filled with wondering fury that her life could be this way, that his presence alone could have stolen from her all she might have been. Her voice came in a scream, as she lifted his body by the arms and shook and shook him, his head flopping, went on screaming after she had dropped him and he cowered on the floor. "You *will* eat! You *have to* eat or you won't grow up!" Enormous and threatening above him. When the voice stopped, when she turned away, he got up, watching her, and went shakily toward his room.

Rosalie sat down at the table and put her hands up over her face. Everything built up in her tore apart and came out in a loud broken sobbing. She let the waves of grief roll over her, lowering her face to rest on her outstretched arms on the table, her dark blonde hair spread across her arms; let it go on until everything was drained from her and she rested empty and still there.

When she could enter his room, she found him sitting on the floor, his head lowered over a small plastic bear that he turned and turned in his fingers. His neck, exposed above his pullover, looked thin and terribly vulnerable. She saw in her mind his head flopping. She went down on her knees beside him and reached to place her hand on his neck, rubbed it gently for a time, unable to speak, feeling the smooth warm skin. It was a monstrous weight in her knowing that of all the thousands of people in this city only she cared about him, that his very life depended on her. He who had not chosen her, as she had not chosen him.

"Aaron, I'm sorry."

He turned his head a little and looked at her from the corners of his eyes. But when she drew him to her, carefully, brought him to rest on her knees, his arms went around her and he pressed his face against her chest.

That night she fed him chocolate ice cream, read to him, held him on her lap. And when he was in bed, the frog beanbag circled in his arm, the stuffed chipmunk next to him on the pillow, she lay down beside him and stroked and stroked his head with her broad soft hand, until his lashes were still on his cheeks.

* * *

Rosalie stares at the patch of blueblack sky out of the window of the plane. Soon they will arrive. She thinks with sudden panic of Jan, who has never lived with children. Suppose she should lose Jan because of his child-presence. She remembers some of the men she has been with, who were stiffly rejecting of him, jealous of her attention, with whom she had felt pulled apart.

In the collapsible tunnel from the plane to the waiting room, she stoops to take Aaron's hand. He lags, and she has to pull him, as the other people hurry around them. But she is glad to occupy herself with him, for her heart beats anxiously.

Her life back in San Francisco seemed almost a dream to her while in her parents' house, where she had closed herself up, become hard and protected. It was as if she had become someone in the last year that they could not possibly know. Now, as she catches sight of Jan standing among the crowd in the waiting room, the last ten days drop away, and she is once again here in her own, her *real* life. Jan looks like a brooding Robin Hood here among all these very civilized families. Tall and narrow-bodied, swathed in her green and black plaid cape, with her red hair chopped off just below the ears, she paces, the cape swinging about her legs in wide flowing movements that brush her faded jeans. Her blunt-toed boots scuff the carpet. She looks outdoorsy, a little rough, and yet somehow elegant. How does she manage that? Rosalie wonders for the hundredth time, the question born out of the rush of desire that courses through her. Jan moves in a decisive trajectory through the crowd, frowning, her hands caught behind her. Then suddenly, seeing Rosalie, she stops, the cape swinging forward in an extravagant swirl, and for a moment her face opens, stunned, and she gazes at Rosalie with a questioning, yearning look.

From behind Jan races Lisa, the little girl who lives with them in their communal household. In her excitement, she almost knocks Aaron down, as she dances around him, thrusting a Christmas package at him.

Then Rosalie is enveloped in the fullness of Jan's cape, held tight, feeling the soft hair against her cheek, the warmth. Released, she looks up into the thin freckled face grinning as if it will split.

And then she feels Jan drawing away from her, afraid to touch too intimately here among all these strangers. Rosalie's body flutters with the need to hold her.

"Oh, I am so glad to see you," she says, the words like a long sigh of relief.

* * *

When they are in the car, moving out of the airport onto the highway toward San Francisco, the children chatter in the back seat, each naming off the Christmas presents given to them by their grandparents. Rosalie looks out at the lights opening like flowers on the rainwet pavement, and breathes the damp air gratefully. But she is annoyed.

"You always pull away from me in public. Even *today...*"

"Oh, Rosalie."

She receives Jan's bony hand with both her own, as
Jan says slowly, "I've told you about the things that used
to happen to Vicky and me... I know you think I'm
paranoid."

"That was *years* ago!" Rosalie snorts. She is weary of
those stories about being a dyke in the old days, about the
hiding, the harassment.

Jan looks straight ahead out the windshield, attending
to the driving.

"It's just that I love you so much," Rosalie explains.
But an uncomfortable inkling awakens in her. Perhaps she
is exasperated less at Jan than at herself for not telling
her family while she was there. She had not been able to
meet the danger: that Pete Mikolsky would take Aaron away
from her if he knew.

There is silence between her and Jan for a while, only
the children's voices continuing in the back seat, and Rosalie
looks out at the body of water next to the Bayshore freeway.
It shudders like a dark jelly in the night, so alien to this
hurtling of machines on pavement, oblivious as the deep
black sky to the human lives enclosed in glass and steel,
streaking forward.

"Was it all right at your parents' house?"

Rosalie jerks in surprise, coming back from the night
to turn and look at Jan's face softly illumined by the dash-
board lights. She tries to think how to communicate the
days in the cramped stucco house, with her sisters and their
children there too, the fighting, her mother's angular silence
like a reproach in the midst of the chaos. And Pete Mikolsky's
low growling voice when she told him about the political
work she is doing now, why she and the others want to
live and work together. "It was bad enough when you got
into that woman stuff! Now you think you can tell our
government what to do!" He sat on a spindly metal deck
chair on the patio, looking out at the littered sand of the
backyard, his fists balled on his sturdy knees, the fold of
flesh pushed up at the base of his skull, under the spiky
gray of crewcut. There was such tension caught in his

massive chest and shoulders that he looked, by turns, threatening and helpless. Sometimes when she watched him doze in a chair, his head lolling, it would seem that round head was not big enough for the great slablike body, that there must be a smaller man caught inside, his head poking up through the hole between the shoulders. But that day, hunching forward in his deck chair, he filled up his body with truculent force, his light blue eyes thrusting angrily at Rosalie, his thick index finger poking the air as he told her, "Rosie, those friends of yours don't know what's what. I bet they sniff cocaine, eh? Take speed, maybe. For all I know, *you do too!* You should be ashamed of yourself—a woman with a son. You should be thinkin' about your *boy.* Providing for him, makin' a nice life for him." He shook his head, turning away from her. "Not hanging around with a bunch of deadbeats." And Rosalie felt the familiar slow crawling of guilt under her skin.

"Hey, was it that bad?" Jan's voice enters Rosalie's conciousness. "You don't want to tell me?" When Rosalie looks up, Jan has turned to glance at her, and her smile, her eyes, are so intensely admiring that Rosalie looks away, made shy.

She wishes she knew how to make a story of it, bring it all here for Jan to see.

They have been driving up the steep side of Bernal Heights now, the shops along Cortland Street showing their blank, locked faces, past the church, the community center, past a group of young men jockeying about on a corner, pushing each other, leaning their heads together to laugh. Now as they turn into Ortega Street, Lisa is bouncing in the back seat.

The children scramble to be first out of the car, and race up the steps to where Maureen meets them at the door, stooping to give Aaron a hug, run her hand over his new short haircut. Rosalie helps Jan carry the suitcases, the bag of toys, up the steps into the entranceway. Around her are white walls, coats hung on their hooks; in the front room a skinny little Christmas tree glows in the dark like a timid visitor. Clover hurries toward her from the kitchen. Sheltered here, Rosalie turns to Jan, slips her arms around Jan's back and lets herself be folded in the cape.

"You're home," Jan whispers.

II

Scrubbing at the caked food on the bottom of a pan, feeling the strain in her shoulders from leaning over the sink, Jan hears Michael's voice from the kitchen table behind her and wonders what Clover and Maureen can find to interest them in his talk. Since Clover became sexually involved with Michael, who lives in a political household in the Mission, he is often here, usually giving his unsolicited opinion. To Jan's great surprise, Maureen, Lisa's mother, seems to have taken a particular liking to this articulate bearded man. Jan doesn't share her interest. His talk sounds like a lecture on the books he has been reading about child development and free schools. Jan has little patience with men who talk as if they are experts on everything, spewing out undigested information on any woman who'll listen.

Leaving the pan to soak, she goes around the table to the bathroom to check on Lisa and Aaron. She is pleased by the two small bodies in the tub: Lisa stocky and square shaped, with a little roll of extra flesh pouching the fine white skin of her belly as she leans over; Aaron slim, with broad shoulders and tanned blond skin. The children seem most complete to Jan when they are naked. They're happily playing now, their heads close together, as they walk a tiny giraffe and a hippopotamus along the edge of the tub.

But the tub is so full that at each of their movements, water sloshes out and runs down the side to the floor. Jan sees that they have covered the overflow drain with a washcloth.

"You'd better let some water out," she tells them.

They glance up at her.

"The floor's getting wet."

Lisa glares at Jan. "No. We like it this way."

Jan is stopped for a moment. She does not like to interfere with them when they are playing so quietly together. Behind her in the kitchen she can hear Michael's voice.

"I know you do," she says. "But every time you get water on the floor it rots a little more."

"We *need* this much water," Aaron says.

"Yeah, we need it."

They lower their heads and go on playing, but Jan can see that they are both tensed for the battle. How she wishes they did not resist so strongly. They make her feel helpless. They are going to drive her to anger, and she does not want to be angry.

"I just told you the floor is rotting and when you slop water on it, it makes it worse."

They pretend she isn't there. Jan looks down on the blond crewcut head, the dark long hair, the two pairs of shoulders close together.

"Take that washcloth off there!"

Lisa's head snaps up. *"You're not my boss!"*

Jan knows how angry Lisa often is at their new arrangement. In a moment she will start shouting for Maureen if Jan doesn't take care of this immediately. It is hard for the mothers to stay out of encounters like this one.

Leaning over, Jan places her hands on the side of the tub and looks close-up into Lisa's round furious eyes.

"Today I *am* your boss, and I'm telling you to get that washcloth off there and let some water out or you're both going to get out of the tub right now and go to bed."

Lisa holds her gaze. She is really formidable, this Lisa, thinks Jan.

A sucking noise begins as the washcloth is pulled from the drain by Aaron and the water burbles out.

Jan straightens up. "Thank you, Aaron," she says, aware that her tone is sarcastic, and immediately judges herself, knowing that sarcasm accomplishes no end but to confuse him. Going back out to finish the pots and pans, Jan feels the tension in her body. As yet, she is never really comfortable with the children, is always standing a little back from them, watching herself. She wishes someone could tell her what to do in each of these situations with them, and at first she thought the mothers might have the key But Rosalie only laughed at her, and then when Jan was hurt by this, Rosalie took her hand and said, "They're just *people*, Jan. And you don't know them very well yet. They always have a reason for what they do, they just can't say what it is, usually, so you have to pay attention."

Jan stacks the last pan on the rack and lets the soapy water out of the sink. She turns to wipe her hands on a towel and leans back to rest.

Michael is still talking. He seems so engrossed in the sound of his own voice that she wonders if he heard her argument with the children. Is it only the *idea* of children that interests him?

Before they come upstairs with Jan—after the battle to get them out of the tub, after the struggle to get them to wipe the water from the bathroom floor—they go to be kissed good-night by the grownups. Lisa crawls up on Maureen's lap, knocking against the table, careless of her knees digging into Maureen's thighs, and throws her arms around Maureen's neck, kissing her roughly again and again on the cheek in a wild parody of passion. Maureen suffers this assault as best she can, and then she tries to loosen Lisa's arms from her neck, but Lisa clings. "*You* put me to bed. I want *you* to put me to bed." Finally Maureen is able to disentangle herself from Lisa's gorilla embrace, and Lisa stands flushed and disappointed before her as she tells her, "It's *Jan's* day, Lisa. You know that. Now go upstairs with her."

Down the hall in the front room, they find Rosalie. Jan stops in the doorway to look at her, a broad shouldered blond woman kneeling amid piles of papers. Rosalie had shown her a picture in an art book, once, a painting by an old Dutch master of a ruddy washerwoman bent over her tubs. "That's me," she said. "No!" Jan protested, but there was a resemblance in the broad hands, the strong arms, the thick light hair drawn back from the wide forehead, the pale eyes and short nose. The painting was an exaggeration of Rosalie's strength, a coarser version of her vitality.

"I didn't know you were in here working," Jan says, as Lisa goes to hug Rosalie.

"Lisa, look what you've done!" Rosalie shrieks, pointing at the stack of papers Lisa has kicked out into a fan on the floor.

This anger surprises Jan, until she realizes Rosalie must be annoyed that none of the other grownups have come in to work with her. How she wishes Rosalie could learn to ask people for help.

Aaron walks dreamily in among the stacks of papers and puts his arms around Rosalie. She holds him for a few moments, rubs the wet bristles of his hair.

"Good night, Rosalie," he says. She has asked him to stop calling her Mama, to call her by her name as Lisa does Maureen—and he tries to remember to do it.

"I'll come down and help you as soon as I've gotten them to bed," Jan tells her.

Rosalie shrugs. "By that time Shirley and the others will be here for the meeting." She does not look up at Jan.

And Jan feels the requisite tug of guilt, even while knowing that she had been busy with the dishes and the children. She turns from the doorway to follow Lisa and Aaron up the stairs, thinking, I'll probably have to deal with this later.

When the children have put on their pajamas and chosen a book and decided, quarreling, that it is Aaron's bed they will sit on tonight, they settle down on either side of Jan. She puts her arms around them, a little awkwardly (she is not easy yet in touching them), and they lean against her.

> "...never tease a weasel
> Not even once or twice
> A weasel will not like it
> And teasing isn't nice..."

Lisa singsongs the rhymes with her, Aaron sits quietly attentive. Jan is amazed at them: from the overbearing monsters of an hour before they have changed into gentle little children. She feels the warmth, the small weight of their bodies leaning against her. They have abandoned themselves to her, perfectly trusting, and she is swept with tendernooo for them. Is this love? Does she love them? She asks herself this sometimes and doesn't know the answer. It is so hard to know in the newness of most of their time together. Now the question doesn't seem to matter. She is simply moved by the touch of Aaron's broad-palmed hand on her thigh, Lisa's voice earnest and soft for once, pronouncing the words.

When the book has been put away and both children are in their beds, Jan leans over Aaron. He puts his arms around her neck and kisses her cheek. "Now me!" Lisa insists. Jan goes to her bed and leans over it. Lisa stares up at her for a moment, then turns her face to the side. "I *hate* kissing!" But when Jan starts to pull away Lisa grabs her and hugs her fiercely.

Holding the little body, Jan feels the child's heart beating against her chest. Something awakens in answer to this throbbing, an inkling of herself as a child, as passionately demanding as Lisa. "Sleep tight," Jan whispers, kissing the soft-skinned ear, and Lisa slowly opens her arms.

Joyce Kauffman

I am a thirty-eight-year-old working class lesbian mother of a three year old daughter who loves to wear dresses, adores Mickey Mouse, and calls my lover (her "other" mother) Mama Marcie, and me Mama Joycie. For the past six years I've been a member of a collective which runs an alternative learning program in a Cambridge, MA housing project; and I am a feminist therapist. I am a very determined person who really does believe that we can learn from our history, that struggle is productive, and that there is hope.

THINK BABY

Joyce Kauffman

Years ago, when I told my mother I was a lesbian, she said, "You're depriving me of grandchildren." I perked right up.

"Not necessarily," I responded brightly, thinking 'This isn't going to be as bad as I thought.'

Then she hissed, "Don't you dare have a child out of wedlock!"

Well, of course, I responded very maturely and said, "I am too going to have a baby and you're just going to have to deal with it!"

It honestly never occurred to me that I wouldn't have a baby. I am a very determined person. When I had this conversation with my mother, I was living with two other lesbians and their four year-old sons. It all seemed very normal to me. In all my significant relationships, the subject of having children was a major discussion—when, how, who would be the father, etc. My assumption had always been that I would find Ms. Right and The Perfect Relationship, settle down and have a baby. For years, I had imagined a certain level of emotional and financial stability and a secure living situation to be prerequisites. I often wondered, especially in the early years of my lesbianism, *how* I would get pregnant. Would I have sex with some anonymous man? Have sex with a gay male friend? "Artificially" inseminate? Who would be the father/donor? In one relationship, my lover and I seriously considered asking her brother to be the donor. The lesbian mothers I knew had their children while in heterosexual relationships and I knew no one who had grappled with this question.

In the late 1970's, I began to hear about the turkey baster

baby boom in California. I was very excited. On a vacation to San Francisco, my lover at the time and I (who fantasized *constantly* about carting around fifteen fat children in a beat-up stationwagon) met with a friend's sister who was about to give birth. What I remember most about her is that she was huge! I immediately repressed any fears of pregnancy and childbirth that surfaced. She was part of a growing network of lesbians having children and seemed confident about the future. I was impressed.

Shortly after the dissolution of my third longterm lesbian relationship, when I was 33, I realized that my fantasy about the circumstances in which I would have a child might not materialize. Taking matters into my own hands, I renewed a conversation begun several years earlier with a gay male friend about having a child together. I told him I was ready. At the time, concern about AIDS was just beginning to escalate. We discussed this and agreed that he would have as complete a medical examination as possible. He was assured that he was healthy, although now it is hard to believe that I went ahead and inseminated without knowing if he was HTLV III positive. My friend later decided to participate in a longterm study by a local gay health clinic through which he would be tested for AIDS virus antibodies at periodic intervals. And, after I became pregnant, he was found to be HTLV III negative. My fears about AIDS have subsided somewhat, but I would certainly advise women to be as sure as humanly possible about the health of the father/donor they choose.

I had read everything I could get my hands on about alternative insemination (which wasn't much). I had thought about my financial and living situation. It was not ideal by a long shot, but I had the feeling that this was the right time and that, in all likelihood, judging from my experience, there would never be an ideal moment. I was single—a state I never imagined I would be in when I had a child. In retrospect, I see that it was a positive thing in that I was completely and solely responsible for this decision. It's likely that this was my first truly independent choice, not in the slightest dependent on another person or on a relationship. I continue to feel very good about that decision.

My friend agreed, it was time. I had been taking my temperature and charting my menstrual cycle for months. A nurse I knew procured a syringe. I zeroed in on when I would next ovulate and we set the date. On a Saturday morning at 10 A.M., my friend arrived. We had coffee, chatted nervously and then he retired to a private room. After a surprisingly short period of time, he returned, said, "Your turn." And left.

I took the small jar of semen and went up to my bedroom. I had told all my friends to "think baby" but had decided to be alone when I inseminated. At that moment, and at many times during my pregnancy and the first six months of my daughter's life, I was proud to be doing this alone. I felt strong, sure, and very much in control of what was happening.

I lay on my bed and filled the syringe with the vaguely familiar smelling semen. Taking a deep breath, I inserted the syringe and pushed the liquid into my vagina. I lay with my legs up and very still for almost an hour, praying like crazy that this would work. It seemed too simple; how could this possibly produce a baby? I inseminated on the following two days and then prepared to wait out the next two weeks for the results.

When I didn't get my period, I could hardly believe it. Too soon, I had a blood test to see if I was pregnant. To say that I was horribly disappointed when it came back negative would be a gross understatement. I called my friend and said we would have to schedule another insemination. A few days later, my breasts ached and I thought I was getting my period. Over the next two or three days, I had a little spotting, but my period did not begin. I was acutely aware of my physical being but didn't dare hope that the test had been wrong. I forced myself to wait until a urinanalysis would be definite and went to a local hospital for another pregnancy test. The nurse told me I could have the results at the end of the day.

It was March 5, 1984, a few days before my 34th birthday. At the end of the day, I nervously called the number I'd been given. Of course, they put me on hold for an unbearably long time. A female voice finally came on the line and said, "Congratulations, you're pregnant." Even remembering that moment now, I fill up with tears. It was too wonderful to take in. After so many years, so many conversations, so many worries... I was finally going to have my baby.

Six weeks after the conversation with my friend, I was pregnant. It seemed that I had been correct—this was the right time for me. The life I imagined I would have when I had a child was not this life, but it was the right time. I felt blessed.

A few weeks later, when I began to feel nauseous and found it difficult to eat, I had to come to terms with another reality. I had imagined my life would change enormously *when I had the baby*, not when I got pregnant. But here I was, sick as a dog and vomiting on a daily basis. I felt horrible and had to cut back on all my activities. Everyone told me it would end after the first trimester and I tried to believe that. There were many days when I thought, "What have I done to myself?" For weeks I ate nothing but mashed potatoes or scrambled eggs and drank only gingerale. Entering my second trimester, I hoped it would end. It didn't. In fact, I threw up the day I went into labor.

The larger I became, the less in control I felt. There was this thing inside me taking up space and pushing my organs around. My ankles and feet were swollen for months. The skin on my face was red and blotchy from vomiting so much. Later in my pregnancy, when I had gained nearly 45 pounds (in spite of vomiting daily), had swollen feet and ankles, couldn't breath deeply *and* had serious heartburn, my fears of childbirth began to subside as my loathing for being pregnant grew. I had been ready to get pregnant nine months before and, now, I was definitely ready to have this child. I had had amniocentesis and knew that it was a girl— even though, being the skeptic that I am, I thought for certain that they had made a mistake.

On November 3, 1984, at 2 A.M. (it always happens in the wee hours), I awoke with contractions. I felt an irresistible urge to go to the bathroom and when I did, my water broke with a huge gush. I shuddered to think of women I had heard of whose water broke in the supermarket! I called my labor coach who arrived shortly afterwards, and we began to call my list of my friends and family. My doctor advised me to go to the hospital. By the time we arrived, at around 4 A.M., I was having contractions just a few minutes apart and was partially dilated. My friends began to arrive at the hospital and took turns holding my hand and encouraging me. Although I had thought I would stand and walk around during labor, I found that I couldn't. I lay on the birthing table surrounded by my closest friends, breathed through the pains and joked and cried during the intermissions. While I was in labor, the rest of the world and everything that was happening in it totally receded. The world became the labor and delivery of my child. It was the most intensely physical experience of my life.

At 9:05 A.M., nine months—almost to the minute—after my first insemination, Rebecca Teme Grant Kauffman was born. She weighed 6 lbs., 10½ oz., was born with her eyes wide open, and, needless to say, was gorgeous. And I, thankfully, was no longer pregnant.

The first six months of Becca's life were a magical time for me. I could never have imagined what it would be like. Even though I had lived with infants and had been around young children quite a lot, I found becoming a mother a challenging, sobering, and humbling experience. The love I felt for this totally vulnerable, tiny human being was overwhelming. The responsibility I felt for her even more so. Sometimes very late at night, after making sure she was still breathing, I would sit and think, like when I was pregnant, "What have I done to my life?" It was (and still is) wonderful and frightening all at the same time.

The enormity of being a lesbian mother and having to constantly deal with a heterosexual world which assumes you are straight is a burden. It is, or should be, enough to adjust to being a mother without this added pressure. There is no way to explain to someone who does not have a child what it is like to be a parent. You simply cannot know until you are doing it. All the preparation in the world won't change this fact. On top of that to have to confront individuals and institutions which, at best, deny your reality, and, at worst, are horrified by your existence, is a total drag.

My life changed dramatically after Becca was born. I could no longer attend several meetings per week, or spontaneously do anything. Before becoming a mother, I had been an avid reader, reading two or three books at the same time, and sometimes staying up most of the night to finish a good novel. When Becca was an infant, I was asked to write a book review—it took me more than 8 months to read the book! Either I was too exhausted to do anthing except watch TV when she was asleep or I would finish the endless chores and be just about to settle down with the book and Becca would wake up.

The logistics alone can make you crazy. Just imagine that every time you leave the house, not only do you have to bring this tiny infant, but you also have to pack a bag with every conceivable item you *might* need—diapers, extra clothes, bottles, food, toys. Going out for the afternoon can feel like preparation for a week-long vacation. Even finding time to take a shower when you have an infant is a major accomplishment.

Certainly during my two months of maternity leave, when I was home alone with Becca, I felt very isolated. I was living alone with her and my life revolved around her schedule completely. I was relieved to return to work when she was two months old. Luckily, I could have her with me at work most of the time for the first eight months. I distinctly remember the first time I left her in someone else's care. A friend had agreed to watch her for a few hours a day while I worked. I arrived— with an armful of baby equipment and a wailing infant. I returned to my office (which was right next door to my friend's apartment) and burst into tears. It is not easy to trust someone else with your child. The reality, however, for most lesbians, particularly for single and working class lesbians, is that you have to work and you have to find childcare. Finding a childcare situation in which you can actually be out is extremely difficult. And, in my experience (three different childcare situations in three years), even where you can be out, it's still not smooth.

It is quite difficult to be out as a lesbian mother in the heterosexual world. Unfortunately, even within the lesbian community, where, relatively speaking, not that many people have children, I've found it difficult to be all of who I am. A friend who is also a lesbian mother, recently commented to me, "I can be a lesbian, and I can be a mother, but there is nowhere I can be a lesbian mother." We lesbian mothers, of course, can and do assert our existence within the community, but the community has a long way to go in terms of opening up to us and to our children.

A lesbian without children has an enormous amount of mobility, spontaneity, and freedom in the world. I became very aware of this only when I had to give it up. The reality of being a lesbian mother in a homophobic and otherwise repressive society did not—and does not—escape me. Countless custody cases involving lesbians threatened with the loss of their children continue to horrify me. And, of course, there is the raging foster care policy debate in my home state of Massachusetts. It is unsettling that, even though I am a mother, I would not be an acceptable foster parent. The realization that the world we live in not only invalidates our relationships, both to our lovers and to our children, but also seeks to deny us basic human rights is sobering indeed. Fortunately, there is a rich history of lesbians and children organizing to confront these inequalities and to assert our rights. I remember watching the "Dykes and Tykes" contingent in the Boston Lesbian/Gay Pride March in the mid-1970's. I remember the debates within the women's movement about children, motherhood and careers. I have participated in and witnessed an evolution of thought which has brought us from painful discussions in the early '70's about male children or the relative acceptance of a woman's *choice* to have children to the current debates within the lesbian community between lesbians "choosing" children and those who became mothers long before the recent East Coast Lesbian Baby Boom. I share the serious concern that we have forgotten our own history and, in so doing, will fail to learn from the experience of others — other lesbian mothers who have, for the most part, confronted these struggles alone and relatively unsupported by our community. I remain hopeful that we can bridge these gaps and that, as a united community, we will continue to confront this insidious homophobia. The lesbian community, too, would do well to examine how children affect all our lives and how we can remain a united community, a community where those of us who are mothers can feel connected, validated, and respected.

During the first six months of Becca's life, while I was still single, I could not imagine how I would ever meet someone. I rarely went out socially. Even beyond that, I could not imagine that I would ever meet someone who would be willing to get involved with *us*. I didn't believe it was possible for the mother of an infant to have a casual relationship with anyone and I didn't want to have a casual relationship anyway. Then I was introduced to Marcie who walked into my life one night and we both knew immediately that something serious and profound was about to happen. Our first date took place on the eve of my first Mother's Day. We—Marcie, Becca, and I— spent Mother's Day together and began our journey towards becoming a family, a journey which has proven to be both joyous and sometimes difficult. But that is another story.

Patricia Roth Schwartz

*I am forty-one years old and live in the
Boston area with my lover, two cats, and a
word processor. I have a private practice in
psychotherapy from a feminist/holistic
perspective. I am also a writer, publishing
fiction, poetry, reviews, and articles in small
press and women's journals. My volume of
short stories is forthcoming from New
Victoria Publishers.*

UNFINISHED BUSINESS: EX-LOVER OF A LESBIAN MOTHER

Patricia Roth Schwartz

Of all the invisibilities and silences I have endured, as a woman, as a lesbian, in a patriarchal, homophobic culture, one of the hardest to take has been that of being the former lover of a lesbian mother. As the part-time caretaker, nurturer, and friend to her two children, officially, I had no role. When I left the relationship, I had no voice, no rights, no options. I lost the children; they lost me.

Jennifer and Brian, (real names and identifying details changed), two pixie-faced, freckled red-heads, ages seven and three respectively, came into my life and heart when I took their mother, Kendra, into my bed. A package deal—but I loved the package. I'd been out for a year-and-a-half or so, still legally married to a gentle feminist man I'd only separated from a month earlier, separated as well from the woman lover I'd had during the last year of that marriage. I knew Kendra slightly through a women's group we both belonged to. She was in the same boat as I, married, but with strong lesbian feelings. Unlike me, she was still actively in that marriage.

To this day, the folly of my getting together with her remains a bit inexplicable. It had to do with something about giving to her all that wonderful understanding about still being married but in love with women which I'd longed for myself but never really got. At any rate, she was desperately eager to come out, and managed to be quite persuasive to a "suddenly-single" dyke who'd just moved all alone into a small apartment with nothing but two cats and a sleeping bag.

I fell for her instant declarations of "love forever," and

fell as well into the cozy routine of her house and household. Her husband worked nights, gave us his tacit approval; I found out later they'd been having threesomes for years with other women. This time Kendra wanted the woman all to herself. I ate meals with her and the kids, did laundry in her machine, went on outings with the whole gang, established an immediate rapport with Jennifer and Brian.

My place in their lives was not just that of playmate or friend. I bathed them, gave them meals, tucked them in at night, read stories, helped with limit-setting ("You can have a carrot—a cookie is not an option."), mediated conflicts. They became an important part of my world and I of theirs.

What I especially loved about relating to them was being able to indulge my sense of play. We cavorted about the house, immersed in fantasy games (Jennifer had a "horse" whom she tethered to the newel post of the stairs), dressing in costumes. We took on projects: brownies, Halloween pumpkins, valentines.

What was hard was trying to figure out my role: not really "parent," but not just "company," either, as the weeks progressed, as Kendra began to use me more and more an an official babysitter. The problems we had are similar to those of all couples in which one is the biological parent of the kids and the other is not. The problem was further compounded by the fact that she and I *weren't* really a couple; she and her husband were.

Our intimate relationship suffered the complications of all such situations: I remember Saturday mornings of frustrating sex while cartoons blared through the playroom wall next door; I remember evenings of crashing early after taking the kids out all day, making supper, cleaning up, having no energy left. None of this, however, was mitigated by the rewards real parents—or even real step-parents— have. I remained always the interloper, the extra, the "other." Kendra began to get angry whenever I asked for more time for me, for us. She especially resented my ability to play with the kids. Because of a painful childhood in which she was forced to take a parental role with siblings at a very young age, it was an art she'd never learned.

In addition, our separate lesbian lives, to which we were able to devote only a small amount of time, were fraught with difficulty. I forced the small women's community of our town to accept Kendra even though she was married. I took her on romantic weekends to The Village to a friend's apartment, visits complete with women's bars, coffeehouses, and bookstores. I gave her access to the erotic dimensions of a woman's love.

As time went by, a great deal happened in the course of this ill-chosen and misguided relationship which was destructive to me. All of that, in essence, is another story, which it is not my purpose to tell here. The upshot of the situation became that, before a year was out, Kendra found another woman lover, a mutual acquaintance, who was apparently less pressuring than I had been about having Kendra consider leaving her marriage. After I found out, I broke off with Kendra completely and irrevocably.

My relationship with her was over and I was glad— but my relationship with Jennifer and Brian was left in limbo. At this time I first felt the real crunch of being an "outlaw" in society's eyes. I had no recourse of any kind, as a divorcing heterosexual would have had. I realize that straight lovers whose liaison is "without benefit of clergy" often exist in the same limbo. Nor was there any support from the women's community. After the initial flutter of gossip, people were anxious for everything to settle down harmoniously, for the two of us to be seen together at parties and concerts—Kendra with the new woman in tow—and for everybody to be chummy.

Besides, there were few lesbian mothers in our circle, and precious little understanding of parenting or the needs of children. I felt crazy with grief and loss. I couldn't call Kendra's house and just speak to the kids. They weren't old enough to meet me on the outside anywhere. I also had no control over what they were told about the situation. When I spoke with Kendra, she told me that the children had been informed that I had been "extremely cruel" to her, and that they were, under no circumstances, to come up to me or speak with me should we all meet in public. Later, she and her husband wrote me a letter saying that I was to stay completely away from the children. Since I had been doing so, and had no choice anyway, it was a moot point.

Of course, the time came when, in a small city, with only a few "alternative" gathering places, we would meet. I saw Jennifer and Brian in the lobby of the YWCA where the lesbian rap group met and where they had swimming lessons. A moment I will never forget was the one in which I had to see, frozen in complete terror, the childish features of the little beings I had loved, cared for, and, not in any way intentionally hurt or betrayed. Apparently Kendra had so thoroughly indoctrinated them into what a bad person I was, and how they would be punished if they spoke to me, that I was only able to carry on a brief, stilted conversation. I realized that to push them further was to split loyalties between myself and Kendra, as the parent whose love and approval they desperately needed. I backed off and grieved in private.

Not too long afterward, Jennifer called me up one evening to say that she had seen a cat, who looked like my missing kitten, Sybil, running through her neighborhood. Now, Sybil had been gone for weeks at that point. Jennifer's home was on the other side of the city from mine. What I think she really wanted was contact, to know that I was still real, to let me know that she still cared, and that, in some little part of her, she felt as lost as that kitten.

Over a year later, I saw Brian at a women's event. He was sitting with a friend of Kendra's while Kendra was off in another part of the building. I spoke to him because he recognized me and not to speak would have been wounding. He said, "Oh, Pat, I almost don't remember you!"

Brian, I remember you—and Jennifer. I don't, nine years later, think of the situation frequently at all. A snapshot of you two hides deep inside an old photo album. I have lived for over six years in a bigger city, have a wonderful new life, a committed intimate partnership, work I love, my writing, and a supportive circle of friends. Therapy has healed many wounds, and given me new ways of relating to others while also nurturing myself. What's left over, I guess, is a profound sense of sadness, not really for me in the personal sense, as this was just one of the hurts and losses life inevitably brings, along with its riches. But that, as a community of women dedicated to such lofty ideals of equality and to making over a cruel and abusive world, we, *too*, so often fall short.

I write this piece for an anthology on lesbian mothering to break the silence of the party not heard from, the ex-lover denied recourse, even to finish unfinished business, to say goodbye, to reassure the children she once loved that that love could continue from afar, even if there were no contact.

I also write because the children cannot speak for themselves. I believe that in this case—and undoubtedly in many others like it—they were treated abusively on a psychological level. What damage was done to their trust I do not know. Their parents' sexual habits had brought at least two other women in and out of their lives before me. Kendra went on to divorce her husband and acquire yet another woman lover for a time. Eventually, she went back to the woman she had left me for. Even though the two of them and the kids settled down in a house of their own, Jennifer and Brian were nevertheless subjected to a great deal of instability in the course of their early lives.

Although I do not now feel that non-monogamy is for me, I respect others' rights to choose it. When children are involved, however, the potential for emotional attachment to a parent's lover is always present. Serious consideration needs to be given to how an abrupt break with someone they've become close to will affect them. Children ought not to be lied to or threatened in order to serve the parent's emotional needs around a breakup.

As far as I know, no further upheavals happened for Kendra's new "blended" family—but I can't help wondering if it came too late. I wonder about my own culpability in any hurt with which Jennifer and Brian are left.

And I have deliberately avoided any intimate connection with a lesbian with young children in the home.

Kim and Carolyn

Kim is a white woman who has been deaf since adolescence. Carolyn is an Asian woman, who is hearing. Earl, their adopted son is an eleven year old Black child who is deaf.

WE ARE FAMILY

Kim and Carolyn

[An excerpt from the transcript of *We Are Family,* a T.V. documentary produced in 1987 by Aimee Sands and WGBH/Boston.]

Narrator:
It's a new idea for many of us—the thought of children growing up with gay parents. But there are an estimated three to five million gay families in the United States. Lesbian mothers and gay fathers are a reality, part of that increasingly diverse institution called the American Family. As gay and lesbian parents become more visible, they are also becoming more controversial. In Massachusetts, gay foster parents have become the focus of debate. In 1985, amid intense controversy, that State virtually banned gay men and lesbians from becoming foster parents. Social workers were instructed to place foster children with relatives or heterosexual married couples whenever possible, except in unusual cases. Massachusetts governor Michael Dukakis takes a strong position on this matter.

Dukakis:
When you're talking about some 6,000 youngsters who, in many cases, are the most vulnerable kids we have, our goal ought to be to try to provide the best possible environment for those youngsters. And all things being equal, I don't think there's much question that a good home with a father and a mother and other brothers and sisters is the best environment.

Narrator:
The Massachusetts foster care policy has been hotly contested by gay activists and child welfare professionals. Civil

liberties lawyers have filed suit against it. But behind this very public dispute are intensely personal concerns about parenthood and family life in gay households.

Carolyn:
I think he acts like a normal child because we've always had normal expectations for him. We've never allowed him to act like a retarded child or an uncontrollable child. We've always expected him to act like a normal child his age. And we're very strict about that.

Earl:
Families are families. Families have rules and they're the same whether they're gay or straight.

Kim:
Being gay isn't the issue. Mothers, regardless of whether they're gay, or straight and married, or divorced with two kids are still mothers.

Interviewer:
This is the story of a gay adoptive family. In 1980, Kim and Carolyn, a Boston area lesbian couple, took in Earl, a Black deaf boy, who at the time was five years old. Kim is also deaf, although she can speak and lip-read. She brought Earl home because he literally had no place to go.

Kim:
I was working in a school for the deaf and he'd been there, living in the dorm, and the end of the school year came. His social worker had known that she had four months, then three months, then two months, then one month, then one week to find a foster home for him for the summer. And she didn't. So the last day of school happened. And there was no cab to pick up Earl, there was no home for him to go to. And so I brought Earl home for two weeks, and then three weeks, and then four weeks.

Interviewer:
Eventually Kim and Carolyn were formally approved as Earl's foster parents by Massachusetts social workers.

Several years later, the two women adopted Earl. This, of course, was before the new Massachusetts foster care policy was put into place. The little boy Kim brought home in 1980 was in deep emotional trouble. Like many foster children, Earl had been bounced from placement to placement for most of his five years, and he arrived at Kim and Carolyn's a frightened and unpredictable child.

Kim:
When we got Earl he was just crazy.

Carolyn:
He was totally crazy. He was supposedly mentally retarded. He was really uncontrollable. I took him to the park once and he didn't want to go at first because he was afraid Kim would never come back. So we went to the park. He had a great time, of course, playing on the jungle gym. And when it was time to leave again, he wouldn't leave, so I grabbed his arm and he started hitting me. He hit me so hard that I had bruises all over my arm. And then he broke away and ran. This was on the Esplanade, right on Storrow Drive with no fence. He ran full speed right to the edge of the curb. And stopped and waved his arms and screamed and laughed. He was pretty crazy.

Kim:
His early life was not real healthy. He was probably physically abused. He was not fed well, we know that. And he still has very high lead levels from eating paint.

Carolyn:
Cigarette burns on the backs of his legs—scars from cigarettes.

Kim:
If he just had high lead levels you would expect to see some neurological involvement; if he was just the result of a pregnancy where toxic drugs were ingested you'd expect to see some problems; but with everything—and then throw in total chaos for the first six years of his life, then you

expect to see a kid that really...really has a lot of problems.

Carolyn:
What we tried to do as parents was first, get the basic be-
havioral things straightened out, like eating appropriately,
eating with a fork. He didn't know how to eat with a fork.
He would eat with his hands. His favorite food was
scrambled eggs. He'd eat it with his hands. Or he started
learning to use a fork, but he'd get scrambled eggs in his
ears.

Kim:
I tell people—it's sort of a joke, but it's sort of true—that
we went through the "terrible two's" with him when he was
seven. The first time we brought him to a toy store, he picked
out zero-to-three-year-old toys. He wanted a busy board. We
bought him what he wanted because it was clear he needed
that. He played with those toys for about three months and
then he was ready for three-to-six-year-old toys. We bought
him Fisher-Price Play People and things like that. He was
six years old. And after a while he moved into age-
appropriate play patterns. It was interesting to me, because
I've studied a lot of developmental psychology, that he had
to go through all the stages. You know, you can't skip things.
In some ways, he's still more immature than other eleven-
year-olds just in terms of still needing more external control
than the normal eleven-year-old would.

Interviewer:
Kim and Carolyn are very strict with Earl. The household's
rules are specific and consistent and Earl can recite them
from memory.

Earl:
No fighting. No throwing rocks. I can't watch TV with
violent programs, and I have to ask permission...I have
to ask my parents for permission. Sometimes I might sneak
and if my parents catch me, then I get punished and I can't
watch TV for a while.

Narrator:
A lot of parents limit the amount of violent TV their kids can watch. Kim and Carolyn are especially careful, though, because of the powerful effect these programs seem to have on Earl.

Kim:
It seems there was a lot of violence in his early life and when he watches a lot of violent TV he tends to obsess on it. It's something that is getting better and I think he's working through a lot in his mind. But still. Yeah, Yeah, we're strict. We're horrible. We won't let him watch *Mr. "T"* and *The "A" Team.*

Carolyn:
Or *Mad Max: Beyond The Thunderdome.*

Kim:
Or go see *Rambo.* You know, he'll walk past the theater and I'll be holding his hand and he'll stare at the poster until he can't see it anymore. But there's no way he's going to see *Rambo.*

Interviewer:
Together, Kim and Carolyn and Earl represent one of those rare foster care success stories. Earl has emerged as a normally intelligent, active young boy. But at age eleven he's just about to turn the corner into adolescence. Doesn't he need a male role model to help him find his way to adulthood? Soon after Earl first came to live with Kim and Carolyn, they began looking for a Big Brother for him. They didn't find a Black man, as they had hoped, but they did find Joe, who's been a regular visitor to the household ever since.

Kim:
He's not without male role models. He doesn't live with a man, but he has Joe. There are other men in his life that are very important to him and that he spends time with. I think kids need to be around both sexes.

Narrator:
Earl is a child who is different. He is deaf in a hearing world; Black in a predominantly white community; and the son of lesbians in a largely heterosexual culture. How does this affect him? What, for example, does he think kids in school might say if they see him in this program?

Earl:
I don't know. Maybe they'll tease me and say, "Oh, your family is lousy, my family—straight people are better than gay people. My family's better."

Kim:
One way to help him deal with being different is to talk about it, and talk about the way the world is, "Yeah, it's true, some people don't like Black people. Maybe they're jerks. If they don't change their mind after they meet you, they're jerks. Forget it. Some people don't like deaf people, that's their problem. Some people don't like gay people, that's their problem." People are different in different ways, and I think he knows that.

Carolyn:
And he sees the same thing happening to us. If something comes up, that someone acts differently to Kim because she's deaf or acts differently to me because I'm Asian, we talk about it. He sees that it happens to us, too, and not just to him. And it happens to his friends downstairs. And he knows that it's wrong, he sees it happening to other people and he realizes it just doesn't happen to him alone. We have a lot of friends that are straight and have kids and really, our family is very similar to theirs. Our house is a mess because we have a kid living here. So you come in and you find an airplane on the table— that's not unusual. It would be if we didn't have a kid. But I mean, it's a normal house. It's a normal house with kids.

Kim:
When the policy first came out, I always felt "shit," we ought to just invite the Governor over here and say: "Come see

our family, you see? We're not molesting this little boy."
I mean, we're just a normal family.

Narrator:
For Earl, the sexual preference of his parents is not nearly
as important as the fact that now he has parents.

Earl:
I think that it's important for families to adopt children.
Because, like...well, there are a lot of children who haven't
been adopted yet. And I feel that gay parents could adopt
those children. And I feel that if gay parents adopted them,
they would feel happy.

Kim:
Earl would not have been adopted if we hadn't pushed and
said: "This kid needs to know where he's going to spend
the rest of his life." And it did make a difference, even though
he'd already been with us for five years. After he was
adopted, I saw some changes in him, didn't you?

Carolyn:
Mm-Hmmm.

Kim:
Just that he knew he was going to stay. I mean, that was
important. One thing was that he got mad at me for the
first time, really mad. The way kids do with their parents.
He said: "I hate you!" during an argument, the way I said
"I hate you" to my mother. People say that to their parents.
Earl never did that before he was adopted. Maybe he was
afraid to. Once he was adopted, he knew he wasn't leaving.
I could get furious with him, but he wasn't going anywhere,
he knew he was staying here. So that made a difference.
The system just lets kids float. So why should they be so
picky about whether or not parents are gay if the kids are
wanted and loved and cared for?

Merril Mushroom

I am a hot Jewish mama, second-generation U.S.-born white Ashkenazi, of Russian/Polish heritage. I was a child of the '40s, grew up in the '50s and have been rapidly aging since I first became a mother eighteen years ago. To date, I have five adopted children of assorted races.

HOT JEWISH MAMA

Merril Mushroom

[for my blood foremothers and my five adopted
children]
I am a Hot Jewish Mama!
My roots go deep
to feed
the family tree.
I come from a long line of Hot Jewish Mamas
who fed and clothed and raised the children,
who pampered the husbands, preserved the families;
who sheltered the needy
and cared for the poor
and nursed the sick
and buried the dead;
who suffered pogroms and faced Christian tribunals
who fought revolutions
and went to the death camps;
who loved their sisters and knew their own magic.
I am a Hot Jewish Mama!
The strength of my foremothers runs full in my blood,
feeds new branches.
Now, new fruit,
not so strange,
grows on
the family tree.

FEAR POEM

maybe
some day
my children will
turn me
in

Connie Chan

I am a thirty-three-year-old Asian American woman who grew up in Hawaii amidst people of many colors and cultures. A psychologist and college professor, I am also an avid runner. These days, most of my running is done pushing a baby stroller or chasing after my partner, Barbara, and our two children, Lee and Malia.

JOURNAL ENTRIES: BABY LOG

Connie Chan

February 9, 1986

Barbara is pregnant! She called after receiving the lab results on the phone. I was so thrilled I wanted to shout and scream and call every single person I knew to announce our great news. We had worked so hard to find this donor that we felt we really *deserved* to have it work. And it did! We are going to have a baby—I counted the forty weeks of pregnancy out on the calendar—in October. What a glorious day this is. I rode my bike to school, powered not by my legs but by our dreams.

At school, it was hard to focus on teaching a class when I felt I was up on the ceiling, flying and repeating to myself, "We're going to have a baby, we're going to have a baby."

Later, Barbara and I went to a Chinese New Year's celebration dinner. Still in the clouds, I whispered to our friends, mostly gay men, "Barbara's pregnant and the baby is coming in October." They were congratulatory, sometimes curious: "How did we find our Chinese donor?" "Hadn't we been looking for a long time for the right one?" "How many times did we try to get pregnant?" The frustration we'd felt for all those months washed away today with the excitement. It even felt easy to talk about the cultural issues: how hard it has been to find a Chinese donor because Chinese men tend to feel an ownership, a sense of responsibility, for their sperm, and no one had been willing. And the only men who would be more open to being donors were gay. With the reality of AIDS, gay men were not, unfortunately, a viable option. Finally, in January, we had found an anonymous (to us) donor with a friend as our go-between. He is a Chinese doctor, perhaps able to see the medical/scientific side of things rather than just the emotional/cultural view. We arranged the insemination through a doctor (our donor's requirement) and joy of joys, glory of glories, it worked! Barbara is pregnant. We're going to have a baby. Today our hard work feels worthwhile—things are coming to fruition. It feels like the beginning of our life as a family.

Sept. 1, 1986

Barbara is now in her eighth month and doing well. We have been busy preparing for the new arrival and are pretty excited. Only a few more weeks to go.

I flew back into Boston after the American Psychological Association convention in D.C. Yesterday I had come back for just one day to inseminate because it was the last chance to try for this month. Then I had to fly back to D.C. for an important meeting last night, and today, it's back to Boston again. It seems crazy to spend so much time and money just to inseminate *one* day, but if I get pregnant this month, I'll have the baby at the end of May. That means I'll get the entire summer off from teaching to be with the baby. It's worth a try. It was much easier to find a white donor than a Chinese donor, so hopefully it will work. We have put so much thought into the timing of our babies, their racial blend, and our family dreams that we'll have a hard time giving up our (supposed) sense of control once the kids do come. We have had to work so hard to make our family dream come true that we do feel a sense of accomplishment already.

I wrote a letter to my parents while I waited for Barbara to pick me up from the airport. It has been one of the more emotionally draining aspects of planning our family: What do I tell my parents? They are very traditional in their views, seemingly unyielding in their expectations of their children. How can they understand that my relationship with Barbara is so strong and so satisfying that we want to share it with children, to enrich our lives and theirs? I feel weak and vulnerable every time I think about my parents' reaction. My life is my own and different enough that I don't share very much of myself with them anymore. Nor have I ever actually "come out" to them. How can I help my parents to understand that my choosing to have a family is very much a testament to them? My choice to create a family is very much related to having grown up in a warm caring one. Because of my experience, I *believe* in spending my time nurturing a new life, much as we kids were the center of our parents' lives. Why is it then, that I feel so scared and so worried? I fear that my parents will not accept my life, my decision to have a family in the way I have decided, that they will reject me after all these years. I have written this letter to them many times over in my mind. Today the words look back at me on paper and I feel satisfied. It represents me; it says what I feel in the only way that I can tell them, in a way I hope they can understand:

> Dear Mom, Dad, and Tom (better to write to all three at once, that way every one in the family knows the same thing):
> I am writing to you because I need your love and support. After much discussion and thinking, Barbara and I have decided to raise a family together. We are very happy and excited about our plans. We have decided to give birth to one child each and to raise the children together as brother and sister. So that the children will share common racial ancestry, and be a blend of our own ancestry, we have decided to have "hapa" kids. Our children will be half-Chinese, half-white, a beautiful combination, we think.
> We are getting pregnant through "alternative insemination" of sperm—from anonymous donors. Barbara became pregnant last January and is expecting the baby in the middle of October. Our days have been filled with

anticipation and preparation for the baby as well as great excitement. I inseminated last month (July) and did not get pregnant, but tried again this month and am hopeful of getting pregnant this time.

I realize that this may seem like a quick decision to you, but we have thought about this and planned it for a very long time. We feel emotionally and financially ready to have children at this time. I hope you will join with us in accepting two new little ones into our family.

Love, Connie

Sept. 4, 1986

These last couple of days have been filled with apprehension and worry. Every time the phone rings I hold my breath for an instant and wonder if it is my parents. I have different fantasies as to how they'll react to my letter—most of the fantasies are good ones but there are the nightmares, too.

It finally actually happened tonight. My brother was on the phone, sounding terrible. His voice was dragging, monotone, but with a nervous quality to it. He got my letter, he said, and wanted to talk. Then he proceeded to say that he and my parents were completely shocked and upset by my letter. So upset that Mom was practically speechless. (At this point, she starts screaming on the phone at me. Unbeknownst to me, all three of them had been on the phone the whole time, though Tom was the only one talking at first.) In spite of the desperateness of the conversation I have to look back on this part as being somewhat funny. Mom knows when it's time for her to enter stage left, I guess. At any rate, they were very distraught and angry. I was ruining my life, they said. "It is a terrible thing to have children without being married. You are destroying our family by doing this. What are we going to tell relatives and friends? Why didn't you tell us sooner? (Because I was afraid you'd carry on like this and I didn't want to hear it.) Why don't you wait to get pregnant? We want you to come home this weekend so we can talk some sense into you. We cannot believe that you would ruin our lives like this. We are so ashamed of you." The conversation then degenerated into hysteria, with my parents alternately yelling and crying, my brother lecturing and whining. This phone call came close to one of my nightmare fantasies. I tried to reason with them, then gave up and did my best not to yell or engage in hysteria as they were doing. When they told me how ashamed they were of me, I just repeated that I was proud of my decision and that I was proud of them for bringing me up to be a responsible person. I told them that I loved them, but I had to live my own life according to my own values. It felt very frustrating. They clearly did not recognize that I was now an adult and needed to make my own choices. My mother made an allusion to the fact that I was a lesbian and how could I live with myself. "We live very well," I answered, "very well." I remember thinking that the old family dynamics were coming through again and I was being treated as the wayward, rebellious child. We were on the phone for over an hour and the call ended only because I told them I had had enough of their repeating themselves and yelling at me. They repeated their desire to have me come home next weekend and told me to call them to make arrangements. "If you love us, you wouldn't do this to us," they pleaded, "If you love us, please come home and stop this nonsense about children." I promised nothing and hung up.

Disillusioned, upset and drained, I was also saddened. Yet another family was rejecting their lesbian daughter and I felt a loss not only for myself, but for my family. *Both* families—the one I came from and the one we were creating.

Barbara and I held each other and grieved for the loss of my dreams of an extended family, of grandparents waiting at the airport with open arms for their new grandchildren. I cried for myself, for my parents, for our children-to-be, for all gay daughters and sons who have lost their families.

And for the parents, sisters and brothers who have misunderstood us, turned away from us, and are missing our company. Later that evening I cuddled up to Barbara and lovingly caressed her round, full belly. "You are entering a hard world," I whispered to the roundness, "but we await you with love and the will to survive and flourish."

October 12, 1986

4:30 a.m.: The phone's ring is incredibly loud and, in spite of my attempts to will it away, it does not stop. My head hurts and I don't know where I am; I only know that I *have* to stop the ringing. Groping towards the sound, I remember that this is a hotel room in D.C. and I'm feeling slightly nauseous. It's Barbara: "Might be going into labor, I'm not sure. Have had cramping on and off all night." Me: "Well, is it or isn't it? I have an important meeting today and I'll be back tonight at seven." As I enter consciousness more, I realize how callous that sounds, "I mean, I'll come home if you want. Do you really think the baby's coming today?" I try to soften my voice while all of me spins with the now-familiar "morning sickness" nausea. I am nine weeks pregnant.

"Yes," she says, "Could you come home? I want you to be here."

7:30 a.m.: Flying this early in the morning is never comfortable; it's terrible when you feel nauseous even *before* the flight takes off. Mercifully, it is a short flight, and not very crowded on this Sunday during the Columbus Day holiday. Barbara is standing calmly at the gate as I deplane. Each time I see her anew I am slightly amazed at how pregnant she is. At the same time I feel pretty excited: we are *both* pregnant in this space and time; what anticipation we feel.

9:00 a.m.: On the drive home Barbara is apologetic, "Sorry, the baby must not be ready to come out yet." I nod and realize that I don't care anymore about the meeting I left— I just want to get into my bed. It's amazing how pregnancy has changed my priorities and tempered my goals for the day—all I want is to get through it with a minimum of discomfort. Forget about deadlines and other essentials.

1:00 p.m.: We wake from our naps feeling refreshed but famished. Fortunately, Barbara's close friend Ellen is here to take care of us and make a big pot of oatmeal with apples. It's a little like a pajama party as all three of us cuddle in bed and laugh about Barbara's false signs of labor. She's feeling fine now, with no cramping anymore. I feel relieved— I'm still too tired to be able to deal with labor after such an early awakening. Still fatigued, Barbara goes back to bed and I read the Sunday paper downstairs.

2:00 p.m.: Barbara's moaning and whimpering upstairs as she sleeps, so I go up to investigate. In sort of a stupor, she complains that her back really hurts and she needs to go to the bathroom badly. Supporting some of her weight with my arms, we maneuver into the bathroom. "It really hurts" she grimaces. "A lot. Feels like labor cramps."

I think we should start to time them. Within ten minutes, while Barbara is sitting on the toilet, she has five contractions, about 2 minutes apart. She's in a lot of pain and complains that she can't move when I try to get her up. My mind starts to race—this could be the start! I ask Ellen to call our doctor's office to report the contractions. Their response is for us to get to the hospital as soon as we can. All this time, I am counting out loud for Barbara *slowly* from one to four, just as we had practiced in childbirth class. She looks terrible and is starting to yell with the pain. I tell her we have to go to the hospital. She looks terrified and says, "no way." She can't even move because of the pain. Ellen yells back that the doctor's office has offered to send an ambulance. We accept. Everything feels like it is happening way too fast. This isn't the way we had rehearsed this little scenario. "Wait," I want to say. The contractions are not waiting. Five minutes later, I look up and there are two firemen in our house outside the bathroom door. Firemen! They stand there, like wooden soldiers not knowing what to do. "Help me get her downstairs," I direct them. At the bottom of the steps Barbara has to lean against the railing, seized by a sharp contraction. Almost continuous, the contractions are getting stronger and stronger. By the time we get to the front door the EMTs have arrived and the firemen are relieved (pun intended). They help me get Barbara onto a stretcher and into the street. At the end of our courtyard there are two ambulances and a long red firetruck in the street along with a crowd of people. "What a spectacle," I have time to think before we are whisked away in a sirening ambulance.

2:30 p.m.: I continue with the breathing and counting while in the ambulance and Barbara starts to feel faint. As the ambulance weaves in and out of traffic, I start to feel nauseous again. Breathing deeply, I try not to think about how I feel and that I want to throw up. Barbara needs me to count and to reassure her. (Who is going to reassure *me*?) The trip is tortuously slow. I make a promise to myself to always get out of the way for ambulance drivers in the future. It's not easy getting through traffic in Boston.

3:00 p.m.: We are rushed into the emergency room. Barbara looks pale; her eyes are glassy, and she is begging for help from every new person she sees. The emergency room nurses quickly determine that the baby's head is not yet crowning and send her up to the labor and delivery room.

3:10 p.m.: The doctor and nurse meet us in the aisle as we zoom into a labor and delivery room. There is a great deal of action and many questions as they put a fetal heart monitor on Barbara's stomach and want to know about contractions, waters breaking, etc. etc. Barbara's not answering, she's in too much pain, so I do the best I can between counting and reassurances. "You're fully dilated," the doctor says. "You can begin pushing." Pushing! I can hardly believe it has happened so quickly. "I can see dark hair coming out," yells the doctor.

"Dark hair, yep that's ours," I want to say. But there's

no time for talk, no time for anything but awe as the baby's head starts to emerge. As I see its head, I think to myself that it's a boy. I don't know how I know, but I do.

One more push and the baby slides out. "It's a boy!" they cry. I just stare, transfixed on the baby and on the fact that a real live human being has come out from Barbara's body. He's small but beautiful.

"We have a son." I squeeze Barbara's hand and kiss her cheek. "We have a son," I repeat over and over in my mind. I like the way it feels. We have a son.

October 15, 1986

Waking up early this morning, I lie in bed alone and ponder the fact that this will be my last morning in such solitude. Barbara and the baby are coming home later today—the start of a new life in this house. The two days since Lee Gregory's birth have been thrilling, fast-paced, and exhausting. I have been filled with wonder each time I've held our baby close to my chest and kissed his head. There is so much warmth, tenderness and love when we touch him. My parents must have felt this way when they held my brother and me: being a new parent makes me feel closer to them. I want to call them and say, "Yes, I understand what it must have been like to welcome us into the world. Thank you for loving me and taking care of me all these years." Even more, I want to share my good news with them, to share how my life has become enriched with this new child. I have called everyone important to me but my parents, whom I have not talked to since that call in September. The impulse to call them is strong, and I go near the phone, but my self-protection wins over. Wonderful news of a baby should not be met by silence or rejection and I cannot risk it.

Instead, I write a letter telling them of the birth, the boy, the changes in my life. I tell them that we are all well, that I miss them, that I'm still the same person I always was, and that I love them. By then, it's time to get dressed and go to pick up Barbara and Lee at the hospital. The baby is coming home with his mothers!

December 25, 1986

Christmas in Hawaii. Just as I've enjoyed it for all these years but this time it's different. Barbara, Lee and I are in Honolulu, as we had made the plans over six months ago, but we're not with my family as I had expected. My parents never responded to my request to stay with them, so we're at a friend's home. The sunlight and warmth are wonderful today. Looking out over the lanai, I can see the familiar landmarks of this city, which I always considered my home. There is a catch in my throat and tears in my eyes when I think of my family. They, too have expressed their sadness at our separation this Christmas: my mother talked of the pain she feels; sometimes at work she remembers I won't be home and why, and she goes to the bathroom to hide her tears. I understood, I said. Sometimes I ride my bike to work and the pain fills me too, catching me during an unguarded moment. I told her it didn't have to be that way, that they could accept all three of us this Christmas. There was only silence and a request to see just me, "no other people." Lee and Barbara are not other people. They are my family, the loves of my life, the joy that greets me each day.

We celebrated Christmas dinner after Lee went to sleep in Alewa Heights, ten miles away from my parents' home. Lee is two-and-a-half months old; I am four months pregnant.

January 11, 1987

Still in Hawaii. These three weeks have passed quickly. It is not difficult to get used to a daily routine of a leisurely breakfast, swimming laps at the pool, naptime in the park, sunsets along the shore, fixing dinner at home. We've been lucky to housesit at a vacationing friend's home so we've established a little family routine with Lee. He is such a delight, so sweet and cheerful, warming our hearts.

Our vacation ends today. Last night I saw my family for the fourth time—alone as they had insisted—and it was awkward again. We went out to dinner and studiously avoided all mention of my pregnancy, Lee, Barbara, or my life in Boston. I felt like I was with strangers, these strangers whom I've known all my life. When I got ready to leave and we said our farewells, they went through the familiar routine of giving me local foods and a flower lei to take back to Boston. I know they still care about me and I wanted to hug them, to plead with them to give my life and new family a chance, to meet my son, Lee. But I said nothing. I accepted their gifts, including a pregnancy Hawaiian blouse, held my tears, and cried on the way home. We'll fly back to reality and Boston later today.

February 25, 1987

Six months pregnant with a four month old on my lap, I'm packing for a business trip to the West coast. I've just finished talking to my parents and need to be productive. While I'm glad that we've resumed our weekly phone conversations again, this one was more upsetting than the usual superficial talk. I can't believe that my mother had the nerve to insist that I not go to San Francisco because "one of our relatives might see me." Her concern about what others might think is causing her shame and worry. I refuse to feel like I'm something to hide. Other conversations with them have left me sad; this time I'm angry.

March 3, 1987

The baby's moving around inside me more and more. It's my favorite part of being pregnant, feeling the squirms and prods. I was dreading yet another confrontation with my mother on the phone, but she asked only about my trip and how did it go? What a relief. Sometimes you *can* win one. I am trying so hard with my parents. In spite of their unreasonableness, I do want to work towards keeping them in my life, and in our kid's lives.

May 20, 1987

Today was my due date and nothing happened. I was sort of hoping to have had the baby by now but I guess there's no rushing the baby if it's not ready to come out. I spoke to my parents on the phone yesterday and told them nothing was happening yet. They sounded uncomfortable when I gave them my pregnancy update. My family has always operated on the principle that if you ignore something enough, it might just go away. They know, though, that this will never go away. Their first grandchild is about to be born: I wish I could share the birth with them, a birth that will transform me (in their eyes) from a daughter to a mother. It is a joyous event that should be trumpeted rather than whispered. In my fatigued, large state today, I started to feel a little cheated by my parents' reaction. There may be some truth in that old saying about a woman wanting *her* mother with her when she has a baby. My need *for* mothering is mixed in with my need *to be* a mother to Lee and to the new baby. So many needs today...

Some of my mothering needs have been met by Barbara and some by *her* mother. She arrived today from Minnesota in hopes that the baby would be born and she could help us out. She's been a wonderful grandmother to Lee and seems to be ready to accept our next baby as her grandchild. I am very glad that our kids will have at least one doting grandmother. She would probably be even more motherly to me if I accepted it, but I'm resistant: I still want to be independent and strong. However, pregnancy and motherhood have a way of wearing me down: I feel much more needy than usual. Fortunately, our friends and my work colleagues have been very supportive; I feel very nurtured and cared for.

May 28, 1987

At 9:19 p.m. tonight, my 42-hour labor ended as the baby

squirted out from my body. I have never felt such an abrupt end to pain accompanied by such a rush of relief in my life. Barbara had tears in her eyes when the nurse cried out, "It's a girl!" We have a daughter! A loud, wrinkled, pink little one. "Your name is Malia Claire," I told her, "you have been long-awaited, and you are welcomed with much love." Barbara and I were able to hold her, kiss her, nurse her (both of us!) for over an hour right after her birth. She is both a result of our hard work *and* a small miracle.

The first person we called with the big news was Barbara's mom, who had returned to Minnesota and missed the birth by four days. "My first granddaughter," she cooed, sounding thrilled. "You did well," she told me. I did, and I was appreciative of her approval as well as her acceptance of Malia and her middle name. (Malia was given Barbara's maternal grandmother's name, Claire, as a middle name in honor of Barbara's mother.)

My long stay in the labor and delivery room was finally coming to an end, and after Barbara accompanied the baby to the nursery, she headed home for some rest.

Alone for the first time in 48 hours, I felt exhausted, relieved, and still excited. Although I wanted to sleep, I felt the need to share my big news so I called a couple of close friends long-distance. Then I decided I really should call my parents. I was a little scared but knew that not only was it the right thing to do, I also wanted to tell them of their granddaughter. They sounded calm, not surprised when I told them the good news. My mother compared this birth with her own labor experiences with my brother and me. It was good to hear those stories. It made me realize that Malia is the newest link in a long chain of children; one day she too will hear my story of her birth. In my exhausted state, I ended the call to my parents without telling them the baby's name. No matter, I thought, before drifting into satisfied sleep, this grandchild of theirs, this welcomed child of lesbian mothers, will make her own name in this world. It is only a matter of time. Time that will soothe the pain, time that will provide the challenge, and time that will see our family grow and flourish.

Paula Martinac

*I was born in 1954 in Pittsburgh to a
working class family, the youngest of three
daughters. I now live in Brooklyn, New York.
I have been writing fiction since I was eight,
and lesbian fiction for the last nine years.
Although I am not a lesbian mother, myself,
my recently completed collection of stories,
<u>Almost There</u>, explores lesbian lives from a
range of viewpoints, including that of lesbian
mothers.*

LIKE MOTHER, LIKE...

Paula Martinac

When Emma got off the plane at Newark airport, her mother wasn't there. She always half-expected her to be standing there, smiling and waving and greeting her like other people were greeting the other passengers. So she was always a little disappointed, even though it was not the kind of thing her mother would do or, in fact, even think of. "You're coming in Friday night?" her mother had said on the phone the other day and almost every time Emma came to town. "Great, honey. I'm going out, but I'll see you late that night or early Saturday." It was usually Saturday, as Emma remembered.

It was a short flight from Boston, and an inexpensive one, and Emma came to New York every other month. She stayed at her mother's apartment on West 16th Street where they'd lived ever since Emma was little. She saw her friends from Barnard and went shopping and to see a play or to AREA on Saturday night. On Sunday morning, she and her mother would sometimes go out for a leisurely brunch and talk about Emma's job at the bank, her mother's graduate classes at Columbia, who they were dating, what books they'd read, and other general chitchat. By the end of the weekend, Emma had had such a good time that she was usually wondering why she'd moved to Boston, but she always went back on Sunday night.

She found a note from her mother when she reached the apartment. "Gone to a forum on Women in Nicaragua. Started at 8, if you get in in time. P.S. 41. If not, see you later. Love, Jessica." She had called her mother "Jessica" for the past ten years or more, but had never really gotten used to seeing it in print. Love, Jessica. Jessica, she knew, would love it if she showed up at P.S. 41 for a political forum. It was only 8:30 and the school was close by. But she would have rather gone out for dinner. If Ben, her boyfriend, had been with her, they would have done just that. She wished the note from Jessica had said, "Meet us at the Odeon." Emma put it down and went into the bathroom to wash her face. She changed from her business suit into jeans and a sweater and settled down on her mother's bed to make some phone calls.

She was annoyed when Alison's answering machine answered instead of Alison. They had made tentative plans to go out. Emma hung up after leaving a slightly curt message and tried Suzanne next. Her roommate said she'd gone to Boston for the weekend. "Would you like her to call you on Monday?"

"Only if she'll still be in Boston," Emma said, explaining that she was just in for the weekend. She tried calling a few more friends whom she hadn't told she was coming into town, but they were all out already enjoying the weekend. Emma pulled on her blazer and went out into the street.

It was almost 9:30 when she strolled past P.S. 41, licking an ice cream cone from Steve's. There was a crowd of women on the street in front of the school, spilling out of the doors, their many conversations becoming one, indistinguishable buzz. She stood to the right of the doors, looking for a face she recognized. Pretty soon she was in a sea of women in blue jeans wearing buttons that said "US Out of Central America" and "No More Vietnams." They were so many types of the same person, she thought—thin, fat, tall, short, white, black, all obviously agitated by whatever had gone on inside. Emma stood watching them, a little afraid that they would sweep her away in their enthusiasm. When she heard, "Jessica, look who I found," she turned gratefully toward the woman who'd put her hand on her shoulder.

"Emma, it's so good to see you again," said the woman, who enveloped Emma in her green trenchcoat. Emma was not sure she would have recognized Laura, her mother's lover, from the last time she'd seen her if she hadn't come up to her first. They had, after all, only had coffee together one morning two months before, and Laura's hair had gotten considerably shorter. It had been shoulder length then but was now only an inch long all over her head.

"Hi, Laura, how are you?" she asked, politely kissing her on the cheek. "Where's my mother?"

"She was right behind me, but in this crowd..." Laura turned and caught Jessica by the hand. "Here she is. This is some crowd, isn't it?"

Jessica hugged Emma tightly. "Honey, you look great. I'm glad you decided to meet us here." She took a bite of the cone. "Cookies and Cream," my favorite," she said, winking at Laura.

Jessica was stunning as always, not beautiful in a conventional way, but bright and dynamic and spontaneous. She always exuded a kind of contagious energy, and her hair and clothes looked as if she'd just run in from somewhere. She took Emma's breath away a little, both literally and figuratively, walking down the street as quickly as she went through her life. Jessica had never had enough time to do everything she wanted to, but she tried very hard. She had managed to cram a lot of events and friends and jobs into the last twenty years that Emma remembered.

"I'm sorry you missed the forum," Jessica said, putting one arm through Laura's and the other through Emma's as they headed toward Sixth Avenue. "It was phenomenal. Presentations by women who recently came back from Nicaragua, with poetry and slides and music. It was really inspiring. Didn't you love it?" she asked, turning toward Laura for confirmation.

Laura nodded less than enthusiastically. "It was well done, but I guess I'm feeling a little inundated with the Women in Central America theme."

"Well, I feel that way sometimes, too, but this was just so moving. Especially the poems. I wanted to go there myself." Jessica turned again toward Emma. "They were beautiful, written by women who'd actually fought in the revolution. You know, it's a whole country of poets practically. That kind of thing really gets to me." Emma smiled weakly and squeezed her mother's arm. "When did you get in, honey?" Jessica continued. "I can't get over how great you look. Doesn't she look great, Laura? I like that haircut a lot. Shorter hair looks better on you, I think, it makes your face look fuller. And speaking of haircuts, what do you think of this crewcut?" she asked, running a hand playfully over Laura's head. "I couldn't believe she did it. Took me a week to get used to it. It's grown out now, you should've seen it two weeks ago."

"I finally tried the Astor Place barbershop," Laura explained. "I think they overdid it a little, but it does feel pretty good. I feel totally butch," she added, putting an arm around Jessica's shoulder. Laura was a tall woman who towered over both Emma and her mother. She was considerably younger than Jessica, probably by about ten or twelve years, but she already had traces of gray in her hair that made her seem the older of the two.

"Where do you want to go?" Jessica asked. "How about Sandolino's?"

Emma said that would be fine, and it was one of the few things she'd said since Laura came up to her in front of the school. It was always that way with Mother and her friends and lovers: they were always coming out of a political meeting or a foreign film or some new lesbian play that made them totally excited and overly talkative. Emma was often included in the plans, Jessica hoping that her daughter would catch the same enthusiasm for political life that she had had as a young antiwar activist and then as a feminist in the women's movement. She had surrounded her daughter with "good people," a seemingly endless string of long-haired, guitar-playing men and women when she was little, and then, when she was an adolescent, of short-haired, guitar-playing women. Emma could chronicle her mother's political transformations through the events of her own life, the fact that at some point they had stopped eating hamburgers and chicken and ate more vegetables and tofu;

the fact that her mother began taking her to Holly Near concerts instead of Peter, Paul, and Mary; the fact that there was first her father and then a lot of men and then almost no men at all in their lives. She was the only girl she knew who had been named for a political figure, Emma Goldman, and who had cats named Sappho and Colette. How many times had she wished for her friend Alison's mother, who wore dresses instead of jeans, even in the house, gave elegant dinner parties for her husband's business clients, and most importantly, acted her age. Jessica had always seemed to be about twenty, as far as Emma could see. Emma had been shocked by Jessica's fortieth birthday four years before, more surprised and incredulous about it than her mother. "I feel great," Jessica had said, and Emma had to admit, she looked it. But she was more a companion than what Emma imagined a mother was, the kind who stayed home, like on television, and cooked and baked and worried about the shine on the floor. It was appropriate that she had almost never called her Mother, except sometimes out of exasperation. "Mother, pu-lease," had been a familiar phrase of her late adolescence, but it had been replaced by "Oh, really, Jessica," after Emma went to college.

"I don't know why I like this place," Jessica was saying, when they'd found a table at Sandolino's. "I've been coming here for years, too. Something about it is like San Francisco and your father," she said to Emma, who didn't remember San Francisco, hardly knew her father, and didn't like the restaurant.

Emma had been born in San Francisco when her father was in graduate school at Stanford, and they had lived there for about four years before coming back to New York, where both of her parents had grown up. Her father had stayed in California, and she had seen him so infrequently since then that he was little more to her than a face in some photographs of her mother's. "We got married too young," Jessica had explained when Emma had asked why she didn't have a live-in father like Alison. "We didn't know each other very well, didn't know what we wanted. The only good thing

that came out of those five years was you—and my
independence."

The waitress checked at their table several times to see
if they were ready to order, but each time Emma ruffled
the pages of her menu and said, a little frantically, "Another
minute, please." Jessica and Laura had already ordered their
food and two draft beers. When the waitress brought the
drinks, Emma closed her menu in a defeated way and said
simply, "I'll take a Heineken." She drank beer rarely,
preferring gin martinis with a twist, and she almost never
ate in coffee shop-like places with menus that went on and
on for pages, mostly, she suspected, to hide the fact that
the food they served wasn't very good.

"Not hungry?" Jessica asked, but she had never been
the kind of mother who worried if her child didn't eat,
especially after Emma reached the age of ten or eleven.
"Emma won't let herself starve," Jessica had pointed out,
when a relative had noticed that thirteen-year-old Emma
was rushing out to a dance with friends instead of finishing
dinner. She was also not the kind of mother who would say,
"You're looking thin," or "You're looking fat"; it just never
would have occurred to her that it was her business to
comment on it.

So the "Not hungry?" was all she said, and then she
started talking about her new Women and Fiction class and
how the professor had been too ambitious in her course plan.
"Of course, there's hardly anything by Third World women
to speak of, just a few thrown in here and there. And not
much mention of the part lesbians played in creating fiction.
I guess I'd just like it acknowledged that Willa Cather was
a lesbian, you know what I mean?"

Emma nodded reluctantly; she was not really sure what
Jessica *did* mean, but Laura seemed to. Laura was watching
Jessica's mouth for every word that came out of it, in such
an obviously advanced state of love that Emma felt a little
embarrassed. She was not sure why, except that on top of
everything—the fact that Jessica didn't cook or bake or wear
dresses or have a husband or act forty-four—she was a

lesbian, too. Emma had gotten used to it, had, in fact, lived with it for over ten years, but it still wasn't something she understood. Emma, for example, thought Laura was an attractive woman, but she couldn't imagine wanting to go to bed with her. What was it that brought two women together like a woman and a man? Jessica had never tried to proselytize and had been very careful not to sway Emma's ideas about sexuality. Emma was eleven when her mother came out to her. "Karen, the woman who stayed over here last night? She's someone I'm very fond of, and I'm going to be seeing a lot of her. She'll be around the house." A long pause. A nervous twitch of Jessica's eye. "Do you know what the word 'homosexual' means?"

Emma had said that some kids used the words "homo" and "faggot" at school to mock out the sissy boys.

"Well, you should never do that, because it's not a bad thing to be a homosexual. It's just different from what most people are used to. And you shouldn't call people 'queer' either."

"Why not?" Emma asked, watching the little beads of perspiration appearing on her mother's forehead.

"It's like 'nigger,' it's offensive, it puts people down who haven't hurt you," Jessica answered in a defensive tone, rubbing the back of her hand over her forehead. Another long pause. "I have to tell you this, because I want you to hear it from me, not at school or in the street. I'm..."

Emma had felt her heart race, not making the connection between the last few minutes of conversation and what Jessica was trying to say. For a moment she was convinced Jessica was dying.

"...a homosexual, a lesbian. I don't expect you to understand right now, and I know I'm botching this up, but if I ever hear you say 'queer' or 'dyke,' I'll...I'll...oh, I don't know what I'll do."

Jessica had left the room, flushed and shaking. Later that day and on several more occasions when she was calmer, Jessica had tried to explain things better, using funny words like "woman-identified." Emma had been totally confused for a long time, and had wondered if she, too, would become a lesbian because her mother was one and didn't used to be. Emma remembered when her mother had had several boyfriends at one time. Maybe Emma would become "queer," too, later on, unless there was something she could do to prevent it.

She worried when, at twelve, she had fooled around with James Lyle after school and he had put his tongue in her mouth. "What are you *doing*?" she asked in horror, sure that she would get some terrible disease from having a strange tongue inside her mouth. Maybe that was a sign, she thought, the first indication that the old saying was right: Like mother, like daughter. After worrying about it for days, during which she avoided James and most of her other friends, she finally blurted out her fear to her mother. Jessica smiled and put her arm around her. "But lesbians do that to each other, too, honey. Do you think it was James you didn't like, or just the tongue, or boys in general? What if Alison or one of your girlfriends had done that to you?"

Emma had to admit that she didn't think she would have liked that any better, that in fact kissing James at first had been sort of nice, until he'd opened up his mouth. "I think my being a lesbian confuses you about yourself, but it doesn't have anything to do with you. You'll make your own decisions when you're ready."

At eighteen, her first semester at Barnard, Emma had decided to sleep with Michael and then decided to keep doing that for a while. Over the next few years, she decided on other boys whom she liked or loved in varying degrees. She never decided on any women. Her senior year, she became engaged to a law student, whom she'd been dating for about a year. But it broke off when he started talking about a baby within the first year of marriage. She'd moved to Boston after graduation, where she'd gotten the best job offer, and spent some time alone before starting to see Ben, the man she was still involved with. Ben worked as a loan officer at the bank where she was in international marketing. They hadn't talked about marriage—she thought twenty-three was still too young—but he was the kind of man she thought she could be with for a long time. They had similar goals. They both wanted careers in banking and money to do all the things they liked. They both wanted a Victorian house with antiques and a sailboat and a summer place on the Cape. Ben was ambitious, something Emma admired a lot, and he'd moved up at the bank quickly since he'd started there five years before, just out of Harvard Business School. He was a little more conservative than Emma was used to, but not old-fashioned in his view of women. He always told her he admired her determination to have a career and thought she would probably be an assistant vice-president at the bank within a short time.

Emma had not brought him home to meet her mother yet; it was something she thought she should work up to. She had told her mother all about him one day over brunch, and Jessica had asked a lot of polite questions without making comments on the answers. Jessica always inquired about him on Emma's subsequent visits home and said she'd like to meet him. But Emma had overheard a conversation between Jessica and Laura the last time she'd been in New York, when they were sitting over coffee in the kitchen and didn't know she was up yet.

"She told me he voted for Reagan, and that that bothered her," Jessica said.

"Well, at least that's something," Laura replied. "At least *she* didn't vote for him. At least it bothered her."

"I know, but how many times have you heard of people in love affecting each other's opinions? We do it with each other in little ways all the time. And she's gotten to be so materialistic since college. When I ask how she is, she tells me what she's bought recently. She had a really liberal upbringing, but sometimes I think she wants to rebel against it, that all along she hated the way I dealt with her." There was a crack in Jessica's voice. "Well, it *is* my doing. I brought her up to be her own person, and here she is. I guess there's no guarantee your kids will want to be like you. I just always thought my way was the best, such a clear choice, that she'd naturally grow up to be a liberal, maybe even a lesbian. But when you think about it, I certainly didn't want to turn out like my mother," Jessica had sighed heavy-heartedly. "Sometimes I feel so stupid, like I should say to myself, she's my daughter and I love her and she's a good peson and who cares if she's turned into a heterosexual Yuppie. God, sometimes I wish I weren't so political, that it didn't really matter to me."

It was one of the first glimpses she'd really had of her mother, the first realization that there was disappointment on both sides of their relationship. Just like Emma had wished for Alison's mother, Jessica had probably wondered, "Why can't Emma be like Alice Rosen's daughter, Terra, who does solidarity work? Or Eva Kincaid's Lisa who's living with her lover at the women's peace camp?" Or maybe she just wondered why, of all possible professions, Emma had to choose banking, the most conservative of all, and actually like it. Why did she value a style of living that was foreign to Jessica? Sometimes Emma wondered, too. Sitting at the table in Sandolino's, across from her mother and her lesbian lover, Emma wondered where on earth she had come from.

They finished their order and Emma picked up the bill to pay for it. "I just got a raise, I forgot to tell you," she explained. "My treat." But she had not forgotten to tell her, Emma had just thought Jessica would take the information in about the same way she would "I missed the bus today" or "Ben bought a new suit." She was right: both Jessica and Laura thanked her and said congratulations, before moving on to the next topic. Ben had taken her out to dinner to celebrate, to an expensive restaurant for fresh lobster. She would never dream of telling Jessica that. Jessica didn't eat lobster and thought it practically criminal to do so. "I can't get past the way they kill them," she'd say. It would only make the disappointment more acute: she wouldn't lecture Emma, just talk about it with Laura that night in bed or the next morning over coffee.

They walked home at Jessica's usual clip, Laura entertaining them with stories of characters she'd run into in the Village. She was very amusing and Emma found herself feeling fond of her. To Emma's surprise, they dropped Laura off at her apartment on West 10th before continuing on home.

"I thought she'd stay over," Emma commented, when they were on their way again.

"Oh, we see each other all the time," Jessica said. "We talked about living together, but neither of us wants to give up our apartment! Anyway, Laura has to get up early to go to a conference tomorrow."

"You're not going?" Emma asked incredulously. She had never known her mother to miss a conference on purpose, and she was sure if it interested Laura, it would interest Jessica, too.

"No," Jessica said. "I have to work on an article about the forum tonight for the feminist newspaper. It's due Sunday, and I promised. What are your plans?"

Emma's heart sank to her stomach. For a minute, she had imagined that her mother was giving up the conference to be with her and had planned an afternoon of shopping and cocktails.

"I tried to reach Alison," Emma said, trying not to sound disappointed, "but she wasn't home. I guess I'll try again tomorrow. I don't have any definite plans."

After a pause, Jessica said, "Maybe I can finish the article early and we can have brunch." She hesitated, wondering if Emma would prefer to make plans with her friends.

But Emma was answering, "That would be great. If you're sure it's no problem."

"I'm positive," Jessica reassured her, already wondering how early she would have to get up to finish the article in time.

They reached the apartment, and Jessica went first to the answering machine. There were a few miscellaneous messages, including one from Alison, and a "Goodnight, I love you" one from Laura. "I think I'll go call her, then try to do a little reading for class. Your old mother's out of the swing of this homework stuff. I never thought going back to graduate school full time would be so hard to adjust to. It's even more tiring than working and taking a class at night, I think." Jessica smiled and kissed her on the cheek. "Goodnight, honey. Nice to have you home again."

Emma started into her old bedroom, but heard Jessica calling her before she'd reached it. "Oh, Emma, I forgot. You need sheets on the bed. You know where they are, right? Goodnight."

Emma grabbed some sheets and a blanket out of the linen closet on her way to the bedroom. She switched on the light and looked at the bare twin bed in front of her. It was just another thing Jessica would never do, for whatever reason. She shrugged, made the bed, and decided to wait until Jessica was off the phone so she could call Ben.

Bonnie Morris

I am a Ph.D candidate in Women's History and am teaching part time while completing my doctoral dissertation on Hasidic women. My roots are Jewish, Welsh, Norwegian, Californian. I was raised by incredibly supportive and creative parents. At twenty-six, I am living in a small cold valley in upstate New York, and am blessed with the companionship of a sweet and brilliant woman. I cultivate lesbian energy through research, political activism, acting, soccer, music festivals and conferences on feminism.

My parenting experience occurred from 1985–1986, when I befriended the young son of a woman I had come to love. This essay is dedicated to her.

LOVING THE FIVE YEAR OLD

Bonnie Morris

When I came out as a lesbian at the age of eighteen, I resigned myself to the possibility of never having children. I had ruled out traditional marriage to a husband, and was not prepared to investigate the alternative options of lesbian parenting: adoption or artificial insemination. For the next six years I buried any maternal longings I had once cultivated.

In the summer of 1985, reading the Old Testament as part of my studies in Jewish History, I was struck by the endless references to childbirth and the strong images of women as mothers. For the first time I realized that I, too, as a lesbian, had the potential to be a great strong Jewish mother. I began to think seriously about having a child someday, and to contemplate the changes this would mean for my ambitions, habits, and schedules.

Within two months a child entered my life. I became involved with a young lesbian mother whose five year old son was very much a part of our relationship. From the very beginning I was struck by my sense of responsibility to Lucky, by my awareness of his concerns and way of thinking, and, certainly, by my own shortcomings in sharing my life or time with him. I spent nearly every other night with my lover, but as she could not leave Lucky alone and b abysitters were hard to come by in our small poor town, I spent those nights at her house in the space she shared with Lucky. Thus I entered into a relationship with two people at once, on their turf, and undertook a curriculum of parenting along with my rigorous graduate school studies.

Lucky's mother is a sign language interpreter who was raised by deaf parents. She, herself, is hearing, as is Lucky, but they communicate in sign as well as in spoken English. The diverse levels of communication in their household fascinated and occasionally exhausted me. One night at a restaurant, the three of us signing and talking, I signed to my lover, "I think you're a good mother." Lucky had observed this, tugged my sleeve, and signed to me, "But *you're* a good mother too." I still regard this as one of the highest compliments I've ever received.

I nearly burst with pride (there's an expression that's fun to sign) when I took Lucky places in public, helped him select a Halloween pumpkin, taught him to light Chanukah candles. At the same time I was aware that I was able to enjoy a share in all his achievements with very little of the responsibility for raising him. His clever mind and quick trust enhanced my feelings for his mother, and I began to respect their intimate bond as nearly psychic in its manifestations. When she and I would make love, cry, or argue, Lucky instinctively woke up, no matter how quiet we had been. He responded to the level of our emotions and to his mother's intensity several rooms away, and would rise from sleep to come snuggle between us. When I spent the night without his prior knowledge he responded enthusiastically in the morning, shouting "My Bonnie's here!" He was also able to express his feelings of frustration when he thought I was spending too much time at his house.

I discovered my limitations as a disciplinarian, my respect for the difficult role of single mom, and my own longings to rekindle the spontaneous creativity of childhood. I aggressively defended the pride and legitimacy of lesbian motherhood, showing Lucky's photo to strangers on the bus like any eager relation, contributing money to his alternative school, and never hesitating over my relationship to him when asked.

The three of us went camping several times in the fall— hilarious experiences wherein I realized that my role as an adult in charge required me to assuage Lucky's natural fears and apprehensions in the dark forest. I had to gloss over my own nervousness, overcome my ineptitude at lighting at fire, cooking outdoors, setting up a tent, reading a map, etc. in order to keep Lucky's anxieties at bay. This necessary capability was just one part of my entire education in "family" life: what is *needed*? What are the practical steps and solutions? Who's looking out for the kid? On a camping trip the line between child and adult behavior becomes blurred rapidly. I scolded Lucky for jumping into the creek in his hiking shoes, but had the laugh at my expense later when I fell asleep in front of the campfire and melted off both soles of my own boots.

While our relationship is close and loving still, when my lover and I broke up I felt a horrible loss: I was separating from not one but two people. I had lost a family. And later I came to feel a keen sense of shame over just how I had come to end the romance; could Lucky ever understand? What must he have thought of me and my behavior? A new person had lived at his house for months and now was gone. Sensitive to his dormant opinions of lesbianism, which were being formulated now and would emerge later in his childhood and adolescence, I wanted Lucky to retain *good* images of me. I did not wish to be blandly forgotten. Eventually I knew that to better understand the dynamics of this special family, it was my responsibility to educate myself about deaf culture and communication patterns in hearing children of the deaf. Plunging into these lessons brought me back to my friends with new humility and love. But while I was trying to sort out my feelings, Lucky and his mother were continuing their own lives and ambitions, and have now moved to another town.

Lucky has just lost his two front teeth, and I cried because I wasn't there.

Donna (Danny) Romito

I am the forty-one year old mother of two grown children. I became a mother (once biological and once adoptive) while married but, since my divorce and entrance into the gay world, my lover and I have raised and cared for both children. I live in a small town in Florida and spend my most relaxing moments up at the ranch with the horses and walking the pastures in between the dairy cows. Next to writing, my second love is dancing and I try to go into Gainesville as much as possible to mingle and dance with the gals.

HIT THE BULL'S EYE

Donna (Danny) Romito

The white sandy beach is 17 miles away and the tourists pass through but rarely stop over. Your average local resident is a down-to-earth, hard working farmer or fisherman with a few professionals and blue collar workers thrown in. The country is just that—country. Jeans and boots are the everyday fashion of necessity, and it's common to see an occasional horse or two tied up in front of one of the local stores.

It would be so easy to say that these were all the things Diane and I were looking for when we left our hometown of Youngstown, Ohio and headed southward to the state of Florida. The year was 1980 and Cross City was a place on the map we didn't even know existed. Now we own a home here in this quaint little town where progress seems to avoid arriving. But this is getting ahead of my story. Let me go back to the beginning.

In 1975 we both became newly divorced women. We met while each of us was still married, fell in love, and decided to be WHO and WHAT we really were inside. Both Diana's divorce and mine involved a great deal of bitterness because we never denied being in love nor kept it hidden. At the time my two children were seven and nine years of age and I took a big chance of possibly losing them, but Diane and I had agreed that there would be truthfulness throughout the relationship... and that included the children.

At the same time we discovered other things: banks wouldn't talk to us, loan companies wouldn't give us the time of day. Along with the two straight marriages went our legal identities. We didn't have BAD credit, just NO credit. There was no longer a MRS. and the MS. was finding it awfully difficult to begin a new life.

Living on a cash only basis was the most difficult thing we'd ever had to do in our lives. Paying the rent and utilities waon't a problem for we had jobs, but emergencies like new tires, medical bills...well...it was rough. The kids had to have school clothes and supplies, and in the summer they always were in need of tennis shoes and play clothes. They weren't dressed like the richest kids on the block, but they were always provided for and were always neat and clean.

In 1977 things began to change. The changes didn't just happen; we made them happen. My family owned a pizza parlor and Diane and I made arrangements to take over a delivery service for my aunt and uncle. Our days began before 10:00 A.M. and kept at a steady pace until well after 2:00 A.M. some nights. The better the delivery got, the better business got, and the longer the hours became. In between deliveries we were back and forth to the house to check on the kids, but most times they were right there with us. Michelle learned to make quite a good pizza and Chris enjoyed walking up to doors to do some of the deliveries. They both enjoyed eating the pizza, too.

Diane doesn't even like pizza but she and I took pride in offering a dependable and quick service. After awhile we were seeing those pies in our sleep.

That same year Diane's foster son-in-law gave us the break we needed. When Diane was married she had taken in a foster child. There had been no agency involved or anything like that, just a matter of friends, circumstances, and a child's need for help. Besides a mother-daughter relationship Diane and Rita became best of friends. Rita and her husband now have three beautiful daughters. They call Diane "Grandma" and me "Aunt Donna."

Rita's husband co-signed a loan for us to buy a mobile home in a trailer park and to begin the establishment of our own lines of credit. Since that time we have had three loans on our signatures alone. That, in itself, is a darn good feeling.

With the support of each other we made it through many

a rough time and in 1980 we decided to move to Florida. Diane was forty-four and I was ten years younger. We certainly weren't young chicks, but off we headed with the children for the sunshine, palm trees, and the prospects of a fuller life ahead. Michelle and Chris kept saying, "Are we there yet?" and they were as anxious as we were to see where our new life would take us.

Ten days after arriving in Florida, on July 10th, we found a farmer who needed help on his barn crew for tobacco picking. We worked the barns that whole summer. Chris went into the fields along with the other boys his age and Michelle helped right along beside us at the barns. In September Diane started work for a lumber yard in Cross City where she "pitched boards" eight hours a day. We moved from the little trailer we'd been living in and rented the house that we now own.

While still working at the lumber yard Diane went to the local drive-in one evening and there she saw a HELP WANTED sign tacked up on the side of the concession counter. She went to the owner and offered him a family deal—she, myself, and my two kids took over management, concession, and the projector. We learned to splice film, repair reels, and cook up a pretty darn tasty hamburger. Michelle learned to put out some good grill meals and Chris became quite good at girl watching.

We ran that drive-in for over two years until it was closed down. Then it was decision time again for Diane and me. We went through the necessary steps and, in 1983, we began our own cleaning and maintenance business. For three years now "D & D" has been servicing the area. The community knows WHO and WHAT we are. We are accepted and we've managed to make a pretty good life for ourselves. Both my children are now in their twenties; Chris is in the U.S. Navy and Michelle works at a local restaurant.

I am the first to admit that Diane and I are the exception to the rule. Things could have turned out *very* differently for all of us. Some individuals cannot divulge their true lifestyle because of certain aspects in their lives. Diane and

I know in our hearts that what we have and feel for each other is good and we are fortunate enough to be able to mentally handle living with society's still archaic views. I was also fortunate to have two children who accepted it from the very first and they have backed up Diane and me many a time. Back when both children were still in grade school in Ohio; a school chum of Chris' was told by his mother not to play with Chris and his sister because their mother and friend were those kind of "queer" people. My son went straight to his friend's mother and said, "I know my mom and Diane live together and I know why— cause they love each other. They care about people and they don't hurt people...which is more than I can say for you." The mother and I stayed cleared of one another, but Chris and his school chum remained friends. I cannot help but be a proud mother.

A friend once asked if we had to do it all over again, would we? If we had to do it all over again we'd do it without a blink of the eye. For every legal battle I remember I also remember the love and support I got from Diane and my children. For all the hard times we've been through I remember the closeness it brought to each of us. For every bad moment, it seems as if a good moment arose from it. When the television quit working and we were without that means of nightly entertainment we found that we became even closer with the kids by spending that time talking with them, playing board games, and learning even more about one another. Many nights I would cry and worry over the possibility of losing my children through the courts because of my remaining true to myself and my lifestyle. I would turn around and there were my son and daughter; they'd wrap their arms around me, hug me tight, and tell me how much they loved me. For all these reasons and so much more, there is no doubt in either of our minds that we would surely do it all again.

It isn't easy. I don't think it was ever meant to be. A very easy way of life is sometimes taken too much for granted. In our relationship no one ever takes anything for granted. There are always too many other outside views, opinions, and prejudices.

Diane will soon be fifty-one and I will be forty-one come October. In the last eleven years we have accomplished so much. If it weren't for the love and understanding Diane and I share for one another I don't think either of us would have done half the things we have. An important part of it all is the relationships of three generations: my parents know, don't quite understand, but accept; Diane and I in our love for each other; and my children's knowledge, understanding, and acceptance.

Each and every one of us has given it our best shot... and we seem to have hit the bull's eye.

Susan D. Eschbach

I am thirty-one, very Aries, and my favorite autumn leaves are the yellow ones with red specklings. My work with special needs children keeps me challenged and hopeful as I watch subtle changes become great triumphs. I write poetry, narratives, lesbian erotica, and social issues curriculums. Presently my rural self is planted in the city where I play rugby, wish for more naps on the grass in the sun, and hope to be a mother in the next year or so.

JOURNAL ENTRY

Susan D. Eschbach

Today I sit with Hara in my roomy kitchen, drinking morning coffee and poking into pink grapefruit sections with the pointiest spoon I could find in the chaos of the silverware drawer. I stare out the window, captured for a moment by the effects of this early November snowfall.

The branches are transformed into white criss-crosses and lattice-work, "like fat, fat white pipecleaners," Hara said in bed this morning as we looked out the window. We are quiet. She reads and sips. I sit with my thoughts, stringing one with the next, weaving whole concepts and then changing the warp for a new pattern. The clock marks our day from the kitchen wall but we are in no hurry. The outside world of schools and work has been called off, bustling Boston delayed.

I am aware of this contented silence, of having my own inner dialogue. I enjoy lingering over my second cup of mocha java, putting my spoon down between bites of pink squirty citrus as I write in this journal that I so often have no time for.

There are no children in this apartment. No one to get breakfast for, no crashing around with toys or books or boots for the snow. There are no shouts about the day off from school or slammings out the door to find sleds or make snow angels. No one is asking me for attention, for help with snaps, for a cup of hot chocolate. I am not reminding anyone about hats or lunchtime or bedmaking.

I am here with Hara, enjoying our relationship, the privileges of quiet, of good coffee, of a day off. Do I want to change this?

I finger the edges of this brown mug, an old one left over from a midnight stop at Perkins Pancake House years ago. It's the last one, having survived yard sales and Salvation Army donations. It reminds me of the years that led me to this kitchen, to this city even.

I've come here with a sense of deep commitment to myself as a lesbian, to be as "out" as possible, to educate others about my life, to help make changes in the texture of our social fabric. Getting here has meant losses. Rural Pennsylvania—beautiful farmland, rolling ridges, deep pines, (conservative, provincial, oppressive)—feels lost to me.

The women I embraced still remain with women but never utter words that describe, define, or celebrate those relationships. We used to sit in diners and bars, country music on the jukebox ("How can I keep lovin' you, when I know that yer not true..."), singing along and bantering with the men whose tractor trailer rigs sat outside. Meanwhile, my "friends" and I played footsie with each other under the tables. We looked meaningfully at each other when the lyrics strummed our hearts. ("I was so lonely, cried for you only, my-y luh-uh-uhve"). We came to Tobey's Country Tavern after our softball games and drank to dissolve the boundaries between us, to excuse our touchings and fumblings, and to contrive a reason for staying the night together.

When I became politicized (sparked by finding Jill Johnston's *Lesbian Nation* in the college library), when I began naming and claiming an identity and stood proudly to announce it, they rejected me. I threatened the safety of their closets. They denied my lover-relationships with them and filled the air with hatred and disgust.

I left to find a place where I could break molds and shape myself anew. A new community, important work, proud relationships, and a decision to stop drinking freed me to pursue this life I now have.

I am thirty years old, soon to be thirty-one. On this snowy day I realize I've been thinking about those door slammings and winter hats for over five years. I've been thinking about night time tuck-ins and pictures magnetted to the refrigerator door. About snow tracks on the linoleum, breakfasts, no days off. About doctors' appointments and diapers and school shoes. About a large size can of Bandaids and extra towels.

These images tug at my belly and pull at my chest. I feel an ache between my shoulders. I imagine pride swelling my cheeks when the snowperson is built or when the handwriting sheet comes home. I imagine irritation set in my jaw and giving a blowy sigh when muddy boots track in. I feel a gnawing fear about night falling and no ruffled head appearing at the door. I feel excitement and a tearful wonder when I imagine listening to first words, first readings aloud, first friendships by these little ones. I fill up to picture a cuddle, a hand held, a tear kissed away. And, I imagine exhaustion, complete and utter exhaustion. Such a fullness of experiences I yearn for, fear shakily, and probably idealize.

I keep up these thinkings and wonderings. I hold a constant vigil, watching over my life. Wondering when I will have the right amount of money, the right sense of stability, the right support system or partner, the right place to live. I am aware that my model is my mother who prided herself on thrifty planning, stretching pennies, finding the best bargains to make Dad's paycheck last as long as the pay period. I feel proud of her resourcefulness for a family of six. Yet, I don't want to be in that position. I've begun to appreciate my opportunity to buy Vermont cheddar instead of Velveeta, and Progresso soup instead of WeisMarket brand. I struggle between believing in the foolhardiness of such purchases and believing that more expensive food is healthier. I wonder how these issues will change, what resourcefulness I will need to fall back on. I have models only of parenting under sacrifices and I wonder which sacrifices will be mine. I want the right answers to the onslaught of questions. I wonder when I will just know.

How can I anticipate the extent to which my life, my

habits, schedules, relationships, inner dialogues will be altered. I expect a seismic shift in my view of the world, a sliding of deeply settled plates that have grounded my daily expectations. I expect a rumbling powerful change.

I try to think of daily manageable specifics. I will get up in the morning long before going to work. I'll brush my own teeth and see to other brushings. Brush more hair than my own. And socks! I barely keep my own matched, especially in the bleary-eyed earliness of a workday. Worry over a fever, anger at some resistance, a flurry of arrangements for childcare may fill my mornings and the space in my mind for mulling about other concerns. I wonder if the space I use thinking about my lover, my colleagues, my mother, my rugby team even, will be filled up with kid-thoughts, or will they all get crammed into the same space, only crunched and tight. Perhaps I'll expand my head, my heart, the stretch between my shoulders, and my belly-groan-and-laugh spot.

I sit here writing at my kitchen table in quiet privacy, feeling gripped with the anxiety of the unknowns and, at the same time, eagerly hoping to work it all out.

The fantasy: the child tucked under a soft blanket with leftover bedtime story thoughts, my lover on the couch reading, finally a calm in the house, and I am writing. A clang startles me as the cat knocks over a bike and I remember holding the back fender, steadying the bike, and slowly letting go as the first ride was taken this morning. I rub my tired eyes and smile. I turn out the light.

I am pulled from this reverie as questions dart back in about how I will choose. There is a new wave of mothering; "lesbians choosing children" we say. This is a lot to choose. No simple answers here. No paths well traveled. In my family there are few examples of discussing choice. Life just happens. People marry, babies come, families grow, and the patterns of generations repeat themselves. No one wonders if it's the right thing to do, for the right reasons, at the right time.

Yet, models are being shaped. Women are doing this

"choosing." I watch.

I watch two-year-olds toddle in overalls around the coffee shop while mommy has coffee and the paper. I hear my nephew on the phone, his high pitched voice describing his day at school, the turkey he made by gluing pumpkin seeds onto a paper plate. I listen as a mother and her teenage daughter struggle to agree on rules of independence. I know women, ten years older than I, finishing the adolescence of their children and beginning new friendships with them as young women and men. What am I considering starting?

The sun outside the kitchen window is liquifying the snow on the tree limbs. Hara touches my arm and I grin. My coffee is cold. It's a great day to walk downtown for some lunch.

Margo

> *I'm fourteen years old, love to go shopping, and swimming is my favorite sport. I'm Puerto Rican and have traveled to New York and Puerto Rico, where I'd like to go back to.*

Shelley

> *I'm fifteen. My favorite pastime is swimming and I run indoor track. I'm really interested in being an artist or art therapist.*

"Tania"

> *"Tania" is fourteen years old.*

ACTUALLY..... IT'S KIND OF BETTER

Margo, Shelley and "Tania"

This interview was conducted in the home of Julia Perez and Cheryl Kennedy. Cheryl is the adoptive parent of Shelley. Julia is the biological mother of Margo and the adoptive mother of Maria. "Tania," who chose to use a pseudonym, lives with her mother, but has been raised part-time as family, with Margo, Shelley and Maria.

Interviewer: Do most of your friends know that your parents are lesbians?

Margo: Probably. They don't say anything about it.

Interviewer: How would they know? How would they have figured it out?

Margo: Because we all live in the same house and they always see us all together, so it's kind of obvious.

Tania: Because of the bulletin board and stuff.

Margo: Yeah, I try and hide stuff when people walk in, but probably most of my friends know.

Interviewer: Do they ever ask you directly?

Tania: My friends don't. My mother's girl friend doesn't live with us. My mom keeps stuff out but I make a point of putting it away when someone is going to come over. Margo's pretty much of a flake when it comes to things like books laying on the table face up! People come in the room and a book is on the bed and Margo's like "Ehhh" and sits on it.

Margo: But nobody says anything, so it doesn't really

matter. It's not really the topic of anybody's gossip.

Interviewer: Nobody cares much about anybody else's mother, right?

Margo: Yeah, they don't really pay attention to it.

Tania: I mean, you think they do, because out on the street you're like, "Ma, don't..... Ma, don't walk near her. Let me walk between you."

Margo: I used to do that all the time. I used to always walk between my mother and Cheryl. I used to make Cheryl walk at the curb and my mother on the inside and I'd walk right in the middle and Shelley would walk next to Cheryl and Maria would walk in front of us. So it wouldn't be really obvious. But it probably was, because we always caused such a scene.

Interviewer: So you're saying you want to hide it and at the same time you don't want to hide it.

Margo: Well, I try, but it doesn't do anything.

Tania: Because her parents, you know, Margo's mother and Shelley's mother live together, a lot more of their friends know. I don't think any of my friends know.

Margo: It's harder to hide it. I mean people say, "Why do they live together?" And you make up all these stories and they don't even fit together so people obviously think that, you know....

Tania: I just live with my mother, so there's not much of a scene created. Once a week I have to stay over at my mother's girlfriend's house and I just tell everyone that it's my godmother.

Margo: My mother tries to make up stories sometimes, but it doesn't work because they make no sense. "Oh my girlfriend, my brother's ex-wife's sister..." It doesn't make any sense so she just says "my girlfriend."

Interviewer: If other kids do find out, even though they don't say anything, how do you feel about that?

Margo: I don't really care. I used to care but I don't care anymore.

Tania: They wouldn't say anything. I mean that's tacky.

Margo: I used to be real embarrassed. One of my girlfriends asked me once and I was really embarrassed. I was like, "No! What are you talking about? Where did you get that idea from?" But it turned out that her mother was gay too, so it was like "Well, what the hell." So I just said, "Yeah, I lied to you a little bit when you came over."

Interviewer: If a kid that you knew said something mean or got nasty about either of your parents what would you say in response?

Margo: It depends on who it was. If it was just a stupid person out on the street that knew who my mother was and knew who I was, but we really didn't know each other—just someone walking down the street saying "I saw your mother and her mother in the newspaper one time" (Editor's note: Julia and Cheryl appeared in a newspaper article on Lesbian Mothers) I would say "Glad you read the paper." But, if it was one of my friends, then I'd feel bad because I don't think that's right. If you don't like the way people are, then you should just keep it to yourself.

Tania: That's kind of like...I mean, they wouldn't like it if you walked up to them and said something about their mother.

Margo: "Your mother has a husband. Hah, ha, ha!" But people don't do that. I don't see it. There's no sense. It doesn't make any sense to do that.

Interviewer: Do you feel different from other kids?

Margo: No, because I'm the total opposite of my mother. So I don't feel different. I don't feel different from anybody else.

Interviewer: And is that OK? Is it good to feel like other kids?

Margo: Oh yeah. I mean I don't know...I used to feel different. I used to be like, "Oh God, can I be her friend?" Because I used to go to my friends' houses and you know, the mother, the father, the little brother and big sister and everything and then they'd come to my house and...it was just like me and Shelley and Maria and Cheryl and my mother and it was totally different than everybody else's lifestyle so like, wow, I don't know if I can be her friend because what if she comes over and she thinks something.

Interviewer: Since you've gotten older do you feel that's less important?

Margo: Yeah. I don't care. If they don't want to be my friend because of my mother, that's their business. They're not worth being friends.

Interviewer: Do you remember how old you were when you were feeling that way you just described?

Margo: Last year.

Interviewer: Really? That's sort of a recent change. What grade are you two in?

Margo: I'm in 9th and she's in 10th.

Interviewer: We'e been talking about friends for a while, let's talk a little bit about families. You're about to have a new family member...how do you feel about Cheryl's pregnancy?

Both: I love it.

Tania: I think it's good.I think it's real good because she's wanted that for a while. She's always wanted a baby.

Margo: Yeah, she considers Shelley her daughter but she really wants to have a baby.

Interviewer: So would you consider it another sister or brother?

Margo: Yeah.

Interviewer: How do you describe your family to people?

Both: Sisters, all four of us.

Tania: Margo thinks up the best stories about explaining it. She tells everybody, "Yeah, me and Shelley have the same father and..."

Margo: No, I say Shelley and Tania have the same father. I say, I have a different father than they do, but we're related because my mother.... Me and Shelley have the same father but different mothers, and Shelley and Tania have the same father but different mothers and so me and Tania are related through Shelley, and Tania's related to me through.....

Tania: And by that time the person is like, "Oh yeah...?"

Interviewer: How will you explain Cheryl's baby? Same father again? Will you say it's the same guy who came around again?

Margo: I say it's Shelley's mother's, but it's a different guy so then we don't have to explain the whole thing over again.

Tania: By then the person is lost.

Margo: They're busy. All these husbands!

Tania: They're lost. They're just like, "That's right, You're sisters. Uh-hmmm."

Margo: "OK, I believe you. Don't explain it."

Interviewer: At that point they really don't need much information.

Tania: A lot of people think me and Shelley look alike. I don't see it.

Margo: They do. They have the same hairdo. Their eyes.

Tania: No, her eyes...Her hair is like...I have Sun-In in my hair and so does she, so her hair is lighter and her eyes are the same color and mine are like green or blue depending on what I'm wearing.

Margo: They look alike.

Tania: The thing is that she's kind of short like me, but she's built different, very different. And it's amazing, see because when we're at the pool people mistake me and I'm like, "No, no, no, no, no..." You'll see. When she comes in you'll see what I'm talking about.

Interviewer: Do kids have a reaction because of your different races? Does that come up?

Margo: No. We say we're all Puerto Rican. That I'm half Puerto Rican, half Black, but that Shelley and Tania are all Puerto Rican.

Interviewer: What are you for real, Tania?

Tania: My mother, she's Jewish, Russian Jews all the way back. And my father I think he has English and French in him. But, lots of my friends are Puerto Rican. In my school it's really separated. All the white kids hang out together. All the Black kids hang out together. And I just happen to hang with whoever I want to. A lot of my friends are Black because I hang with Shelley and Margo and a lot of their friends are Black.

Margo: But it's different because Shelley hangs with more Black kids than I do and I hang with more white kids than Shelley does. It never really made a difference to us, the color, ...if you were purple or yellow.

Interviewer: It sounds like you were brought up that way.

Tania: Yeah, your awareness is more if you're raised by lesbians than if you're raised by straight parents or...especially straight white parents.

Margo: I think that's just the way it is. It seems like it's that way with a lot of families, not only white people. It's Black people, Puerto Rican people, Chinese people, too. I mean if you have a Black family, they don't teach you, "I want you to go out and get a white boyfriend." And you don't see white families saying, "I want you to go out and get a Black boyfriend or a Puerto Rican boyfriend..." You just don't see that.

Interviewer: Your family outside this house? Is that what you mean?

Tania: Yeah, she calls Cheryl's mother Nana.

Margo: I call her Nana. And Shelley calls my grandmother Abuela, you know, in Spanish. I think they'd prefer me to go out and get a Puerto Rican boyfriend rather than a white boyfriend. And I'm sure Cheryl's family wants Shelley to get someone white instead of Black or Puerto Rican, or whatever. I think it's just like that.

Interviewer: Do you feel judgment from your extended families about being in a lesbian family as well as the race stuff?

Margo: In my family, sometimes from my uncles. Not all my uncles, because some of them really consider Cheryl their sister, their blood sister. But two of my uncles, I don't think they accept my mother for what she is. I'm sure they'd prefer her to go out and get a husband and get married and have four kids like they do. One uncle, he really treated Cheryl bad. He didn't respect her at all. I mean he knew her name but he'd find a way to aggravate her. He'd call her "Charlie."

Tania: And Cheryl's the kind of person that will say, "No, no, that is not my name."

Margo: And they corrected him all the time, but he just felt he had to aggravate her. My other uncle, he's not really like that. He didn't really treat her bad, but it was just like... they didn't really pay attention to her. Like she wasn't even there.

Interviewer: Do you ever wish your mother went out and

got a husband?

Margo: I used to, but now I know...they're so aggravating. My father is a very aggravating person. I try hard to avoid him. You know, being brought up in a family with two women instead of a man and a woman, it's different. When I go to visit my father it's like, "What? Who are you? What are you talking about?"

Interviewer: It's true. It is different. If you were giving a message to the world about it, what would that be?

Margo: Well, when most people think about having kids living in a family with lesbians and gay men, they think, "Oh God, they're going to grow up gay. They're going to grow up to be lesbians. They're going to get AIDS." You shouldn't say because her parent is a lesbian she's going to go out and get a girlfriend, too. I wouldn't choose it for myself but, if that's what a person chooses to be, that's what they want. You can't tell them, "That's gross. Go change your lifestyle." I don't think it's anybody's business what goes on in anyone else's life.

Tania: You know, if you take the kids who grow up in gay families and you take the kids who grow up in regular families, I bet you the percentage is the same of those who come out gay and those who don't.

Margo: A lot of times when you have straight parents you turn out to be gay. It just seems like that. In Gay Pride marches you see, "My mother's straight, but I'm not." But you don't see straight people walking down the street saying "My mother was straight and so am I." You don't see that. So people go around saying, "Oh your mother's a lesbian so you're going to be a lesbian too." But so far, I'm not. I don't think I'm going to be.

Interviewer: Do you think if you got older and it turned out that you were attracted to women it would be OK with you? Like if you were twenty-five or thirty?

Margo: If that's what I wanted, then it would be fine.

Interviewer: Would you raise kids the way you were raised?

Both: Yeah

Tania: A little different. I wouldn't be as strict.

Interviewer: Otherwise, you think they did it right?

Tania: I think the best part about it is, you're more aware. You're not as closed in. You don't think, "That person's that way—Ugh." I think gay people get that a lot so they're going to teach their kids not to do that. I think a lot of straight people aren't going to tell their kids, "Don't say 'Ugh,' because that's the way that person is."

Interviewer: And so, if you're a straight person, when you grow up and then you raise a kid....

Tania: My children aren't going to be prejudiced. If there's anything I can do about it they're not going to be prejudiced against anyone.

Margo: And if I have a kid and my kid turns out to be gay and that's what my kid wants to be, I'm going to support him as much as I can. I'm not going to say, "No, you are my son! You cannot be gay. Please don't be gay. If you're gay don't bring your boys into my house." I'm not going to do that. I'm going to tell him if that's what he wants to be that's his business. I'm going to support him as much as I can. I'm not going to think any different of him. People say straight people are regular and gay people are irregular, but that's dumb. The Bill of Rights says people are equal. But if people are equal you can't say some people are regular and some are not. It doesn't make any sense. A lot of my friends see a boy walking down the street and say, "Oh look at the way he's walking. He's a fag." Sometimes there are girls who are really close and they hang together and only with each other. People say, "Oh, lezzies, lezzies." Sometimes that bothers me because it's like they're saying it about me, Shelley and Tania.

Interviewer: When people say that, do you ever say anything back to them?

Margo: Somotimoo. Somctimcs when they ieally keep it up I just say "Why...that's wrong." I always tell people that. I always say, "That's wrong."

Interviewer: Do you think people are changing? That people are becoming more open?

Margo: No, because if you take the way kids are now, where did they learn it from? I mean, if you find a kid that says, "Ooh, gay people are nasty. My mother said to stay away from them," if you find a kid that grows up in a house like that they're not going to grow up to be open to things.

Tania: Maybe eventually most people will be pretty open, but there are so many people that aren't. I mean, yeah, there are lots of people that are gay and you can tell by Gay Pride and stuff.

Margo: You can even see gay couples walking down the street. *Interviewer:* When I meet kids like you, it makes me feel hopeful.

Margo: My mother says that all the time.

Interviewer: She's right. You'll become adults and you'll have good attitudes. You'll raise kids that will have good attitudes. People like you can try to make changes.

(Shelley joins us having returned from her job at the mall.)

Interviewer: Shelley, one of the things we asked earlier was if there was a message you'd like to give to the world about being raised in lesbian families.

Shelley: I would say that I want the world to know that it's not contagious.

Interviewer: That's what they said too.

Margo: It's not a horror story.

Shelley: And it's not that bad. Actually it's kind of better. I've looked at different families with the mother and father and they don't really communicate well with the child. They don't have long conversations about important things, not just things like the birds and the bees and stuff like that, but stuff that will help you with your life. And I've never seen that. I go to my friend's house and her mother and father are really cold in terms of relationship toward her. She wishes she had parents like I do.

Interviewer: So you all sort of said the same thing that it's not contagious and that there are ways that it's better. And that you'd want to raise your kids like you were raised.

Shelley: It's really true that when your parents are lesbians or gay (or if they have lesbian or gay friends) you're more likely to get a more rounded sense of the world and, you know, you won't be so prejudiced.

Anonymous

We choose to write this piece anonymously. This is not our preference but speaks to the realities of the day. Our child is not yet legally adopted in the courts, and the laws and homophobia in this country are such that we risk loss of our daughter if we reveal who we are. Also, the adoption agency we worked with is one of the few that works eagerly with single parents and if we came out here we would run the risk of jeopardizing future adoptions for lesbians. The process of writing this piece, of affirming what we went through to become parents was wonderful. The fact that we have to publish anonymously is devastating.

ADOPTION: THE REALITY FOR ONE LESBIAN COUPLE

Anonymous

FIRST MOTHER'S STORY

I wasn't going to do this—have a child that is. Growing up, I had very definite ideas of who I would be as an adult, and those ideas never included children. I remember lying in my tent in the back yard with my best friend. We were both twelve and we were seriously discussing the future. We agreed we would never get married. And, of course, we knew that we certainly would not have children, since we had no intention of marrying. We didn't even discuss the option and discard it. The idea was nowhere in my mind. I was going to be a professional (the profession changed from time to time from lawyer to astrophysicist to teacher) and I was going to live in Chicago (the place to go when you grew up in a small community in the midwest) and drive a convertible with the top down, my left arm out the window, smoking unfiltered cigarettes. I was going to be a woman of substance. I certainly wasn't going to tie myself down with a husband and raise children. I saw what that had done to my mother. No thank you.

Yet, here I am at the age of thirty-nine, walking my twenty-month-old daughter from the subway to her day care center. Not thinking about my dissertation (which is in progress) or the book I hope to write (about adult education) but rather worrying if I have enough diapers and wondering if I should pick up her bottle when she drops it or have her pick it up. What is the correct developmental response? And which response keeps the bottle cleaner?

How did I get here? For years I have known that when

I am in a room with adults and children I am the adult on the floor with the kids. Their games were always more interesting to me than the adults'. But I just chalked that up to lack of confidence in my ability to talk to people. Furthermore, I wasn't naive. I knew that having a child involved a lot more than rolling around on the floor with one at a party. I think I first started giving serious consideration to the issue when my sister had her son. She was thirty-three at the time, and I had thought she would never have children. She had been my role model for a professional woman (albeit married) and now I found that her decision to have a child was challenging my decision not to. Then my best friend, another competent woman whom I admired, adopted a little girl, and again I had to think about my own choices.

Like my sister, my best friend was married and therein lay a major difference between her life and mine. It's all well and good to think about having children but, if you're a committed lesbian who never sleeps with men, you don't just have a child. You have to act in very conscious ways and that means first overcoming any ambivalence you have about being a parent. And, spending time with my best friend only heightened my ambivalence. My lover and I would visit this friend and her husband three or four times a year, and they looked terrible. They were always exhausted and they spent so many hours negotiating who would take care of the baby and who could leave the house and who was responsible for getting a baby sitter that I was overwhelmed just watching them.

When we would return home after visiting these friends, we would spend hours talking about what we should do. Should we become parents or not? We made long lists of the pros and cons although we could never figure a way to weigh the factors. What we did notice was that the con list was long. We finally concluded that no rational person would ever become a parent if they thought about it long enough. Who would knowingly give up that much? We were both in careers that meant a lot and required full time commitments. Still, we took turns being on each side of the ambivalence. Some months she would say she wanted to have a child and I would say I didn't. Other months we would switch positions. I finally concluded that the only way I was going to become a parent was by accident, and those accidents don't happen very easily for lesbians. I used to imagine that someone I knew would die and I would have to parent their child. The option was remote and not pleasant to consider since I didn't know anyone I wished dead. Mostly the image made it clear that I would readily accept parenthood if it were thrust upon me, but I wasn't ready to choose it for myself.

The issue, however, didn't go away. First of all, the new baby boom started hitting the lesbian community. Up to a few years ago, the only lesbian mothers I knew were those who had had children in heterosexual relationships before coming out. Gradually, I started hearing about and then knowing women who were making the choice as lesbians. One of our best friends talked about getting pregnant. She wanted to choose the "father" but raise the child with her lover. Another friend started exploring adoption.

These women's actions were a major factor in helping me resolve my feelings. I was fascinated with their process. I would talk for hours with them about the pros and cons of adoption and artificial (or alternative) insemination with known or anonymous donors. Gradually, I started to know that I wanted to do this, too. My lover, however, wasn't so sure. We talked endlessly about what it would mean, what we would gain, what we would give up. And we agreed at first to pursue the adoption option. Several weeks later I went back to the midwest to spend Thanksgiving with my family. One day my sister and I were in a restaurant watching all the women with children. Surprising even myself, I blurted out to her that I wanted to adopt a child. The even greater surprise was her response that her husband might be able to arrange an adoption. He is a lawyer whose firm handles the adoptions for a local hospital. I was excited beyond description. It all seemed so easy.

That was perhaps the only time easy was ever used in the same sentence with any events that followed. I contacted an adoption agency that would do the necessary home study. I, of course, had to put myself forward as a single applicant since lesbians are not a legally recognized unit and, more importantly, lesbians and gays are actively discriminated against in our attempts to have children. My lover and I had agreed that we would avoid the political issues and be in the closet in order that I would be found a "fit" adoptive parent. After all, we reasoned, once we had the child, it would be ours. (We still think that decision was right, but it was a painful one.) I had the home study done, completed the other necessary requirements and contacted my brother-in-law. When could I expect a child? He seemed far less enthusiastic than my sister. Did I know how expensive this was likely to be? I said I did and was ready to pay all necessary costs. He stated again and again that he didn't know how long it would take but he imagined no more than eighteen months.

My lover was sure we would have a baby in six months and we started planning our lives accordingly. I arranged to have no work that summer so I could take care of the baby in the first few months. We contacted relatives to borrow a crib and other basic equipment. Worse than that, we started hoping with every phone call that we would receive word that a child was on the way. We knew that we might hear at the last minute that a woman had checked into the hospital and wanted to give her child up for us to adopt, or we might get two or three months notice. Our whole lives were focused on hearing the news that there was a baby for us.

The months dragged on. Six months went by, then nine months, then a year. Gradually we started freaking out. Would this ever happen? We started sensing that for us it might not.

My brother-in-law was in a partnership with his brother who was clearly less than enthusiastic about placing a child with us. Would he make it impossible? We did not know.

Also, the law firm was suddenly being contacted by far fewer women who wanted to give their children up for adoption. The situation looked hopeless.

During this period, I had not stopped thinking about giving birth. In addition to knowing that I wanted to be a parent, I also felt a strong, almost indescribable desire to give birth to a child whom we would parent. One day when I was feeling especially hopeless about the adoption, I realized that I needed to give more room to my desire. My lover was less certain than I was, although she said something very important. "If you want to give birth to a child, I would never say no." This started a new period of hope and activity. We were both clear that if I chose to be inseminated we wanted to do that with a man whom we knew. Neither of us wanted to choose to bring a child into the world whom we would have to tell, "We have no idea who your father is." When we talked about potential donors we quickly agreed on a man we knew and had very positive feelings about. We wanted someone who would be involved in the child's life in the role of uncle but who would have no desire to control how we raised the child. We needed someone whom we liked and trusted.

The man was married to a friend and colleague of mine. Wasting no time, I talked to her the next day at work. I was extremely nervous. How do you tell someone that you think her husband would make an ideal sperm donor? I had no idea what her reaction would be. To my delight, it was extremely positive. She talked to her husband and he too was positive about the idea. They were agreeable for several reasons, perhaps the most important of which was a strong political commitment to overcome the oppression of all minority groups, including lesbians and gays. The four of us met several times to discuss the idea. We drew up an agreement that summarized our understanding of each person's expectations and role. We went ahead with this knowing that the donor would have more legal rights and responsibilities than my lover. We trusted each other to live up to this agreement and we agreed that we believed in our contract more than in the supposed rights guaranteed by a court of law.

Then began the next hard time. The four of us got together twice a month during my fertile period. I was carefully monitoring my temperature and the consistency of my fertile mucus. Twice a month, two days apart, we would inseminate. And then we would wait. Sometimes we were hopeful; sometimes we were skeptical, but the result was always the same: I didn't get pregnant. And I was devastated. Everything that we could control had gone so well. We had a wonderful sperm donor. The four of us had come to agreement on extremely difficult issues. The vibes were good, but the results were nil. We did this for over a year. Again, I was starting to panic. I knew that some women had taken years to conceive, especially with artificial insemination, but all my friends were conceiving after one or two tries. The self hatred I felt was intense. Although the feelings were irrational, I was convinced that I had failed. Each month it got more difficult to inseminate and each failure to conceive was more painful. I was thirty-seven years old. Was that too old? Had I waited too long? I had no way of knowing.

After about a year, we started hearing encouraging news about the international adoption possibilities. My lover and I had always agreed on one thing: getting a child was more important than giving birth. It seemed necessary to consider adoption again. Now, however, the decision was more complex. Any month I might get pregnant, and that was clearly my first hope. We also had two other people to consider. The sperm donor and his wife had made a major commitment to our desire to have a child, and I felt that we had a commitment to them as well.

I heard from the adoption agency that they had a new source in Latin America. The country required prospective parents to go there for a month. Few people could do this. If I could, I would be at the top of the list. We barely hesitated. Of course I would do this. But I was not prepared to give up all hope of getting pregnant. We continued to meet monthly to inseminate. The donor and his wife were extremely understanding about our feelings, and they were disappointed. They had looked forward to the role we had agreed upon. They especially hoped that I would get pregnant before we heard from the adoption agency. But that was not to be. In March we got the call. There was a child for us in Latin America. "What sex?" I asked. A girl. "How old?" Twelve months.

Three years after my conversation with my sister, we had news of a child for us. But the hard part wasn't over just yet. I went to Latin America in April to see the child and sign various legal papers. In the meantime, the rules had changed. I had expected to be able to bring my daughter home with me, but that was no longer the process. Instead, I had to return to the U.S. without her, and we had to wait five months for the courts there to approve the adoption. We didn't know why it took so long. "Court procedures," we were told. In many ways the last wait was the cruelest. We now knew that a real human being was in the world waiting to become part of our lives, yet she was thousands of miles and many months away.

Finally, she arrived. We went to the airport to get her with three carloads of friends and family. After the interminable five months of waiting, the plane was exactly on time. The door to the passageway opened and, shortly after that, the escort walked out with our daughter in her arms. I started crying as I walked forward to get her.

Now she's here and I worry about what to do when she drops her bottle. I can't believe how consumed my life has become with these mundane matters. But I'm so glad. Truly, being a parent is just what I want.

SECOND MOTHER'S STORY

I am the youngest of three and had no experience raising children. I was never interested in having any, although I was raised to get married and have children, as if by rote. My mother was a woman overwhelmed by the task of raising children in an oppressive, isolating suburban environment. My unconscious wish, therefore, was to not do what my mother did. Part of my answer to doing things differently included the acceptance of love feelings inside me for other women.

I have known since I was a small child that I was a lesbian. I denied this reality and went through my "heterosexual phase." Coming out later was a culmination of fears, doubts, and finally, acceptance and serenity. Following a number of unsatisfying relationships with women, I came to the conclusion that I deserved to be in a committed, long-term relationship that offered me some security, passion, and intellectual challenge. I am now in such a relationship.

My lover and I typically polarize around any issue. She takes one side, I the other. I have become accustomed to our pattern and view it as a lucky dance. When she began to talk about having a baby, I saw myself turn my head and face in another direction. The problem was she didn't shut up. My deep love for her eventually illuminated one clear choice: "If I truly love her, I want her to be happy and have in her life what she wants for herself." Happiness for my lover was having a child, and I had chosen her to spend my life with. Part of my own maturation process has been to accept as spiritual gifts things put in my path that I would normally be closed to.

My wishes, however, were not truly selfless. When I had pictured my future, it included children. A number of my friends had children and I had loved knowing them. I pictured a kitchen full of activity and noise and hub-bub.

We were able to clarify early on what our priorities were: the most important thing was getting a child. Our goal was to become parents in two years by one of a number of different options. She had a strong urge to have a child biologically, but I did not. My interest was in parenting.

We talked to other lesbians who had children and who were in the process of getting children by various means. I think had I told only straight people about our desires we could have gotten really screwed up. Lesbian mothers in this culture are considered deficient. Heterosexuals, no matter how lacking as parents, are considered better off. Every gay person, except one, encouraged us, without strange innuendos, such as, "What will the child call you?" as if the name a child calls someone determines the quality of the relationship.

I cannot stress the importance of gay people saying, "We know you will be good parents." The self-doubt and fear of getting our baby was overwhelming to me at times and I had to keep checking in with my friends to hear them say, "You can do it." A process that in heterosexual culture is supported by an incredible number of rituals and acclaim is just unfolding in gay culture. Our friends gave us a shower that celebrated our relationship as much as our baby. I am very grateful to our gay community for this acceptance.

Parenting has been, on the whole, much less scary than I had thought it would be. When I met our child, I had an incredible sense of what she needed, almost psychic. My capacity to mother is stronger than I had thought. There are terrifying moments for me when she is upset and I have tried everything. I get really scared that something is horribly wrong, and then she sleeps. I have discovered that I really have a great many strengths. I have a relationship that supports me in my every move, friends to reach out to who applaud my every effort, and a work situation where people care about me. I am still oppressed as my mother was by being a woman and doubly oppressed as a lesbian but the need to reach out for my daughter's sake has become paramount.

The struggle, of course, is to fit it all in. Mothering is a time consuming job, an unpaid low status occupation that is supposed to be second nature. I am lucky to have some money and material items that make the job of mother much less of an isolating experience. I have day care of the highest caliber. My family has not disowned me; they are supportive and sweet with our child.

So we keep on, fitting in work and childcare and mothering and working to share our strengths and love with others. The adoption of our baby is incredible when one looks at all the forces working against it, the discriminatory social laws and "well-meaning" folks who think anything is better than a gay parent. Our child is from a foreign country and is of a different racial heritage—that brings other forces to bear. There are political questions about our adoption that abound and criticism from many realms. I firmly believe that spiritual forces meant for this child to be with us and that our health as a family will prevail. I feel grateful to have spiritual principles upon which to base my life and the life of our family.

My role in the adoption was a major one. However, due to the present reality of adoption agencies and homophobia, this had to be hidden. Part of my role was to be the worrier. Let us not pretend worrying is unimportant. I fought many psychic battles with my inner critic and oppressor and then shared that with my partner. I believe that allowed her to grow through my experience without expending her own energy on the same. I also provided half the financial fee, gave moral support to my lover, and did other nuts and bolts kinds of tasks. We feel sure the adoptive worker knows of our sexual orientation, although it was not mentioned. I have very mixed feelings about the way the adoption went forward with us in the closet, as I know this helps perpetuate the system. It is a compromise and we would not have gotten a child had we not compromised in this way.

Life with our baby is work work work and some very special moments that I wouldn't trade for the world. She is a willful little child and quite a fighter. When she cries, every bit of energy is in that cry. She is a beautiful child and she is learning to hug. She spent her first many months in an orphanage in either a crib or a walker, without enough stimulation or personal attention. When she arrived here, she was way behind developmentally. She is growing by leaps and bounds and I am proud of her every move.

I am in many ways a typically defensive new mother. I feel that I am right about our child and at the same time

I feel I am wrong about her. Everything she does is a new experience, the first illness, the first cold, the first time waking up in the middle of the night, etc., etc. I ask for a lot of help with my daughter, and having a baby has really tested the trust between my partner and I. Luckily, we agree on many things. We agree we need time away from the baby, that we want our friends and family intimately involved with her, and that we want to share childrearing. I have a strong ethic of fairness, and we divide the work fifty-fifty.

I thought I would be jealous of my lover and the baby. I have found, to my delight, I am not at present. I am pleased when she loves the baby and the baby loves her back. There is no tug of war between us, and we are working together to provide a life for her. I consider all that we do as work including childrearing; and therefore there is not the separation as in some heterosexual relationships where the work outside the home is work and the childrearing is zero.

As a couple, the baby has made us look to the future in terms of what we would like for our family and community. Our friends, including those who are new parents, join with us in this looking-forward. My feelings and thoughts of love for our baby have at times reminded me to act more positively in my relations with others. Her own perfection challenges me to see through negativity and reach out towards that which is ideal in us all.

Cecilia Pinhiero

I am Portuguese and Spanish and an eighth-generation Californian. I am thirty years old and was raised in a Catholic family. I am the biological mother of my, now, six-year-old daughter. I work as an instructional technician in an elementary school in my home town. I am very active in A.A. and live the spiritual steps of A.A. in every part of my life.

CECE

Cecilia Pinhiero

My name is Cecilia but ever since I was a kid they have called me Cece. How do I begin to tell you what it is like for me now in this phase of my development as a spiritual being and a single lesbian mother? Being a lesbian mom is the greatest gift of love and learning in my life, but it has not always been this way for me. I have fought long and hard to become the woman I am today. A lot of my fight was with myself.

In 1978 I moved from Santa Cruz, California, to, of all places, Willard, Ohio. I was just 20 years old, tryin' to soothe my soul. But I was on a hard path. I started drinking wine a lot. I felt very alone. Every night I would come home from work at the candle factory, drink a bottle of wine and pass out. This went on for a year.

Then I met a man. He was crazy. He had been in Vietnam and he was still angry. I thought I could calm the beast that lived inside him, so we got married. I remember vividly a telephone conversation with my sister prior to my marriage. She said, "You better go through with this wedding, Cec, you never do what you say you are going to do." I took this as a dare and no one at that time dared to dare me to do anything, 'cause I would do it.

Well, the marriage didn't work out and my being a closet lesbian was only part of it. He and I never talked about it, we didn't know how to communicate. Somehow we both knew I was a lesbian. When I was twelve years old I had a girlfriend. She was my first woman lover; we explored each other's bodies and it was pure and innocent. A wonderful feeling. Then she discovered boys and it was over. This was tucked far away in my mind somewhere. As for him, he wanted to be close and intimate, in the beginning anyway. The thing of it was I could never let him in. We could never reach a place of intimacy. He could never touch my soul or get into my heart. So he beat me up physically and mentally. The last straw came one afternoon when we had been drinking too much alcohol (which we did every day). He called me a lesbian and beat me up real bad for that and nothing else. He had decided for himself that I was a lesbian because of my attitude toward him. He knew this was a painful area for me, he could see it in my eyes. He kicked me when I was down, every time I tried to get up he would kick me more. Then, suddenly, he dragged me up by the hair into the bathroom and made me look at my bloodied face in the mirror and said, "This is what you are, look, do you like what you see?"

He wanted something from me that I could not give him. I still shiver at the thought of that day. He was brutally cruel. I pray that no one ever has to go through what I did.

I sought help and left him. I went to therapy at the battered women's shelter. Everything was okay for about three months. But I had this gnawing hole in my gut that was driving me nuts. One day he called, and I went back to him.

We moved to a small town in California below Yosemite. I took up jogging and being alone a lot. I got a dog, a cat, and a pet goat. They were my friends and my constant protectors. One day my husband flipped out and destroyed everything. He shot my goat, destroyed my record collection, and demolished everything in the house until there was nothing. I had nothing, emotionally, spiritually and materially. I was truly alone.

I made a choice. I left him. I felt a force in my life that I did not understand. Soon I found out that I was pregnant. I felt a calm, a peace, a reason. I have never heard from or seen my ex-husband since.

I now had a reason to live, a child was growing inside my body. I moved back to Santa Cruz. I was 23 years old.

My sister became my birth coach and I had natural childbirth. On November 20, 1980 I had a baby girl whom I named Tamara Ann. She became my life force. Time moved on. I got Tamara and myself settled into a trailer in a park and I adored being a mother. Then one day when Tamara was fifteen months old, my sister said to me, "You can't be a single mother, Cec." I thought for a moment and then felt my self-esteem and self-worth fly out the window. She destroyed me with words. She said I needed a man, so she set me up with this guy who was a coke dealer. She knew what my weaknesses were. I always wanted to escape reality and drugs seemed a good way out. I got into drugs, so I weaned my baby when she was seventeen months old. I didn't want the drugs to go through my milk to her. The wonderful, intimate bond that nursing had provided for me was severed. I became an addict.

Soon I met Joanie; she was an addict too. She was not just another woman, I had known her before. We grew up together, we lived on the same street when we were kids. We had a lot of catching up to do. We became lovers. This was almost paradise for me. I fell in love with her very deeply, but she was married and it just didn't work out. We spent one summer together. I became obsessed with her every move and she was just playin' around with me. She told me to split. I was devastated.

I had such plans. I felt so awake; we were going to teach our children what life and love were really about. She had three kids of her own that I had taken care of.

I wanted to die if I could not be with her and I tried to kill myself. It did not work.

I have done a lot of soul searching since that time. I also began recovering from drugs and alcohol. I was an addict/ alcoholic so I went to a recovery house. My daughter went to live with my mother for the longest nine months of my life. When Tamara came back to me we had to start over. She was four years old and we began to build a clean and sober life together. I came out as a lesbian and it was like coming home for me.

The first hard issue I had to face was the wanting and desperately needing some kind of recognition. No one says, "Wow, that's great, you're a single lesbian mom. Wow, that is something to be." They just don't give you anything. My family sort of slipped away from me, so I sought out help from therapy and my lesbian community who were sober and clean members of A.A. Without the network of lesbian support I never could have made it through those crucial times. My daughter and I have grown a lot since then. We go to therapy together to learn to communicate, and we lead a simple loving life. I work with children as a Teacher's Aide in a special education class, and I run a cafeteria at the elementary school that I went to when I was a kid.

Tamara is my greatest gift and my most painful struggle. I teach her and she teaches me. I have learned to set limits with her, which has been hard for me because Peter Pan is my hero and I have never wanted to grow up. (Wendy, where are you?) Tamara and I are two separate human beings. This was hard for me to accept because we were merged for so long. Through her and a power greater than myself I have learned to love myself. We talk now and she tells me how she feels and I tell her how I am feeling. I am truly blessed; she is a wonder and only six years old.

I have had two lover relationships with women in the past two years of my new clean and sober life. Tamara has stood by my side in whatever decisions I have made and seems to adjust to changes much more easily than I do.

For today, my main identity revolves around mothering. The mother-child relationship has been the primary source and experience of love for me. This is a great gift. Loving has become a part of my being, part of the way I choose to live, part of my work and my play. I believe that Tamara chose me and I her, that she really wanted to be born into the world.

I feel that through being a lesbian mother I can make my contribution to peace and love on earth. Everyday when I wake up I thank our great mother earth for another day. I live for today, one day at a time. Coming to love myself has been a process and I practice meditations. Saying them to myself in the mirror each day has helped to heal the little girl that lives inside of me. They go like this:

> Cece,
> I love you, I'll take care of you, You can trust me, I'll be there for you, I'll be there even when you die.

> Cece,
> It is not what you do, but who you are that I love. You are special.

> Cece,
> I see you and I hear you.

> Cece,
> You don't have to be afraid anymore.

Jay Reed

I am a sixty-year-old second-generation fugitive from a Mormon/Presbyterian background who is the mother of five children and the former co-parent of two. I have been a teacher, secretary, office manager, campus housing inspector and freelance legal courier. A graduate of the University of California, Berkeley, I am the author of a book of poems, Infinitude (Page/Wand Press, 1986), lover of long walks, hot showers and baroque music.

NIGHT SOUNDS

Jay Reed

I never got used to it. Even though I'm fourteen now, a freshman in high school, and consider myself reasonably intelligent, there are some things that resist a deeper knowing; or should I say there is a stubborn reluctance to grasp things someone we trust can't afford to have us know at a particular time?

My earliest memory of the sound is as a very young girl, awakened from first sleep, my bedroom windows open to the unusually warm air of a fragrant spring night. It begins as a low, insistent growl, getting louder and stronger above the rustle of twig-snapping tumbling, hisses, scurrying, becoming a drawn-out yowl, swelling, climbing and suddenly twisting sharply into an abrupt painful screech that slashes the darkness like new chalk on a blackboard...

The first time, with heart thudding under my pink cotton crepe pajamas, I pad down the long hall to my parents' room and crawl in between them for security against the breath-taking terror. I snuggle sandwiched between hairy and silky skin, rocking their stillness with my sobs. Mommy instinctively gathers me into the shelter of her warmth. Daddy, muttering, but roused to the situation—always the instructor—says, "Don't be scared, Trini; it's only cats mating." Mating. I tuck the word away for later, comforted.

My mother and I share the same name: Katrina. I used to think it was from lack of imagination. Now, I believe it's because Daddy wanted to show that we both belonged to him: his wife, his daughter—branded, first and last, big and little. But there are no guarantees; never mind the names. They decided to separate. Well, Mommy decided;

Daddy didn't want to. He cried and went from wine to scotch to Transcendental Meditation to EST. Mom started asking her friends to call her "Rina." It was almost like having a name all to myself at last. But I didn't want things to change; after all, they were married, weren't they? Mated.

We went to live with another family for awhile in a large, spacious house with many rooms, and at first it was fun because other kids were there, too. My dad called it an artificial arrangement and said it wouldn't last: two women together with all those kids. He gave it five years; it lasted two. Sometimes I used to half wake to sounds of arguments, shouting, ragged wailing, but I burrowed down into my own slumber for refuge, not sure that Mommy would be in her own bed if I wandered in to look for her.

When we moved the next time, it was to a tiny house Mom called a fixer-upper; some day she'd add an extra story so there would be a bedroom for herself. In the meantime the living room sofa was her bed. It was like camping. Mornings she could stuff her thick sleeping bag and pillow into a big bamboo basket, put the round, silvery East Indian tray across the top, and the whole thing turned into a coffee table.

Lots of people came to visit, now. Mom was so pretty with her gold-streaked hair, her changeable green eyes that could darken with trouble like clouds going across the sun. But she didn't get angry much anymore. Someone was always coming around to make her laugh, to make her get out the wine and they would get silly. Sometimes men came, but she seemed only to be playing with them: teasing and coy, but not serious, making sure they wanted her but not wanting to give them any more than the fun that was in the playing. With men, having kids around was a help, I overheard her tell a friend; it kept things light. With the women, there was more talking, more touching, and they always wanted to stay so late they had to spend the night, so as not to drive home after drinking so much, Mom said. My girlfriends spent the night, too, sometimes, or I slept over at their houses. Everybody wants a best friend.

One night, when I was about nine, Mom's special friend, Janice, who had been over all afternoon, was staying late. Looking back, I see it was a time of revelation, but I was not ready to have revealed what I was not prepared to understand, what Mom could not yet handle having me know. In a way, this period in our lives reminded me of when my parents still lived together in the sprawling house under the oaks and our grown-up friend, Jack, would stop by after his work, hours before Daddy got home. He would sit around drinking wine and playing *Pong* on the TV. Watching Mommy fold laundry, peel vegetables, fix Steven's bottle, he would give her a one-handed pat or hug every time she passed where he was sitting, coax her to join him, sit down, have a glass of wine, relax, kick back. Mom liked to keep moving, but she also liked to have Jack there, making her feel special. He always left to go home to his own family before Dad stepped off the bus, right in front of our house.

Mom's friend, Janice, was like Jack; she sat around and talked and drank a lot, watched Mom work, patted and hugged her as she passed, urging, "Rina, slow down, have some wine, kick back, relax!" Sometimes she stayed for dinner or came back when Steven and I were in bed, after her evening work. Rina loved company.

The night I remember, I was again in that first layer of sleep, in that tiny house where Steven and I had a bedroom but Mom did not. Suddenly I was awake and did not know why; my skin prickled with alarm, but I couldn't pinpoint the source. Then I heard murmuring, a crescendo of cries rising like the scales I labored over every afternoon at the piano that served as room divider between our living and dining areas. There was something about the sound that triggered echoes from deep in some buried memory. It began again: eerie, indefinable—a sound for which I had no vocabulary, yet which struck a note of old, almost familiar fear.

Now chilled, I left the cozy haven of my bed and headed along the short chain of small, one-level rooms, aiming for my mother's expected, reliable reassurance. Dark from drawn blinds, the house was lit only at its farthest end, toward which I was guided by the cold, flickering glow of the silent television—a glow which cast its spooky light on a scene that finally paralyzed me in shock.

I have tried to recall that scene a thousand times, to make it add up to what I was told at the time. It does not compute. I stumble from my bed toward the living room, no doors in the way. Hoping to find my mother on the sofa, I note its stark emptiness, stripped even of cushions. The bluish light of the TV jerks and shifts, playing over a bumpy mass on the floor: all the sofa cushions and pillows, formed into a wide platform upon which I see the pale curve of a bare back and shoulder, discolored in the dim light and strangely fluid as if swaying under water, moving, moving— the right arm seeming to be stirring something beyond my view. Above the ghostly gleam of a fleshy back and jiggling shoulder, the hair is a dark, wavy shadow, nothing like my mother's straight, sun-shot blonde hair. And as I make out the angles to be legs, I realize there are more than two, or that the two I see are from different bodies; and out of the center of this pile of movement comes a sound dragged like a violin bow across untuned strings: a cry more piercing than the wildest howl of a female cat in heat, pinned down and thrashing in the bushes.

The forward drive of my own body at that instant connects with an invisible roadblock of confusion, and stops; but my voice, already sent ahead, calls, "Mommy...?" too late, before I can smother it. There is a startled scramble; a blanket flaps like a huge, dark wing. I am suddenly a frozen tower of jelly, while at the same time a flush of heat rises to the roots of my hair; I feel blinded, glued to where I stand.

A voice which is Janice's reaches my ear at the same moment I'm aware of her hand, a bit firm and sharp, clutching, turning my shoulder and steering me back in the direction from which I came. Words shower over me, insistent, attempting to be soothing, but with that undertone of annoyance grownups use when they are trying to persuade you of one thing while distracted or reacting to something else.

"Did you have a bad dream, Trini?" Janice prods, her nearness a wall.

"I...I heard a noise...It woke me," I tell her, sensing it is *my* behavior that must be explained, is out of line, to be tolerated only if I can be calmed, convinced of my own error.

Janice laughs, relieved at picking up the cue for her response. "Oh, that was just the TV you heard. I guess we had it up too loud. Sorry, baby. It's okay, now."

She does not let up the pressure on my shoulder as she applies her other hand and playfully chugs me like a train back into my room. Where is my mother during this dialogue? Does Janice want me to think Mom is asleep or watching television without the sound on? Why is Janice acting like a father, when I want to curl into my old safe harbor, my mommy-nest, the curve of her warm, tickly lap?

That happened when I was in fourth grade, so naive. Now, five years later, my best friend tells me a secret. Her mom is a lesbian. I tell her my secret. I think mine is too, but she can't talk to me about it. My friend and her mother discuss everything—even *this*—right from the beginning. My friend tells me that when our mothers had dinner together a few weeks ago, hers told Rina that she thinks I know—and isn't it about time to level with me?

In our family we do a lot of pretending. We all protect each other, for fear of making somebody uncomfortable. Sometimes it makes me lonely. Mom finally did talk to me a little bit about all this—not much. She said it just means that she feels emotionally closer to women than to men. So what? So do I. There must be more to it than that: why they want to sleep together so many nights, be together all the time. My mom smiles a lot and laughs in a silly way when she's embarrassed. I know when to shut up.

The one thing, though, that makes me kind of mad, is that for all those years, I needed to believe Janice and not to believe what I heard and saw and felt. There's never been a sound on TV like the one I heard that night. I think I have a lot more to find out, but I guess I'll just have to do it on my own.

Rose Romano

As a thirty-seven-year-old, single working mother, I have been solely responsible for my daughter's care almost since her birth, supporting us as a typesetter. I write poetry and have had work published in _Earth's Daughters_, _Common Lives_, _Sinister Wisdom_, and _Home Planet News_. A third-generation Italian-American, I will be publishing my own literary journal, _La Bella Figura_, to be devoted exclusively to Italian-American women, with a special welcome for Lesbians.

LA FAMIGLIA—STRAIGHT OR GAY

Rose Romano

I grew up in a working class Italian family in a big city. It never occurred to any of us to question what our parents were: our parents were our parents, our standard for judging the rest of humanity, entitled to our respect whether they earned it or not. As our parents, they were, by definition, good enough for us. It was up to us, as the children, to try to be good enough for them.

Because of this attitude, I don't think I'll ever dare to come out to my father (even though he already knows); however, I came out to my daughter as I came out to myself.

I left my husband after only a year and a half of marriage. I have one daughter. For me, coming out was a gradual process, with several sudden realizations to mark my progress. This was also the way I came out to my daughter. There was never a big speech, with silence before and after. It was just a slow realization on her part, the way other children learn that their parents are straight. And several times I've had to remind her, since television, children's books and movies seemed to make her forget that mothers can be gay.

I remember when, a few days after I'd mentioned something about being a lesbian, she came to me and asked me what a lesbian is. She was six years old. I told her a lesbian is a woman who loves and marries another woman. She was thrilled; her whole face lit up. She told me she wanted to marry me when she grew up.

When I told her we couldn't get married because we're family, she was very disappointed. But she was back again in a few days with a new plan: she'd marry a woman just like me.

And I remember when she was seven years old and she saw me kiss my lover good night. This took place in my lover's apartment, so it was a real kiss. My daughter's reaction was to hang her head, pout, and mutter, "Mommy never kisses *me* like that." To this day, I don't know whether she was jealous of my lover for having me or jealous of me for having a lover.

Gay people are often asked whether they think their children are more likely to be gay than the children of straight people. And gay people often answer that most gay people have straight parents. That usually stumps the questioner, but it doesn't really answer the question.

I didn't know, when I was six years old, that there were women who marry women. At the age of thirteen, the idea of my being gay was just unavailable to me. I accepted my lack of enthusiasm for the prospect of dating boys as another sign of being immature and a hopeless nerd. If my mother had been a lesbian, I would have know I had that option, too—that even a working class Italian could be a Dyke.

So, when people ask me whether I think my lesbianism makes it more likely that my daughter will be gay, I just say— "Yes, thank the Goddess."

So far, I haven't had any of the problems lesbian mothers often have. In fact, although my daughter became engaged to a boy at school in the third grade (hopefully, it's just a phase), my lesbianism seems to be helping her grow up happy and well-adjusted.

She seems to think that I was inspired to love women after she was born when I realized how wonderful she is— as though she thinks that I decided, if I can't marry her, I'd marry a woman just like her. To her, being a lesbian means being strong, being smart, running fast, climbing over fences, and riding a bike with no hands.

Then there was the time my daughter and I were looking in the window of an art gallery at a painting of a woman wearing only a long, flowing black skirt and two silver serpents wound around her breasts. My daughter remarked, "Look what she's wearing on top," apparently thinking it was silly. I answered, "Mmmmmm, I'm looking." She laughed and said, "Oh, Mom," the way she laughs and says, "Oh, Grandpa," when my father tells her the same senseless jokes he used to tell me.

But I know some problems are coming. For example, I bought her a t-shirt that says "Women of Strength." She refused to wear it because she was afraid people would think she's a lesbian.

Now, at age eleven, she's asked me what's going to happen when she invites her friends to our apartment and they see me kiss my girlfriend. I told her I wasn't planning to kiss anyone in front of her friends—not a very good answer. But I don't have any answer at all to that question. I have no idea of what to do. And, what will probably make things even more difficult for both of us, I resent having to come up with solutions to problems that shouldn't be problems in the first place.

Or maybe that attitude will make things a little easier. Maybe if we can remember that problems of acceptance aren't problems within us I'll be able to keep my head and my daughter will continue to be well-adjusted and more-or-less well-behaved. Maybe I've managed to impress her deeply enough with the Italian feeling of family so that she'll accept me even if her friends don't. Maybe she'll realize that bigots aren't worthwhile friends anyway.

Or maybe not. But then, children don't come with guarantees, whether their parents are gay or straight.

Christine Ratzel

I am a raised and recovering Catholic, a working-class woman whose family were shoemakers in early New England. I have identified as a lesbian since the mid-seventies, and I am presently going to graduate school for social work.

I have written several articles about lesbian and gay parenting, I lead workshops for lesbian mothers and their children with my oldest daughter, and I have begun a national newsletter for and about lesbians and their children. I hope to write a book about children raised by lesbians. Interested mothers and children may write: PO Box 267, Amherst, MA. 01002. SASE.

DIFFERENT DRUMMERS KEEP THE BEAT GOING

Christine Ratzel

I've just landed in Eugene, Oregon for a much needed ten day respite. My mom is having radiation treatments, fighting her third onset of cancer in as many years, this time in the lung. I've been driving two hours a day to Boston to be with her, rushing back two hours to Amherst to make classes at the University three times a week and going to a spirituality class the fourth night. I work the graveyard shift as a residential counselor for deinstitutionalized adults four nights a week and I am the mother of two teenage daughters. One is a sophmore at an upstate New York college and the other will graduate from high school in June. She still lives with me.

Being a single parent is hard and being a lesbian adds some to that. My daughters have been raised with the knowledge of my lesbianism. They were seven and nine when I left my marriage. I'd been identifying as a lesbian for two years prior to its termination.

So, here I sit in this woman's home in Oregon. The womanfriend I am going to stay with is skiing with her lover for the weekend and will be here later to pick me up for the two hour drive down the Pacific coast to her mountainside cabin. I look forward to our sharing our energies and space with one another. And I am comforted by the generosity of the woman who picked me up at the airport as I am reminded of the community women naturally have with one another, and I am warmed by our sense of family. I didn't even know her name a few hours ago and we already feel free enough to tell our stories to one another. She is a straight woman and a single parent with a five-year-old son. I tell her some about me and my life back in Massachusetts while she prepares a delicious meal for all of us. I feel at home in this quiet house on the other side of my world, thousands of miles from Massachusetts.

I read the announcement in *Women of Power* asking for lesbian mothers to submit stories about their experiences. While in the air somewhere over the Rocky Mountains, my mind immediately began typing the words in the sky. We need to tell our stories, share them with one another.

What can I tell? What do I have to share? I think many of us often ask that about subjects we feel touched by. And then we say we will sit and do it, write it out someday; but often we don't or simply can't because there isn't time to sit and collect the thoughts, much less put them down. I realize I have three days before I have to submit this to meet the deadline so I decide I am going to take the time.

I am a lesbian mother. Is that like being a teenage werewolf? The statement seems a little ominous in that context. It has been ominous in societal terms. As a mother who is a lesbian it has been difficult to relate in both worlds. The straight community doesn't condone my lifestyle and would shun my children as well as me were it a commonly known fact in their social, political and even spiritual worlds. In some cases the revelation could be life threatening because of the homophobia in the culture. School would be difficult for them. Their friends would be few; they are anyway as we have had to choose carefully who to trust with the knowledge of my choice of who to love. Certainly they have had friends over the years, but there have been only a handful we felt we could trust with the information that I choose to love women. It is all very well to be politically correct and tell the world, but the choice is not totally my own when it concerns my children and we must make this decision together. Until they were/are old enough to understand, I have had to think it through alone.

The lesbian community hasn't always been the support I had thought it might be. Often because of being a mother and because I have been married, I have not been accepted in my community. The community I came out in was the hardest one. Women who had been in marriages were almost nil and those with children were even more scarce so there was little support for paronting. Raising children was seen as being tied to the institutions of the patriarchy and not politically correct.

I was perceived as the woman who had children who was trying to be a lesbian. It warped my image of community for some years. I had turned away from the coffee klatching neighborhood gossip parties to be ostracized in the loving, supportive, nurturing women's community. Support systems didn't exist and still don't to a large extent. Biological families are a primary source of support in the heterosexual society, yet, as lesbian mothers, we often find not only non-acceptance, but total exclusion from the family. A lover may not be perceived as a welcome family member and families become split, keeping grandparents from grandchildren, children from parents or siblings from one another. The lesbian family is essentially isolated.

We remain cut off in our neighborhoods because of the necessity for secrecy. This is beginning to change as some women venture into the public eye in school settings and as open lovers in the community. We still struggle for recognition and acceptance, difficult to achieve in all areas of society. While heterosexual families can ask for just about anything in a new place—from babysitters to sex thera- pists—a lesbian mother moving to a new area generally can't go to the next door neighbor and ask for the telephone list of local lesbian families.

The heterosexual concept of supermom takes on a new configuration when it is used to describe a lesbian mother. In terms of this society, she is a single parent often working outside the home, usually attempting to gain skills or education for job advancement and economic stability while raising children and doing all the tasks included in the "het" definition of the supermom ethic. At the same time, a lesbian mother is encumbered with the added chore of educating both communities about herself and her family, combating invisibility in both worlds and learning how to live her own life in a different way.

The prevailing myth in both lesbian and heterosexual communities is that lesbians do not have children. It is assumed by heterosexuals that lesbians do not want to have children or to raise them. The lesbian community hasn't supported the concept of family since women have been trapped in the roles of wife and mother in the past and have used the greater part of their energies to raise the chidren and protect the patriarchal concept of family.

The invisibility of the lesbian family makes it difficult for the entire unit to survive, let alone thrive. The general lack of acknowledgement of the lesbian partnership in a primarily heterosexual society can put a strain on the adult relationship as well as on the family as a whole.

Part of the invisibility comes from the lack of language to adequately describe the relationships involved. What do we call it when two women are raising children? Does their sexual relationship matter? Sometimes the women are not sexual partners but are raising their children together. What do we call that? Co-mothering? Co-parenting? What do children call the non-biological parent?

Existing societal structures are not open to lesbians and our children. Churches function as support structures to families but, according to most traditional religious faiths, lesbianism is unacceptable. Organizations like the YM and YWCA's, Girl and Boy Scouts, and social and athletic clubs also function as support structures for families. Yet, in order to join as a family, two lesbians may have to pose as sisters. If a mother wants to lead a scout troup, she may need to stay closeted. Childcare for her children may depend on secrecy as well.

The lesbian mothers I have met over the years have been struggling to survive economically, as well as spiritually and emotionally, and have understood the chore it has been.

My daughters and I have found places where we have received support as a family. As an example, both of them have accompanied me to Michigan for the music festival for two consecutive years and worked at the concession stand, having the time of their lives. We've enjoyed our growing times together in the communities of women where we have been able to be ourselves.

My oldest daughter's biggest fear the last time she went to Michigan was that someone would try to pick her up. She doesn't identify as a lesbian. It helped to have the Saint's collective there (they ran the concession stand at the festival). Merry, one of the members, spent a lot of time kidding her about how she should try it, she'd like it. They bantered back and forth all week about the pros and cons of their respective choice of partners and we all fell in love a little that week. Both daughters have fond memories of those years and of the Saints.

My youngest daughter is quiet about my lifestyle. She says she doesn't have a problem with it, but does not necessarily want to talk about it with people. I sometimes wonder what she harbors in her silence. Certainly she hides her feelings. I know and have felt the anger there. She has seen lovers enter and leave my life who have had relationships with her as well as with me. The pattern has been promises of continued contact which have proven to be shallow and she has been left with the emptiness of lost commitment and must feel abandonment again.

We had an argument as she dropped me at the airport this morning. As we rushed for the gate, she complained about my leaving her again to "go off on a trip without her." She forgets the last trip I took included her for five days and she doesn't think about the real and the good reason she hasn't seen much of me in the past twelve days. My mother has needed me and I can't be everywhere for everyone all the time. She forgets that sometimes. I feel guilty sometimes, but not nearly as much as I did years ago. I know I am doing all I can, the best way I know how. But it doesn't always help. I am reminded of how it must be for her.

She has seen a lot of leaving in her seventeen years.

Her dad, me, in returning to work and "never" being home again, the three lovers I have had in the past eleven years and her sister's decision to stay in another state with her dad when we moved 5 years ago, have all meant people have left her world on some level, in some way. It is not easy for her. We don't always find the time to talk about it, and when there is time, she is not always willing to let me in. She has to want me to reach her and sometimes she doesn't want me there.

My oldest daughter has been very supportive of me. She has expressed a desire to co-lead workshops with me for lesbians and their children. We are presently looking for funding and creating a workshop format to address issues we want to discuss. I am asking mothers and their children about their ideas. It isn't an easy task, getting them to agree they will come to a workshop to deal with the issues. There is a good deal of internalized homophobia, hurt and fear of what each will hear from the other when they sit down together. Yet, whenever I talk about the subject or my desire to write a book, I am told how much the need exists and how I must keep going and I am encouraged to do it.

There have been times, too, when she hasn't been as clear about wanting to support me. One Sunday afternoon several years ago my lover and I were doing a family project with the girls and she leaned over and kissed me on the cheek. My daughter saw this and got up and left the room. She'd seen open demonstrations of affection before, but I sensed immediately that something about this time was different for her. I followed her upstairs and knocked on her door.

She had her head buried in her pillow and I went over and sat on the side of her bed and gently put my hand on her shoulder. It was as though I had sizzled her with a branding iron as she rolled over and jumped off her bed. This little eleven-year-old was very angry and hurting too. "Why can't we be NORMAL? We're not a normal family!" she screamed at me.

I stood silently as her face got redder and the tears

streamed down her cheeks. After a few moments I asked, "Can I talk with you about it yet?"

She didn't answer, but closed her eyes and lowered her head. I went on. "It's true, we are different. Who I choose to love is different from what you have been taught is normal out there in the world. But do you think I am sick?"

She turned to gaze out of her bedroom window. "No," she said quietly.

"Well, do you think Liz is?" (Liz was my lover at the time.)

"No."

"I don't think we are either but a lot of people out there do think that and that makes it hard for all of us." I continued, "I am sorry that the world is like that because we all have to live with it until we can change it and that's going to take some time." And I added "Honey, I need to share something important with you. What you saw downstairs was the love that exists in this house being shown to people and shared with people in it. It is normal to do that when people care about one another. Does that make sense to you?"

"Yes," she said.

"Thank you for listening," I said.

Then she asked if she could spend some time alone so I left her to her thoughts. She came downstairs later and we finished our project together.

We have had to work out the appropriateness of demonstrating those feelings in the house over the years and we've always done well with it. When their friends have been there we have always respected my daughters' wishes about not showing overt affection. We have had many discussions about pamphlets, flyers or books about lesbians and lesbian events being left out or postered around the house. It's been like getting them to wash the dishes or pick up their clothes and there have been times we have stopped in midstream and wondered who was the parent here anyway, but it has fostered an easy flow amongst us. We have learned about our humanness with one another. We are bringing two worlds together and finding ways to harmonize despite differences. There is the age difference, the relationships of mother/daughter, straight versus lesbian issues, closeted versus open issues. My oldest daughter has made a point of telling her boyfriend(s) when the appropriate time presents itself in their relationship. My youngest has not yet had the opportunity to make this decision. I did tell one of her boyfriends and it was mutually accepted by everyone. All of these issues have come up and been worked on in the daily situations we have found ourselves in. We have all been personally politicized and have learned and grown a great deal as a result. My daughters continually tell me how they have learned about life in ways their peers may never experience in a lifetime of living. They have compassion, understanding of the human condition from firsthand experience. The injustices in the world are understood sooner in some cases as they have experienced the *necessity* of discernment.

They have learned a healthy respect for me, for themselves and for the authority in their world. It is not necessarily a given that what the authority figure says goes. Questions get asked and discussion ensues, decisions get changed. My daughters' word is to be heard and respected.

It hasn't always been easy and it never will be totally easy. We are learning all the time and are aware we have to struggle to keep growing with one another. We love one another and aren't afraid to be angry when we need to be. The honesty we've come to share and are continually learning how to share with one another has given us a strength and a bonding I will cherish for my lifetime, and I think they will too.

The struggles don't end. We keep on dealing with problems. When I read the first version of this to my oldest daughter, she picked up on the fact that I'd used her name at least three times. She said she'd prefer I not use it. Internalized homophobia prevails. We still feel a necessity for secrecy and hiding on some level. While I feel I have made inroads by living openly as a lesbian within my family structure and out of it wherever I felt it possible, there is still more to do to change the attitudes in the society at large. The steps we are taking are making a difference. My daughters are aware of choice in areas I did not even know existed when I was their age. We are changing the world together.

Amy Wolfe

I am an eighteen-year-old Jewish woman, born and raised in Brooklyn, N.Y. I am now in my freshman year at college where I am planning to major in Women's Studies. My goal is to be a writer and an actress.

MY MOM

Amy Wolfe

My mother's a wonderful person. She has a Ph.D. in environmental psychology. She teaches, has written a book, and many articles. She is forty-five and she is a lesbian.

My mother never sat me down and told me she was a lesbian, it was just a part of my life. I never resented her for it, but I did resent the fact that I could never tell anyone about her. It's so stupid to judge someone on their sexuality but it's even crazier to judge someone because of their parent's sexuality.

When I was younger it really hurt me. I couldn't understand why people would hate my mom. I've tried to figure out why and I've come to the conclusion that people don't like change. It scares them. The fact that my mother doesn't feel the need to conform bothers people. I think all people would like to be nonconformists in one way or another. The fact that my mother isn't afraid to do what she wants, no matter what people say, makes them uneasy.

When I told my friends I was writing this article they thought it was important to talk about my childhood. I don't see why. My childhood was the same as anyone else's. I fell down and scraped my knees; I cried the first day of school and I sucked my thumb. The only thing different about my childhood was that I was taught that people are people. Their sexuality, race, sex, cultural background and religion do not matter. My mother taught me to be open minded, not to make quick decisions about people until I know them.

Many people assume that my mother tries to force me to be a lesbian because she is one; this is not true. If I came home and told my mother I was straight, gay, or bisexual it would be fine. People never consider it force when straight parents try to impose their sexuality on their children. Many straight parents wouldn't accept their children if they came home and told them they were gay.

I think part of the reason why some people hate gays and lesbians is because they are insecure about their sexuality. They are afraid to deal with it, God forbid that they find out they're gay.

A popular misconception is that lesbians hate men and that because my mother is a lesbian I've missed out on having a male role model. Many times I've heard people say that lesbians are disgusting and that they are man haters. I always get angry when people say things like this. It shows their ignorance.

Recently my mother and I participated in a radio talk show about gay parents. The interviewer asked me if I thought I missed out on anything not having a man around the house and how do I deal with men, since they are forty-nine percent of the population. My answer was that I didn't think I missed out on anything, in fact I think I've gained a lot. My mother has taught me to deal with people as individuals. Because of her, my relationships with both women and men are even more meaningful.

This may all sound surprising to people but that just shows how much we all have to learn about the world and the different people in it.

*Thanks to Shayne Trotman for helping me write this article.

MOM

You are a train
screaming through the dark,
a lion
protecting her young,
a library
giving ideas,
knowledge.
You are a raindrop
conducting a storm
the sign of life
twice over
my triangle
You are as deep
as purple and
as sweet as
chocolate.

Ellen Grabiner

I was born in the Bronx in 1950, but have lived in New England for the last fifteen years. I am a painter who has supported my work as an artist by teaching, cooking, astrological counseling, and waitressing. I live with my lover and son in our new home in Cambridge, Massachusetts.

ALEX

Ellen Grabiner

December 1984

The labor and delivery room is designed to be homey: curtains, a couch, chair and ottoman. But the institutional clock on the wall belies the room's domesticity. Staring at the clock, I am aware that only an hour ago I was sound asleep. Yet the events of those sixty minutes have taken on a timeless, slow-motion quality.

My attention is drawn away from the clock by a hand on my ankle. I look over to see the resident. There is something about his touch that makes me feel seen.

"Are you married?" he asks.

"I'm a Lesbian. This is my lover, Susan. I inseminated."

I am stunned by my lack of hesitation. As a beginning Lesbian I had resigned myself to coming out over and over again. But these debuts were colored by a trace of apology. An explanation often accompanied the fact that I had chosen to love a woman. I then reached a plateau when everyone knew and coming out happened rarely and only if I really felt like sharing intimate details. I was luckier than most. No one cut me off; everyone seemed to chalk my choices up to being one of those sensitive artist-types. Even my brother, a Seventh Day Adventist, convinced that my Lesbianism is indeed a sin, maintains that my sins are no worse than anyone else's. He loves me still.

But then I went and shook up everyone's preconceptions (no pun intended) by deciding to have a child. This, a perfectly normal and acceptable avocation which I was unwilling to tackle in a normal and acceptable way. The most telling response to Lesbian motherhood was the woman

who called a midday T.V. Talk Show in which Susan and
I were panelists. "You can't have your cake and eat it too!"
she said. 'What did she mean?' we wondered. Surely she
wasn't saying, 'If you are not willing to suffer being in an
intimate relationship with a man, then you can't have any
of the goodies. If you want to be a Lesbian fine, but don't
think you can also have the joys of having children. That's
pushing it.'

Yet, lying on the table, hooked up to an I.V. and fetal
monitor, I don't feel like I'm pushing, shocking, explaining,
or apologizing. I am just answering the resident's question.
I consider that I might be in shock. I brace myself for the
reactions of the resident and nurses.

"You must have wanted this baby very much."

I feel touched by this young man's consideration. I know
he knows that, for me, getting pregnant was not just a matter
of forgetting to insert a diaphragm. I am relieved not to
have to deal with homophobia in addition to everything else.

I resume my clock watching. Alex's heart beat is loud
and steady on the fetal monitor. According to the portable
ultrasound, my membranes are still intact. That doesn't seem
possible. I can still hear the splat, splat, splat of what I
thought was water on the floor. It was pitch dark. I awoke
with a sense that something was not right and immediately
felt a gush of fluid. I ran for the toilet with my hands between
my legs, trying to keep from spilling all over the floor,
thinking that my membranes had ruptured prematurely. I
turned on the light. Blood was pouring out into the toilet.
I had to believe it was water breaking. No one loses this
much blood and survives. Susan was on the phone calling
the doctor. I was stuffing a towel between my legs trying
to keep the blood in.

The two units of blood have just arrived. I don't quite
understand why it took as long as it did but I am glad that
it is here, just the same. The resident has explained the
possible dangers.

"You may develop a rash, feel itchy...in some extreme
cases..."

Everyone is busy preparing for the transfusion. I am watching the clock even more diligently for I've begun to notice what I believe are small, regular, painless contractions. They are about five minutes apart. I hope that I am hysterical. They are now about four minutes apart. I pray that I am imagining them. I know they are being recorded on the fetal monitor. No one else seems to be concerned. (This is a strategy I often use to calm myself. When I fly and I am convinced that we are falling from the sky I remind myself to look at the flight attendants. If they are remaining calm, I am firm with myself and insist that we are not falling despite what my bodily sensations seem to indicate.) I remember all the pregnancy, labor, and birth books that I devoured over the past four months. I remember that when contractions are close and regular that's when you hop in the car or call the cab. That's when you are in labor. I am only twenty-six weeks pregnant. I am not ready to be in labor. I am starting to panic.

"I am having contractions. They are regular and about two minutes apart." (I exaggerate, hoping to get someone's attention.)

The nurse places her hand on my belly and joins me in my clock watching. After several three minute intervals, she informs the resident that I am indeed contracting regularly. While I am sure this means the impending delivery of a not quite baked baby, the resident remains calm.

"Your uterus is irritated from the loss of blood," he announces. "It's quite common, but of course it's important to stop the contractions. There is a drug called terbutaline. It usually works in cases like these. However it will raise your pulse and the baby's. We need to do an EKG to check your heart. If that checks out, we will need to give you some morphine to calm you down since your pulse is already quite elevated."

As I try to listen to what he is saying, I am aware of only one thing. I may lose Alex. And I've never really had him to lose. I know he is a boy because during one of the many ultrasounds he spread his legs wide as if to announce his arrival. I know he is active and kicks often. I imagine he likes to kick. I imagine that he has been aware, throughout this frightening pregnancy, of my need to be reassured. Each time I bled, he would move just enough to let me know he was well and alive. He passed each ultrasound with flying colors. I know he is twenty-six weeks old, maybe two and a half pounds. I know that this is very young and very small. If I go into labor I know there is only a very slim chance that he will survive.

As I lie there attached to the EKG, I review the pregnancy. I was one of those lucky women who had two, maybe three good weeks. The first three months I was so nauseous I couldn't move and didn't, except, of course, for running to and from the toilet when necessary. At eighteen weeks I had my first bleed. I was sure it was a miscarriage. When I found out it was placenta previa I was relieved, but in the weeks following my panic escalated. I wouldn't sleep at night (my first, second and fourth bleeds all happened when I was sound asleep) and constantly checked my underwear. I was sure that every little drip or discharge (and in pregnancy these are many) was blood. But most difficult was the psychic battle. I felt as if I didn't deserve to have a baby. Where did I get off thinking I could just inseminate, get pregnant and have a baby? I didn't feel big enough, strong enough, loving enough, old enough or good enough to tackle something as monumental as caring for the life within me.

The resident is preparing to give me the morphine shot. "Morphine was used to slow contractions before we had terbutaline. It won't hurt the baby," he explains. I expect to feel familiar feelings. I expect to feel ripped off about having such a lousy pregnancy. I expect to feel panicked about losing Alex. I expect to feel pissed that I can't have what I want. What surprises me is that I feel calm and somewhat sad. I make a conscious decision to be with Alex. I tell him that I love him and that I am grateful for the short, yet powerful, relationship we have shared.

"I *must* be in shock," I think.

I turn on my side and look over at Susan. She looks grey and worried. I smile at her.

"Get some rest," she says taking my hand.

As I drift into my morphine induced sleep, I realize the contractions have stopped.

* * *

September 1987

I trudge up the stairs, anticipating how good my bed will feel. It's been a long day. I wince as I reach the point on the stairs where I can see the top of the desk, littered with bills, old drawings, a belt buckle and duct tape. We are moving. We are buying the middle floor of a three family house just ten blocks from where we live now. In the studio, boxes filled with my paints, brushes, and pastels are piled high. Susan and I share some doubts as to whether we will actually be packed and ready for the movers on the first.

At the top of the stairs, I decide not to allow my gaze to linger on the desktop. Instead, I turn my back to it and walk into my bedroom where I am confronted with yet another stack of boxes. I am one of those people who cannot pack without thumbing through each book, journal or stack of drawings. The accumulation that has occurred over the seven years since my last move is astonishing. I squeeze my photo albums and old calendar books into cartons designed to hold Playmobile and Gund toys. I am drawn to my pregnancy journal. I begin reading about my decision to get pregnant, about my trip to California to visit my cousin Cary and her two-month old daughter Dena. I read about my first visit to Dr. Q. My terms: I want to inseminate on Friday. (It was Wednesday.) I want a Jewish donor. I want the baby to be able to know his biological father. I want to inseminate at home. His terms: You *can* inseminate Friday. We have no Jewish donors. We have a policy of strict anonymity for our donor's protection. You may inseminate at home. We settled. I didn't get pregnant. He found a Jewish donor. I was happy. I got pregnant on the third try.

I find a letter I had written before I even inseminated. "Dear Alex," it began. I knew I wanted to name my baby Alex. It's a Jewish tradition to honor the dead by naming our descendants after them. It's a way of keeping their memory alive. My father's name was Alex. The letter goes on to welcome this baby and to explain the special circumstances around his/her birth. It is a naive, idealistic and loving letter. I feel proud to have written it.

I flip through photos; me inseminating, doing a shoulder stand to assist the sperm in their long journey; me, pregnant, on the top of Mohonk Mountain with Mom and Liz; me, more pregnant, in the shower at the hospital, during my five weeks of bed rest; Susan, looking haggard and me looking puffy, holding up present after present amidst oohs and ahs at the baby shower; me, huge, standing sideways the night before my C-section.

As I tape the box shut, I remember the first time I felt Alex move. I was eighteen weeks pregnant. Cary called from San Francisco and said "I don't want to pressure you. Have you felt the baby yet? It feels like gas," she giggled. I had heard like a feather, like a fish, but gas? "Only it doesn't move around. You'll feel it three maybe four times. Right in the same place. Then it sort of fades." It couldn't have been a more accurate description. Lying on my side in the waterbed the next mornning, I felt one, two, three, then a fourth fainter little bubble of a touch. It is still thrilling to remember it.

I slide the box under my desk, kick off my shoes, turn out the light and lie down. Something hard digs into my ribs. I turn the light back on and draw back the covers to find an entire set of blocks. My irritation dissolves as I remember my morning with Alex. His sing-songy "Mom-mee, Mom-*mee!*" greets me each day. I bring him into our bed, where Susan and I doze. Allie sucks on his morning bottle. He'll occasionally disturb our slumber to ask a pressing question: "Mommy, what comes after seventeen?" or to share his process, "Uh, I'm thinking about, uh, a walk to Central Square." It is those morning moments I treasure most. Each day I am amazed at his being, awed by his perfection and delighted in his presence. I am grateful.

I pick up the blocks, and once again turn out the light. I hear Susan's footsteps on the stairs, but I am too sleepy to call out.

Linda Marie

I am a white Northamerican woman. My children's father is originally from India. My children are now in their twenties. I think it is a more open world for lesbian mothers than when my children were born. I don't say we are fully accepted members of society, but at least we have been introduced.

I have written numerous articles, short stories and published a novel, but I tire of calling myself a writer.

UNRESPECTABLE WOMEN

Linda Marie

The sun is shining through a tear in the curtain—I've thrown nearly everything out or given it away—so, I have only a few boxes of things left. I have to beg him to keep them in storage for me. He is buying a house and taking my children with him as well as all of his own things— OK, OK, so he has convinced me that I am not a good mother. Not because I am a lesbian but because I am without skills to find work that I could support these children with.

My eleven-year-old son peeks in the door. My body created him, held him, and I loved him before I ever knew who he was.

"Mommie, if I bring you some coffee, will you wake up?" he asks me in his high voice. He's up before everyone else and feels lonely, so he brings coffee, then sits on my bed. We talk. I tell him I want to know everywhere he will be today—in case the Fonz comes to visit, I will know where to find him. I don't care what he does so long as I don't hear about it from some adult later on.

I try to use the bathroom but my daughter's using it. "Don't get blood all over," I tell her. I know she's on her period and loves to play with her new blood. She wants to know if she and I will be going anywhere today. She's into hanging out with me and my friends since she got this new body of hers— before that, she was content with girls her own age. I tell her "yes, yes" and that I will be leaving tonight.

I go downstairs to the kitchen. The cousin I'll be living with, who came to take me to Louisiana with her, is sitting with her lover and my friends, sipping coffee and chatting.

The goldfish that I have transferred from silver salad

bowl to fish bowl is almost dead. It is in the middle of the table and everyone is watching it intensely. I change the water again and the fish perks up—a few hours from now it will act as though it's dying again. This changing bowls has been going on for days.

I spend three nights on the bus to Louisiana, and it will take forever for the memory of my children to fade. I'm afraid to be on my own and I wonder what will kill me first, hunger or loneliness. I can still feel my children's bodies pressed against mine. I still hear myself whispering to them when I leave, "I love you, good-bye, be good."

Cousin is sitting in the back of the bus with her lover. I am sitting in front because I like to feel like I'm driving. My legs are swollen and I am sitting next to a very large woman who has a case of diarrhea of the mouth. Not only does she talk non-stop but when I begin to doze she hits me in the ribs with her elbow and says "—now ain't that sompton what so an so—."

While we are riding through the desert, the bus begins to act up. The air conditioning breaks and the many babies and small children on the bus are sick and puking everywhere. One woman holds two babies on her lap for three nights. The bus driver sees she only paid for one seat and says "Stack 'em up, lady—someone wants to sit there!" There are never any empty seats for her children.

Cousin and her lover and me rent a dressing room for 25¢ in the Houston bus terminal. We stretch out on the floor and groan, then get back on the bus a half hour later.

Finally we are in cousin's trailer in Louisiana. I am at one end and cousin and lover are quarreling at the other end. Then, they are making love, making the trailer tremble and sway.

We leave the next morning to pick up cousin's little daughter from deep-deep-down-in-the-woods cousin's house. The house is a shack on cement blocks and leans to one side as though it were trying to get under a tree and away from the hot southern sun. Chickens are squawking and being chased through the shack's curtained front door, out the swinging door in back, by a small boy with his arm in a cast. A small girl removes her teeth for me—to show me she already has false ones like my aunt, her grandmother. She is ten years old and her dress hangs oddly on her.

Woodscousin is very loud—SHE HAS NEVER HAD TO LOWER HER VOICE. And if we were sitting under a tree in a city, instead of here in the country, her voice would echo from block to block. "—so anyway," she is telling us, "I was down thar digin this har ditch with two other guys an the boss calls me outta the ditch and tells me I'm fired! No reason. So he done tol the union I was leaning on my shovel chawing the fat with the boys—plus know what else he said? That I wasn't able to do hard labor—like six kids ain't hard labor—well, I knew I had it licked—the dude that was arbitratin was black an if he don't know what dis-crimination is no one does. Look here what he wrote: 'The boss, Mr. Gesas, is obviously anti-woman and fired Mrs. HampiJane O'Tool for that reason.' LORD! I'm gettin eight months in back wages!"

We all congratulate her. Her husband is undressing me with his eyes and batting flies from his sweaty shoulders. Cousin Hampie's youngest brother arrives in a rickety old truck and announces his mother wants to see me. I ask to leave at once. They all laugh. Youngest brother drawls real slow, like he's been chewing, drinking and smoking pot. (He has been.) He says, "Ya'll sceared she gonna bet ya over the hade with the bible—well, ya'll better hurry an leave cause she done packed up er bible an she be a walking right through here." He points to a path cut through some thick brush.

So cousin, lover, daughter and me are back in the trailer. This time the three of them are quarreling. The clock on the wall rings after an hour and the daughter sleeps and the lover goes out and gets herself plastered, leaving cousin and me alone. It is pleasant. I wish *we* could be together—just her and me for awhile. We color in her daughter's book and talk about everything we remember ever doing together and we laugh and feel sad sometimes too. I suddenly wish woodscousin was here. Then this cousin and woodscousin and me would all go to the bank of the Mississippi and honor the birthplace of our grandmother — who gave birth to so many — who also gave birth to many who are to this day creating more lives.

It is late and lover falls through the door with two other women — lover and two women are Cajun people and sometimes speak in two tongues. One woman is upset because cousin's daughter took *her* daughter's underpants down — they are both ten years old and I didn't see what the problem was or what business it was of adults what children did in the privacy of their own space. The woman is outraged. "We don raise ar keds likka dat!" she tells me. She's an ex-con up for armed robbery, an ex-prostitute, and, as far as I could gather, a madam living and sleeping with two of her lovers who are women. (I personally found this woman to be colorful, charming, absolutely fascinating, although her politics sucked!)

Now cousin and lover have it out over how daughter should be raised until lover passes out and the two Cajun women leave. The next day I leave with a small bag and a change of clothes (I told cousin and her lover and daughter that I would be back in a few days and I haven't heard from them since.) I occasionally wonder how my two pieces of luggage are, and — I suppose I should call San Francisco and see how my children are doing. But — I don't know if I want to be alive to them. Perhaps it would be better if they think I am dead.

I leave cousin to visit friends on a faraway island. There is always something to learn on faraway islands. I get on a small plane, as small as a large bird, and fly away.

There are children outside and inside of me. They are all over me. I can hear them while I sleep. They are swinging, playing, laughing, crying. I can hear whiny little voices — "Mommie, mommie!"

I am on an island — far, far south. In spite of that there are probably more yankees here than there are on Cape Cod. Once, some five years ago, some friends and I were musing over what happens to older lesbians — where did they go? We knew they existed and must be somewhere but we were between thirty and forty years old and the oldest lesbians we knew. It is an absolute high to discover there are at least two lesbians over sixty on this island—two big-sisters.

One big-sister is a great white heron and I follow her long graceful legs each morning through a quiet path to an opening at the sea. The great white heron sister tells me of her life and I tell her of mine while we tread salty waters together. She does magic—jumping into a mysterious circle that is on the path where we are walking, she held one hand in the air, the other on her navel and leapt into the circle and I did the same after her.

I'm a cockroach, we have both agreed, because the pre-historic cockroach has lived through everything.

Other big-sister is a duckling. Her feathers are so soft and tempting, but when I try to come close, she squawks and runs away. I love to watch her in the kitchen. It's hers and she knows where everything is and she flits from one side to the other, mumbling and grumbling as she does. It is peaceful here, it is quiet. There are only three creatures on a sandy island watching a watercolor sunset—they are a great white heron, a duckling, and a cockroach.

I'm supposed to leave tomorrow. I want to hug big-sisters' legs and beg them to let me stay. I don't want to go back to any confusion—I am tired—I know now. Ah! I will forget everything and start a new life. I know it will not be easy but I *will* do it.

I go to San Francisco first, where my children are. The bus goes through town from the bus terminal. I hold my head down and cover my eyes as the bus passes through town. In case I would see my daughter windowshopping. Or perhaps my son riding his skateboard. I might not be able to control the urge to jump down from the bus and grab them up in my arms. Where would we go? How would we live? I feel ill as I did once when I had a miscarriage. I was going to stay but I can't. I can't pretend I don't mind that my children are not going to live with me. I have to leave and I don't really decide where to go. I simply end up in Seattle. I go far away from friends—loved ones—pain.

I don't know if the goldfish died because I have not been in touch with anyone for many weeks now. I am living in a basement—I can stay for twenty more days until I get paid. I work for some dreadful disease, getting $3 per hour, 5 hours/ 5 days—I am down to $30 to last until I get paid. I am staying at a charity house in Seattle and the people are tired of being nice to people in trouble—besides they've had some bad experiences. I have promised to slip quietly to and from my room and ask no one for anything. I have looked for housing with women and either they want someone to make a lifetime commitment, or they don't want strangers—.

I want my daughter to run across the street and get a paper—I like to read my horoscope. I'm worried sick about her crossing the street. There are so many things to worry about— the incestuous feelings I have for my son—the fish dying—the fear that someone will rape my daughter—never again having a kitchen where my friends visit and have coffee—never having a home—being destitute—worrying about the children eating junk food and watching too much TV. I worry that I will never be able to outgrow the dependency of fifteen years of knowing where everything in the kitchen is. But if I had stayed, the fish would still have died.

I think—I don't have my children—that is, they are not with me, but—no matter what happens they will have the silent memory in them that they began their lives inside of *me* and they were nursed at *my* breast until they were a year old. I gave that to them, and I can not be richer for them than that. What I have given is more than all the men in the world with all the power and money can give. This is what I am left with.

But it is not depressing because I am going to become like a cockroach. They are everywhere—every kitchen is theirs. They're anarchists and look queer and have a foul breath to ward off enemies. A cockroach has whatever size wings she wants. She immediately cleans herself after man has touched her because she finds his touch so offensive. She lays her eggs in a magical shell and hides them—that is all she does for her young. We have outlived other prehistoric creatures. We own the night. We do not travel in armies like ants, who are predictable, but scatter like guerrillas. Man has tried many methods of destroying us— from stepping on us to using chemicals that destroy everything. I will not die or go away or forget. Me and all my sisters are becoming as strong as cockroaches.

Margery Nelson

I am a fifty-nine-year-old lesbian feminist writer and mother who lives and works in San Francisco. (My children, all adults, live in the east). Over the years, I have been politically active in the women's movement and the peace movement and have made many changes in my own life. I support myself as a hypnotherapist.

THE MOTHER AND THE LESBIAN

Margery Nelson

I don't say I'm a lesbian mother, because I don't think of myself that way. I'm a lesbian AND I'm a mother. These two separate parts of me have been at war during most of my life. The mother in me used to be terrified of that lesbian. Denied her. Tried to stamp her out. Even tried to kill her. I thought I was insane. I never set out to be this lesbian feminist activist. I remember myself splitting down the middle, the lesbian and the mother ripping my body apart, a violent tear that left each side bloodless for her own valiant struggle to survive alone. Tormented by society's bigoted preference for the mother, the lesbian emerged resentful and furious about all the closeted years, the squelching of her energy. The mother, feeling conquered by the lesbian, was confused and heartbroken at leaving her children behind with their father and losing her home. Shut out by the homophobia of her former world, lonely in the midst of a movement of young, single women, a movement in which most of the other women were the ages of her two daughters, her son.

First I was a mother and then I became a lesbian. But that's not how it worked inside of me. The lesbian was around all the time I was growing up, only I didn't recognize her.

THERE IS A PART OF ME THAT LOVES ADVENTURE AND DANGER, LIVING ON THE EDGE, TAKING RISKS. THIS IS THE PART THAT LOVES WOMEN. I'M THE LESBIAN. I'M THE ONE WHO BECAME A FEMINIST AND A POLITICAL ORGANIZER. I'M THE ONE WHO LEFT HER CHILDREN AND HER HUSBAND BEHIND AND SET OUT TO HELP CREATE A MOVEMENT

OF WOMEN.

I WENT TO CAMP AT 12, FELL IN LOVE WITH THE COUNSELORS AND LEARNED ABOUT THINGS LIKE FREEDOM AND BREAKING RULES. SEX WAS NOT A POSSIBILITY, BUT SOMEHOW, SURROUNDED ONLY BY WOMEN, MY GUILTY FEELINGS ABOUT ALL THOSE "ABNORMAL" LONGINGS DIDN'T SEEM TO MATTER SO MUCH. I LEARNED TO IDENTIFY BEING WITH WOMEN WITH FEELING FREE.

High school was a nightmare. I stumbled through it waiting for summer to come around again, numbly doing what I was told, being a good girl, excelling at studies. That made me different too. Girls weren't supposed to be smart. I felt like a complete outsider. A fat girl. An alien.

THE ONLY THING THAT MADE HIGH SCHOOL POSSIBLE WAS MY LOVE FOR MUSIC AND THE MUSIC TEACHER. I PRACTICED FOR HOURS. AT CAMP AT THE END OF MY JUNIOR YEAR, THEY TOLD ME NOT TO COME BACK, SAID I WAS A TROUBLE MAKER, AN INSTIGATOR.

World War II had just ended. The boys were coming home. Time to push women back into their place. Our culture, our leaders, my parents and teachers preached at us that real women want to marry and stay home and have children. Any other kind of woman was sick, pathetic, depraved.

I WAS SOME OTHER KIND OF WOMAN, ONLY I DIDN'T HAVE A NAME FOR ME.

In my senior year of high school, I went on my first diet. The doctor gave me amphetamines. My friends and I knew it as speed. I stopped studying so hard and let my grades slide. By the end of the year, I'd met an ex-marine and fallen in love. We married on my nineteenth birthday.

I SLIPPED INTO A DEEP HOLE, SLIDING DOWN BELOW HARD ROCKS, SLIPPING AND SLIDING, NEVER FINDING BOTTOM.

When I started having dizzy spells, the doctor said, "There is nothing wrong with you that having a baby won't cure."

I HAVE TO DRILL A HOLE IN MY CHEST TO LET OUT THE BITTERNESS. IT POURS OUT WITH SUCH NOXIOUS FUMES THAT I GAG AND CHOKE. I WILL DIE FOR LACK OF FRESH AIR.

That young mother, still a child herself in so many ways, gentle and scared, aching for love, longed for a world that would accept her, where she could be herself.

I wanted babies to hold against my body, to feel their warmth, to share their sweet kisses, to play with. They accepted me. They reached out their arms for me and made me feel safe. Even when screaming all night with their pains and their fears, their unconditional need of me was magical. I was normal.

My children were beautiful and I was normal. Dressed up in an adult woman's body, I could even pretend that I didn't have to be afraid anymore. For awhile, my fantasies about women stopped. The labor of my first child, shocking in its intensity, its length, its reality, hurtled me into that new world over the threshold of my screams and agony. I knew I would never be the same.

This new world, a women's world, was the oldest one there is: women helping women, holding screaming, puking babies, quieting them, holding sweat-drenched hands and sharing pain; women teaching women to survive, always imperfectly, but doing the best they could.

A scar grew over the hole inside of me. Loving my baby and the two who followed after her, I was everything I was supposed to do and be. Women were my friends. I was accepted. I was acceptable. Everything in the culture told me this was true.

AS LONG AS I STAYED IN MY PLACE.

I loved my babies as I had wanted to be loved, pouring my heart out to them, nursing them, giving them what I could never imagine getting for myself, trying to make them safe in a world gone mad. In the midst of the horrors of the cold war, I found a magical time of sweet breath on my cheeks and soft kisses.

A new persona arrived and thrived: **SUPERWOMAN.** On her knees scrubbing floors to make them really clean, sewing curtains and clothes for the children, clothes for the dolls, baking and decorating wondrous cakes for birthday parties, driving the children to the doctor and to school and to music lessons and ballet, she took over the family. She welcomed her husband home at five every afternoon with a smile. She hustled everybody off to church, sang in the choir and taught Sunday School. She dieted and lived on coffee and cigarettes.

Knowing herself by the condition of the things and people around her, superwoman wanted her house and her body to be perfect. Her standards merciless, she was always watching, always wary, lest she might slip up. Although doubting everything else about herself, she believed herself to be an adequate judge of perfection. Judging was part of the role.

And thus, her own feelings were irrelevant.

I remember putting on the role like a cloak and wrapping it around me, layers and layers of it, that had to do with how to set the table, what kind of food to feed my husband and children, how to dress and, generally, how to behave. The more I dieted to be thin, the more layers of my role I wrapped around me.

HER MIND CERTAINLY WAS NOT DEVELOPED. SHE DIDN'T KNOW BEANS ABOUT THE WORLD. ALL THAT MATTERED TO HER WERE HER JUDGMENTS AND THOSE OF HER FRIENDS, WHICH SHE ACCEPTED AS VALID WITHOUT QUESTION. SHE WAS SO SHELTERED AND SO NARROW AS SHE TRIED TO BE ALERT AND SENSITIVE TO THE NEEDS OF EVERYBODY AROUND HER EXCEPT ME. I HATED HER. I HATED THAT WOMAN WITH A HOLE IN THE MIDDLE OF HER. SHE PUSHED ME DOWN THERE SO

DEEP I ALMOST DIED.

All my life there was a longing, the sense of something missing, an awful ache inside; anxiety about practically everything. I thought that children would satisfy that longing. And they did: when they were very young, needing me, unconditionally loving me.

The experience of having children was unlike anything else I've known in this life and the experience of having one, and then two, and then three children was different, too. Those babies pushed me to grow up along with them. I had to learn about things like patience and selflessness. I wasn't born that way. They taught me with their howling needs. Living in a world of women and children, I learned.

NOT HAVING THE VOCABULARY, I COULDN'T SAY, "I AM A LESBIAN. THAT IS WHY I LOVE WOMEN." WHILE SUPERMOM WAS CARRYING ON, THEY KEPT ME SHOVED DOWN IN THAT SUFFOCATING HOLE. WHILE SHE WAS CARRYING ON WITH ALL THOSE OTHER HOUSEWIVES—WITHOUT TOUCHING ANY OF THEM —I BEGAN TO THINK I WAS INSANE.

I remember a day when I looked at my marriage and knew that it had spoiled, although I didn't understand why we were growing apart. He went to his air conditioned office while I stayed home in a sweltering house in southern Texas, cleaning and caring for the babies. He'd come home wanting me to want him and at some point I had begun to fake it. For how many years after that did I still try to be a loving wife? I remember screaming at him just because I had to scream at someone.

After my babies slid off my lap and took up their own pursuits, I became sick. Dreadfully sick with a tumor on my thyroid, hepatitis and a kidney infection, my whole body broke down and stayed that way for a long time.

I wanted to die. As I saw it, I had a choice between death and insanity. There seemed to be no other way to go. But just as I began to feel something stirring in me, I tried to stamp it out. I tried to kill it.

THAT SOMETHING WAS ME. I WAS LOCKED UP. *When supermom said "I don't know who I am," the shrink pontificated, "The problem is that you like to be on top during intercourse."*
I DECIDED TO GO BACK TO SCHOOL, TO FINISH COLLEGE. THAT WAS 1960 AND WOMEN WEREN'T DOING THAT YET. BUT I PUSHED. IT HAD BECOME A MATTER OF SURVIVAL.

I remembered driving to the local college campus in the early sixties, feeling terrified. I had forgotten so much. Even about decimal points: what do you do with them? What do they have to do with anything real?

Why didn't I get a divorce? Strike out on my own with the children? It was unthinkable. From my narrow perspective, there was nowhere to go. Falling in love with my husband, marrying and having children was the only acceptable thing I'd ever done. How could I walk out on them just because I was troubled? Everything in the culture said it was my fault. How could I leave my children when they were young? There was no choice about that. I had no marketable skills. I didn't know any lesbians, or even any single mothers. Because I knew myself only as a wife, mother and student, there was no part of me to take over and guide me. Turning again to music, I learned to play the guitar and taught my children to sing with me. I grew my hair long and wore long skirts. I became an earth mother.

I LEARNED SOME GREAT SONGS. AND THEN IN SOCIOLOGY AND PHILOSOPHY CLASSES, I READ ABOUT ROLES AND ROLE CONFLICT. I DISCOVERED SOCIAL THEORY: KARL MARX, SOCIAL CHANGE AND SOCIAL MOVEMENTS, A POLITICAL WAY OF LOOKING AT THINGS. THE WORLD OPENED UP.

THE CIVIL RIGHTS MOVEMENT BLOSSOMED. BETTY FRIEDAN WROTE *THE FEMININE MYSTIQUE.* FREEDOM WAS IN THE AIR AND I BREATHED DEEPLY.

Meanwhile, superwoman still had to prove she was normal. She had an affair with a man who taught her she was not frigid after all. She worked compulsively at her studies, took a research and teaching job and tried to demonstrate that she could be liberated and still be a good wife and mommy.

I HAD TO CUT LOOSE AND GO EXPLORING. I HAD TO CUT LOOSE.

I won a three year fellowship to a university two hundred miles away. Defining it as the housewife's equivalent to the G.I. Bill, I accepted.

AT THE UNIVERSITY, I BEGAN MEETING LESBIANS. WOW. BUT NOW, MUCH OLDER THAN THEY, I WAS THE SUBURBAN HOUSEWIFE AND MOTHER THAT MOST OF THEM WERE REBELLING AGAINST. EVEN THOUGH I WAS REBELLING TOO, MOTHERHOOD MARKED ME AS SURELY AS IF I'D BEEN BRANDED. AS I DISCOVERED MY LESBIAN SELF, I ALSO BECAME A WIFE GONE ASTRAY, A WOMAN WITH CHILDREN. I COULD NOT BE A REAL LESBIAN.

Superwoman became super commuter. Traveling back and forth between the university and home to be with my children, I began to have the sense of meeting the other half of myself on the highway.

I never stopped being a mother. It was built into my body, in my sagging breasts and the belly that never did flatten after my third child, a ten pounder, was born. It was built into my character, (a certain long suffering, martyred stoicism and a bizarre tolerance for inane behavior in the young).

BECAUSE I DIDN'T KNOW HOW TO BRIDGE THAT GAP IN MYSELF, I DIDN'T KNOW HOW TO CROSS IT TO OTHER WOMEN, EITHER. I COULDN'T GET RID OF THE MOTHER OR INTEGRATE THAT ENERGY INTO A MOVEMENT THAT WAS YOUNG, SINGLE AND CHILDLESS.

THE YOUNG WOMEN I MET IN THE SIXTIES AND
SEVENTIES ACCEPTED ME AS LONG AS I WAS PASS-
ING. AND PASSING IN THAT CONTEXT MEANT NOT
BEING A MOTHER, NOT BEING MY REAL AGE, NOT
HAVING EXPERIENCED MY LIFE.

As they raged against their own mothers, even though
I understood that rage (wasn't I filled with it?), I could not
bear to think that my daughters might hate me as ve-
hemently as this. Feminist dumping sessions left me feeling
terribly isolated. In this movement of women I needed so
desperately for my own survival, there seemed to be a little
understanding or space for a woman who was both a lesbian
and a mother.

My attempts to speak of my loneliness met with embarrassed silence or heartless remarks like, "You're better off
without your children." My isolation compounded the
longing for my children.

AS I GREW STRONGER, THE CONFLICT BETWEEN
ME AND HER GREW MORE INTENSE. I DISCOVERED
MY ANGER AND RAGE AT A SOCIETY THAT FORCED
ME DOWN INTO THAT HOLE, THAT FORCED ALL
THAT DENIAL OF ME, OF MY LONGINGS, MY NEEDS.
I TURNED ALL THAT ANGER INTO POLITICAL
ACTION.

THE FIRST WOMAN I MADE LOVE WITH TOLD
ME THE NEXT MORNING HOW MUCH SHE WISHED
HER MOTHER WAS LIKE ME. ALTHOUGH I KNEW SHE
WAS TRYING TO BE KIND, I FELT HURT AND TER-
RIBLY SEPARATE FROM HER.

More illness and wracking pain. Once again looking
at death, fearing and wanting it, I still felt uncontrollable
guilt and sadness over leaving my children, even though
by this time they had all left home, too.

I WROTE MY DISSERTATION ABOUT THE RADI-
CAL SUFFRAGISTS WHO PICKETED THE WHITE
HOUSE AND WENT TO JAIL. ALICE PAUL, WHO WAS

THEIR LEADER, TOLD ME THAT IN ORDER TO UNDERSTAND THEM, I WOULD HAVE TO BECOME INVOLVED MYSELF IN POLITICAL ACTION. DIVING INTO DEMONSTRATIONS AND ENDLESS MEETINGS, I DECIDED SHE WAS RIGHT. MY LIFE AS AN ACTI-VIST, CHALLENGING THE EXISTING ORDER, BEGAN TO MAKE A NEW KIND OF SENSE. AND THEN I MET ANOTHER WOMAN MY AGE WHO WAS ALSO MAKING GREAT CHANGES IN HER LIFE. SHE WAS A CAREER WOMAN, SINGLE, WITHOUT CHILDREN. AT THE TIME, SHE SEEMED LIKE A MISSING PART OF MYSELF. WE FELL IN LOVE. OUR SUPPORT FOR EACH OTHER HELPED US BREAK AWAY FROM THE PAST. WE MOVED TO SAN FRANCISCO TO START ANEW.

Although my body started healing, there was a hurt place in my heart that remained untouched.

AND EVEN AFTER MANY CHANGES, THE MOTHER HUNG AROUND, POPPING UP WHEN I LEAST EXPECTED HER, FEELING MISERABLE, STILL LONGING FOR HER CHILDREN.

Sometimes it seemed as though all I could do was weep. Heartbroken.

PATHETIC. I INCREASED MY POLITICAL ACTIV-ITY, BECAME A POLITICAL ORGANIZER.

No matter what I did, the difference in age continued to separate me from younger women. One group of radicals told me that all my experience made me "too eclectic."

My body, though beginning to heal, continued to break down in illness, forcing me to look more deeply into myself, to examine this fundamental split in my identity created by the same social reality I and others were trying to change.

I began to realize that, in spite of all the political rhetoric about being a movement for all women, there were fundamental problems in the way we were organizing. Like the superwomen housewives, we feminists were judging each other constantly, listening carelessly, holding our ideologies above the reality of who we were.

I stopped dieting and focused on accepting my fat body, my age and my disability. I found a healer, a woman who pushed me into searching beyond, beneath and around all the roles I'd played until I found my own center. Taking my hand, she went with me into my terror, into that awesome void where I discovered that my lifelong yearning was for the child in me who dressed up in the costume of a woman and then lost her way. And when I picked her up and held her, crooning the same old lullabies I'd sung to my babes, I found my creativity bursting up like healthy shoots springing out of a compost heap. Searching for strength, I discovered a deep abiding peace, courage for long nights and days of frustration and sometimes overwhelming problems. Life gave me a gift.

Now, when I think about the part of me that is a mother, I remember how that naive child, filled with cultural dogma about how to behave, was pushed by life to grow out of her own ineptitude. When she looked around, who was there but other women. Some were lesbians. Many were not.

These days, I think about childbirth as a metaphor for me giving birth to myself in middle age, going into that pain over and over again, laboring through the threshold of agony and isolation to create new life.

When I visit with my daughters and son, my life lights up with sparklers. They accept my sweetheart and they all have loves of their own. They all seem so much better able to cope with the world than I ever was. And yet I see empty places in them, hollows, that tell me they have suffered from that split in me. Perhaps, they carry an ache for a time when they were babes and their child-mother held them and promised they would be safe with her. And a rage that it could never be.

As younger lesbians have babies and raise families, it becomes easier to talk about being a mother, and now, as I hear about their trials with younger women, and with their own daughters, I hear a wheel turning. My present lover, like most of my friends, is younger than I. I am still the oldest one at most of the gatherings I attend and am still acutely conscious of the existence of ageism.

Writing and my garden help me keep my sanity and sense of humor, while my profession as a hypnotherapist carries me to the edge of life where I meet other women in their pain and go there with them, knowing we can both survive.

And more and more, I hear an ancient voice that says: I AM THE MOTHER AND I AM THE LESBIAN, TOO. I HAVE LOVED WOMEN THROUGHOUT THE AGES AND HELPED THEM TO CARRY THEIR BURDENS. I WAS THERE AS YOU LABORED, TEACHING YOU ABOUT SURVIVAL AND I AM WITH YOU NOW. I AM AN ANCIENT WISDOM. I AM THE LIFE FORCE, THE LIFE REGENERATING FORCE. I AM STRENGTH. I AM COURAGE. I LIVE IN EVERY WOMAN. I LIVE IN YOU.

René Cliff

I am a thirty-one-year-old Black poet, writer, and teacher's assistant who lives with my two-year-old daughter in Sacramento, California. I am currently working on a collection of poems entitled <u>Hands On The Pulse Of Life</u>. I work with handicapped children and adults in regular classrooms and in resource centers.

I enjoy playing bass and guitar at jam sessions and I love spending time at the beach.

*René Cliff is a pseudonym.

CHANGING SEASONS

René Cliff

Three years ago while stirring spaghetti sauce, I said to myself, "I'm a lesbian." I have always known I was a lesbian since a very early age.

When I was sixteen, my mother introduced my family to Denise. Denise was a teacher, forty, very attractive and new in town. Her husband wouldn't be joining her for another month, so I gladly kept her company in the afternoons. Her furniture hadn't arrived yet, so she sat on a cot, and I lay on the carpet grading papers. The throbbing between my legs drove me crazy. All I wanted to do was embrace this woman. When Denise left town six months later, my little teenage heart was broken. There were other women too whom I felt attracted to. I didn't know how to express these feelings, so I repressed them.

Standing there in the kitchen that evening, I could feel these repressed feelings coming to the surface. I repeated the word "lesbian" softly again, and checked my watch. Tonight I'd see Karen (my lover), while my husband attended evening college. I had encouraged Robert to go, thinking this would slow his drinking down.

Karen and I met years ago in the bathroom of our junior high school. She looked like a flower-child, straight out of the sixties. Her long, auburn hair hung down the back of her suede fringed jacket. Her family moved to another neighborhood a year later. I never forgot her captivating smile, nor her expressive hands that seemed to be directing her own symphony. Karen was to come back into my life, but this time she would be involved with my brother-in-law. We were cruising around one night when Karen told me about a recurring dream she was having. In this dream she was always making love to women. She asked if I ever had such dreams, or thoughts about women. I said yes, and we smiled at each other slyly.

Two months passed after our reunion and we drove to a motel and made love. I thought I had died and gone to heaven.

Tonight I felt like a silly teenager in love for the first time. I couldn't wait to finish dinner so I could go to her. Sometimes our lovemaking was so passionate that we thought we'd explode into a million pieces, into each other's being.

I sometimes had to reassure Karen that I didn't turn to her because my marriage was failing. I had simply fallen in love with her. Other times we would sit and say nothing and that was enough. When Karen was pregnant, I was her support person when she went into labor. She squeezed my hand and I said, "I wish I was laying there." She gave me a painful smile and said, "Stop crying, it will be your turn next." Karen gave birth to a baby boy early that afternoon.

It was painful leaving Karen in the evenings to return home to an insensitive husband I didn't love anymore. Society had brainwashed me into heterosexuality. It took years, but I decided that I would wake up from this hellish nightmare. So there I was, a Black, middle-class woman having an affair with a woman I dearly loved and wanting a child.

Robert and I had gone through infertility work-ups for almost two years. We had seen four doctors in all. I was put on Clomid, a fertility drug that increases a woman's chances of becoming pregnant. Finally, Dr. T. suggested that Robert stop drinking for a period of two to eight months. The alcohol was having an effect on the motility of his sperm. After this suggestion was made, Robert continued to drink even more. We began to argue a lot (later he dropped out of college), and I put the thought of our having children on the back burner.

Robert's behavior became so erratic that I was literally

afraid to sleep next to him. I began to find spoons in the bathroom and mirrors laying around the house. I knew then that Robert was deeply involved in drugs. One night I returned home to find the ten-speed and a garden rake locked in the bedroom with him.

I walked to Karen's in the dark cursing every step. When I returned home the following morning, I packed a small suitcase. I called my mother and explained that I was going to file for a divorce. She suggested that I not alert Robert to what I was going to do. I agreed. Robert came home after work with an attitude, so I kept out of his way. I had lost my driver's license and asked him if he had seen it. He ignored me and walked off. I said, "Hey, I'm talking to you." He chased me into the bedroom and hit me in my left temple, knocking me on the bed. When he let up off me, I grabbed my jacket and the ten-speed and made it down the steps.

Robert heard the door open and came after me. To my surprise a police car happened to be sitting next door. I looked at our car that Robert had blown the engine in, and dropped the bike next to it. While I explained to the officer what had just happened, Robert took off on the bike. The officer waited until I got my suitcase and watched me walk down to the neighborhood bar. At the bar I could use the phone, have a drink, and decide in what direction to go.

The muscles tightened in my neck. My anger began to direct my actions. I called Ron, a close friend, and had him drive me to the hospital. I had an abrasion on my left temple, a bruised jaw, and my doctor prescribed muscle relaxers, and #4 codeine for the pain.

Ron was very patient with me after we left the hospital. He drove me around town until I decided to go to Karen's. I walked into Karen's an hour later. She said, "Girl, I was wondering how much more you were going to take." Shortly thereafter, I got a restraining order, attended a dissolution workshop, and did my own divorce. I was so elated when the divorce was final that I said to Karen, "Let's string some beer cans on the bumper, and put up a JUST DIVORCED sign."

It had taken me all this time to realize that my marriage failed not only because of Robert's substance abuse, but also because my deepest feelings of love belonged to women. I parted from Karen within the year because of her drug abuse. I prayed that both Karen and Robert would someday be free of drugs.

After I left Karen, I went for long walks, did a lot of reading and began to frequent the gay bars to dance away my frustrations. I became involved with a very kind-hearted woman that I had met in the bar. Things didn't work out between us, so I moved out of her place and moved in with one of my relatives. Five months later at the Broadway L.T.D. (a mixed bar), I met a woman who also wanted children. We sat on Katrina's bedroom floor one summer afternoon discussing our future goals which were similar. Those goals were to finish college and have a child. It felt good to have something in common with someone at this point in my life. I pulled myself together and decided to return to college.

Karen had introduced me to David a few months back. David was dark, well built, and his cat-shaped eyes seemed to stare right through me. When he began to take an interest in me, Karen explained that I was relating to women now. He told Karen, "That's okay, I think that women loving women is beautiful." David was always glad to see me and went to great lengths to cheer me up. We went for long drives in the mountains, played pool together, and eventually became good friends. I had discussed my desire to have a child several times. One night he came out and asked me if he could volunteer. "Besides," he said, "it's better than making a trip to the Sperm Bank." We had been shooting pool that night and one thing led to another. I was very nervous because I hadn't slept with a man in ages. I wasn't sure how I'd feel afterwards. We made love that night, but the magical feelings just weren't there. When I make love to women, the promise of total bliss is enough to fulfill me.

In July of '84, I almost fell off the couch when my doctor informed me that I was pregnant. I was really shocked. For two years my test results had come back negative. Plus,

David and I had slept together only once. I saw no reason to terminate my plan for college because I was pregnant. Autumn leaves crumbled underfoot while I prayed I'd make it through Humanities without getting sick again.

Camille arrived after fourteen hours of labor on a beautiful March afternoon. I felt very blessed when my doctor placed her on my stomach. I looked up to her father and my mother, and somehow managed a tired smile. I didn't even require stitches after Camille's birth. I'm not sure, but I think the redraspberry tea I drank throughout my pregnancy eased a lot of the pain. I raised the blinds in my hospital room and the world was blessed with one more precious miracle. My thoughts skipped to the future. Some day I'll have to explain to Camille that her mom is lesbian.

Camille didn't stay a baby long. At seven months, she was running over my feet in her walker. At nine months, her walker was history. I ran into Katrina again at the Take Back The Night rally. Katrina had lost four children in the past due to her diabetes. She proudly announced that she was five months pregnant. She now has a healthy son. We had each reached one of our goals.

By Camille's first birthday, we moved out of our cracker-box apartment in the Lavender Heights district, into a two bedroom duplex. Anyone passing by our huge window might see Camille with her thick, black braids, and cocoa brown eyes peering out. Camille is magnetic, drawing both children and adults to her. When I was pregnant with Camille, I constantly spoke to her. I'm sure this has something to do with her early development in sitting, walking, and talking. Her ability to memorize information blows me away.

As a new parent, I have learned many things from Camille. Since her birth, I have begun to focus on myself more. I give everything I do a little more thought because I want to be able to respond in a constructive way, to any given situation. It's important for me to confront everything I fear since I don't want to pass my fears on to Camille. For example, I don't swim very well, so it's a must that we both learn to swim.

Being a lesbian mother, I know I'll have problems to deal with. Although I don't have to contend with an ex-husband, or custody battles, there are still problems. I have come out to only one family member, so the rest of my family doesn't know I'm lesbian. It hurts me deeply to hear comments from my mother like, "The Lord will send a good man and a good daddy to you." It's sad, but I'll never come out to my mother. She would only throw biblical passages at me. The Judaeo-Christian tradition has taught the world that homosexuality is immoral. Biblical passages in the past have been used to discriminate against minorities, Jews, and women. It's a tragedy that so many gay people are rejected for following our natural homosexual responses.

It is also difficult at times to find a lover who will accept my child. While visiting the Blue Moon, a women's bar, a woman gave me a puzzled look when I showed her a picture of Camille. I'm no mind reader, but she was probably thinking, "This woman is supposed to be in gay life, and she has a young daughter?" She might have been wondering if I was still involved with men. I have met some gay women who weren't very trusting of women they thought were bisexual. I explained to her that I will always be involved with women.

There is a new breed of lesbian mothers out there, and we are many. I recently heard of a lesbian couple who have both been artificially inseminated, bringing two beautiful children into their relationship. The lesbian mother of the '80s is a foster parent, adopts, has been artificially inseminated, has selected a male friend to father a child, or has children from a previous marriage. Either way, all of us are women loving women and our children.

It is late October and tonight I'm dancing with my new love. The straight bar I sought refuge in, is now a women's bar. As I dance at the Blue Moon on the same date I left my husband three years ago, I have much to celebrate. As the seasons changed, I grew into the new lesbian mother.

Sue Silvermarie

*At the age of forty I have a lot in common
with my seventeen-year-old. I'm making a
career change (mail carrier to social worker)
and feeling my way into a new identity, much
as he is. Back when I was pregnant, unwed
and straight, my choice to have and raise
my son was made in the face of stiff opposition. After he was born, I married a man
who had been a Catholic priest. He was not
the father. I came out as a lesbian and left
the marriage when my son was two. I had
a great deal of support from a co-op group
of mostly lesbian mothers over the years, and
for three years we lived with a wonderful
friend who co-parented with me. This friend
who was never my lover took my son in later
on for an entire year, while I lived elsewhere.
The rest of the years David and I raised one
another alone. I am white and my son is half
Brazilian. I've been a poet and performer for
the past fifteen years.*

SINGLE MOTHER

Sue Silvermarie

"There was an old woman who lived in a shoe.
She had so many children she didn't know what to do.
She gave them some broth, without any bread,
And whipped them all soundly, and sent them to bed."

In Mother Goose
an old king is a wise one.
But an old woman
means a used one.

Yes of course
she was worn out.
She had such a crazed look
Welfare wouldn't even
let her into a project.
But she was resourceful.
She found a big synthetic boot
big as a boat
dumped by the company as a gimmick gone wrong,
and had her kids haul it to the hills
on a roller-skate device.

Most of the time
they managed to get by.
The kids
played Robin Hood in the forest
and taught themselves
useful things like reading trees.
She herself
was a specialist in writing spells.

No money there though
so she gathered herbs by day
to sell at Saturday market,
and moonlighted as a witch
when the kids were asleep.

Most of the time she managed
to get by.
But once in a while
she cracked under that ax
of responsiblity.
Naturally
it was one of the cracks
that got into Mother Goose.

A cold night in the old shoe.
No bread, nine kids
and every one of them
overtired as owls at dawn.
Her nerves were raw
as she ladled that broth.
Then the whole shoe rocked
with some new ruckus
and enough was enough.
She whacked the nearest with her wooden ladle
and lined up the rest at her lap
to be fair.

They ran howling to their loft
and she had to endure
that splitting chorus for another hour.
Finally
she dragged herself to the door.
The hills, her only comfort,
this night stood like
accusations!
And she didn't, NO she didn't,
she didn't know what to do.

1975

SEVEN YEARS SATISFIED

We each
are boomerangs
returning home. We fly
sure of perfect catch, into one
bearhug.
We laugh, rippling,
bonding also in sound,
our babble a chime and echo.
The room tumbles with us
as we lose our roles and
ages, feed our equal hunger
as we
wheel, as we whirl.
Such a shining of eyes
then, when we can stop to see it:
yours, black
as the gleaming
Brazilian midnight when
I felt your life take root in me;
my gaze
chestnut brown, flushed
and rich with fresh vision.
How a month apart can startle!

David
So many threads
you dangle from and spin
to me. Little acrobat how
we risk
the ropes and fly,
the weaving between us magik.

First night

I let you sleep
with me, and let myself,
secrets and ghost stories acting
lattice,
like elastic
verbal presents
given and clambered across.
Next day
we speed on bikes
parting the air, sucking
the air like flames. You ride ahead
buckled
into your black
cap, an aviator
with red plastic glasses and fringed
pink gloves.
Exotic child
my mothering's as odd
may it be as artless, as your
fancies.

I fathom you
anew tonight and smile
as you teach me chess. I cherish
your glee
of expertise,
your generous cues, the
calm of your glance in strategy.
Nearness,
like a sea mist,
lifts to show me clear deeps.
I see I am in love with you.
Seven
years satisfied,
suddenly separate,
you arrive across the table.

You claimed
my womb without

announcement, on the night
in July your kind claimed the moon.
I know
I pulled your tide
choosing you as surely.
Tonight I sense one cycle draw
complete,
one begin. We
move to new relation.
I mark your widening course, I feel
myself
shifting orbit.
Seven years satisfied
I am, watching you reach beyond me.

1977

JOURNAL ENTRY

December 28, 1982

David's hands are larger than mine now. They hold mine strongly now, not as once when they rested like tiny birds inside my hands, not as once when they held on to one of my fingers and could find no fault with me. He has hands now of a young man, beautiful hands that are long and graceful, and quite suddenly I know that this child will someday take care of me with these hands.

Hands that are just beginning to give and take in the world I live in, they seem to me to be alive with gifts. He has healing hands, creative hands, this I sense for the first time. Power and innocence in my child's hands. I love this boy who has come into my life and reaches out into his own life now, with these hands. Shaping his own life, trying the weight and texture of ways to live, his hands show me my own hands gone further. His hands will reach where I have not. These hands that seem to me to be perfect will touch and feel pleasure and pain. These hands that are larger than mine though he's only twelve years old, will elongate even more as both of us grow older. When my hands are very veined and wrinkled and wise, his will enfold mine easily. This is the miracle.

Lee Swislow

I am a thirty-eight-year-old biological mother, raising my son with my lover of six years. I am the daughter of a Jewish father and Catholic mother, raised Catholic. I work as a nurse and think constantly about whether to have another child.

J.J.

Lee Swislow

The March on Washington . . . Our First Separation

For a while I agonized over whether I should bring him. In retrospect, I don't know how I could have even considered it. It would not have been any fun to drag fifteen-month-old J.J. down to Washington, spend much of the day standing around, do a little marching, and then go back to Boston. Of course, it was terrific for me. I had been to the Gay and Lesbian March in 1979 and this one was bigger and better. But J.J. would not have appreciated it in the same way.

Once I decided not to bring him I was okay with the decision. I was even a little excited about being on my own, briefly, being a childless woman once again. Although I was going to be gone for only thirty-six hours, this was to be our first real separation.

It wasn't exactly that I missed him. There were moments when I wanted him there, like when I was hanging out on the Mall and imagined his excitement at being able to run in such a large, open space. But these were only moments. I enjoyed being there alone (meaning not with my child but with my adult friends).

Yet I was acutely aware of how entwined my life is with his. In the last fifteen months we've been to many demonstrations and social events together. Always he is there to take up any empty space, and to add to already full space. I talk about him, I talk to him, I watch over him. In being so much a part of me, his existence obscures the challenge of knowing and simply being myself.

I love my son deeply and passionately. And I also see how much work it will be for both of us to loosen our very magical connection.

A Handshake and a Baby

Neither Joe nor I are into contracts. Partly it's personality and partly it's politics. He's a principled anarchist, while I'm a socialist opposed to most government structures. Besides, I think a contract is only a statement of how one is feeling at that particular moment. Conflicts that arise in the future have to be resolved in the future. For me, the most important thing was knowing that Joe would never take me to court. On that issue, I have no doubts.

Darlene and I wanted J.J.'s father to be someone we both knew and liked, and someone who wanted to be involved with the child. We had minimums and maximums on his level of involvement. The minimum was that J.J. would know that Joe was his father and that they would have regular, if infrequent, contact. The maximum is a little looser. It will depend on how much they like each other and how much time they want to spend together. That's a dynamic I can't control. The limit is that Darlene and I are the parents and we make the basic child-rearing decisions.

I knew Joe would have no trouble with any of this. I first met him doing union work at the hospital where we both worked. Later, he was head nurse on my floor. We've been friends for six years. He is not a very possessive person, and that extends to his sperm. If I wanted to have a kid and he could help me, he thought that was great.

It took me six months to get pregnant. During that time Joe kept track of my cycle, would check to see if I got my period, and would write down in his calendar the days he was coming over to visit and jerk off. We had a corner for his favorite sex magazines. He used my pyrex cup as a receiving vessel. Even now I feel good every time I cook.

Still, despite all Joe's sweetness and conscientiousness during this process, I felt incredibly dependent on him and vulnerable during this time. I didn't want to ask for or do anything that might make him angry. After all, at any moment he could decide the whole thing was a drag and he didn't want to do it any more. Even though the fear was all in my head (Joe was totally committed to the process), it was, at times, almost consuming.

Now I have J.J., Joe comes over once a week to babysit. Generally I go running. For right now, it's working great.

The Little White Boy With Soul

Originally Darlene and I were looking for a Black donor so that I would have an interracial baby, one that would reflect our interracial relationship. We initially asked Joe's lover, who is Black, rather than Joe. But the more we talked with him and the more he agonized over possibly being the father, the more clear our priorities became. The donor's commitment was more important to us than his race, since we wanted an involved father. Joe was clearly the one. Naturally, Darlene still wishes J.J. had a little more color.

Darlene grew up in Boston, and has a huge extended family here. Her mother is one of fourteen children. Darlene has an aunt, uncle and cousin who are gay. Everybody is out and accepted. Similarly, I've always been welcomed as Darlene's lover.

People in Darlene's family were pleased and supportive when they learned I was pregnant, even if they were unsure about the mechanics. (I think Darlene explained that to them privately.) Darlene introduced them to the language of co-parenting, a phrase she had only recently come by. (Her mother calls that kind of language "Cambridge talk.") The word co-parenting was new, but the idea of women raising kids alone was not. Many of her aunts and cousins have kids, and few of them live with the fathers. And so, although Darlene and I see J.J. as our own little miracle, to Darlene's family, he is welcomed and loved as just one more kid.

Because Darlene's family lives in Boston, while my parents live in Florida, it is her family that J.J. sees most. Darlene's mother sits for him often, and her sister babysat him for six weeks before he was old enough for daycare. That's when they started calling him "the little white boy with soul."

At this point, I think it's more a prediction than a reality. It's still early to tell how much soul he has. I do know, however, that Darlene and her mom are both pleased at how much he likes grandma's cooking. They don't think much of the tofu and veggies I feed him, and like to see him grubbing on fried chicken and yams. I like to see J.J. feeling safe, loved and at home with Black people. I hope it's a feeling he never loses.

A couple of weeks ago I was walking through Central Square with J.J. in the backpack. We passed a particularly large boom-box playing loud rap music. As J.J. started bouncing in the pack, I thought, maybe he will have soul.

Could this be Co-Parenting?

While I was pregnant, Darlene was thrilled to tell people she was going to be the co-parent. She was glad there was a word for what we were doing. Although she had a language, there were no real concepts to go with it. She didn't really know people who were co-parenting, she didn't talk to her friends about it, she didn't go to a support group for lesbians thinking of having kids. None of this is Darlene's style. She figured we would deal with raising the kid together when he arrived.

Although she didn't have a very clear idea about the co-parent's role, she had a very clear idea about the mother's role. For Darlene, the mother was the one with ultimate responsibility and ultimate authority. Other people could be very involved with a child—aunts, grandmothers, friends, cousins— but in the end, the kid still had one mother, and she was the one with the power.

Before J.J. was born, Darlene would say, "If we broke up, would you still let me see the baby?" I would answer, "But, Darlene, this is our child, not mine." She would reply, "You know what I mean." Of course, I did know what she meant. Certainly if we broke up, Darlene's access to the child would be limited by what I would allow. I would have the baby; she would have only my good will and intentions to count on.

My ideas of co-parenting were hardly much clearer than Darlene's. Although I'm more likely to discuss things in advance, and to talk about them with my friends, I, too, really believe you only know how to deal with a situation when it happens. Eventually J.J. arrived, and Darlene and I became his parents.

I first tried breastfeeding J.J. when he was about fifteen minutes old. I was awkward and unsure; he was a natural. He immediately found my breast and started sucking. I'm not sure he stopped for the whole next month. Although we planned to have Darlene give him bottles occasionally, it was easy to keep putting it off. I didn't want to start pumping my breasts until I was sure I had a good milk supply. I didn't want to give him formula because I thought that might interfere with my milk coming in well. Besides, the whole idea of sterilizing bottles and preparing formula seemed complicated and difficult during those already stressful first few weeks.

Darlene didn't push the bottle business either. She hates to be in situations where she is not totally at ease, and this little newborn made her somewhat anxious. J.J. was frequently fussy, and the only thing that consistently pleased him was nursing. For both of us, it was much easier to just let me take him, nurse him, and comfort him.

When J.J. was about six or seven weeks old, we started aggressively trying to give him a bottle. I would go out, leaving Darlene alone with J.J. and a freezer full of breast milk I had been conscientiously pumping. J.J. had no interest in the nasty rubber nipple Darlene was offering him. He would cry, he would fuss, or he would just go to sleep. But he would not drink from the bottle.

After a number of tries, Darlene was ready to give up. So was I. I'm sure we could have forced the issue and eventually won, but neither of us had the heart for it.

Darlene felt that I was the mother, and that if J.J.

wanted to nurse that much, then that's how it should be. She couldn't imagine her role being equal to mine, particularly with a newborn. She was also having a hard time coping with the tremendous increase in responsibility that comes with being a parent. Letting me be the only one that could feed him guaranteed that I would have most of that responsibility.

And I was willing to take on that responsibility. I was thirty-seven years old, I had been waiting a long time to be ready to have this child, and I was completely into him. As much as I wanted to raise J.J. with Darlene, in the deepest sections of my heart, I believed (and truthfully, still do believe), that I could parent him better than anyone else.

For me, that's the heart of our co-parenting conflict. I don't say the words out loud, I don't use them in discussions with Darlene, but in my mind I say—He's my child and I know what's best. Because Darlene doesn't believe she should have equal responsibility and control, because she won't fight me for that, I don't have to face whether I could really give it to her. I say I would prefer more equal parenting, but those words have not been put to any test.

Actually, Darlene and I don't have many conflicts about raising J.J. I knew, from having seen her with her nephew over the four and a half years we were involved before J.J. was born, that we had different parenting styles. I sometimes think she's a little harsh, and she thinks I do far too much reasoning and talking. But I think that's okay. I'm pretty easy-going and I think kids are adaptable. I know J.J. will learn a lot from the different ways of loving, playing and disciplining that Darlene and I have.

Right now we're comfortable with our roles. What's most important is that Darlene loves me and J.J., J.J. loves Darlene and momma, and I love the both of them.

Jan Clausen

I am a writer, political activist and "non-biological" lesbian parent. My poetry, fiction, and critical prose have been widely published in the U.S. and Great Britain. Recent books are The Prosperine Papers, a novel (Crossing Press, 1988) and Books & Life, a collection of essays (Ohio State University Press, 1988). I work in the Central America solidarity movement, and transcribe tapes for a living.

ERICKA

Jan Clausen

"Ericka" and "The Birthday Party" are excerpted from Sinking, Stealing, *a novel. When Rhea dies suddenly in a car accident, her ex-husband, Daniel, wants custody of his daughter and the options open to Josie Muller, Rhea's lover, are few.*

When things go well with Ericka, I feel terrific, easily inclined to congratulate myself on my powers of nurturance. When they don't, I feel rotten, a washout as a parent and perhaps as a human being. All my L.A.-nuclear-family spawned pessimism about the prospects for constructive relations between the generations comes flooding in, inclining me to hark back to the drastic views of a certain early radical feminist who denounced the enterprise of motherhood as so inherently oppressive to adult and child alike that she proposed infants should begin their careers in test tubes and grow to maturity in some similarly antiseptic setting.

In the days when we lived together, I used to oscillate frequently between these poles of enthusiasm and alarm, and could never decide whether Rhea's comparative equanimity should be ascribed to a different temperament, or to her relative security as the official Mother. Since Ericka's birthday weekend, I've found myself back on the old see saw. Something, somehow, shifted for me then: it became plainer to me that I wasn't about to capitulate quietly to the forces of circumstance, wasn't going to give up on her without a fight.

I imagine I notice a change in the weather between us already, though I haven't held my famous parley with her father. Sometimes, wonderfully, we seem much closer; at others, only more intimately at odds, wrangling and sparring like a pair of crochety siblings. It's almost as though in order to fight for her I have to fight her first. Fight her, and perhaps myself.

Case in point, our initial interaction when she comes to spend a weekend, Daniel having elected to park her with me while he and Brenda travel to Cleveland overnight on some unspecified business:

To begin with, of course, conditions are, as usual, far short of the ideal. From one point of view the extra time with her is a windfall for which I ought to be grateful, but my gratitude is marred by irritation at having had the offer of it sprung on me midweek, requiring me to cancel dinner plans with Luce and reminding me that I'm viewed in certain quarters as a glorified babysitter. Still, I'm quite prepared to put the best face on things—until the front door buzzer jerks me awake at 7:30 Saturday morning.

I stagger into my robe and wait at the top of the stairs while loud, deliberate thumps gradually ascend. *Fee, fi, fo, fum*, seems to be the general tone. At last my erstwhile child heaves in sight lugging her overnight case as though it were a serious burden. Impeccably dressed this morning, her hair well-brushed, barretted, she leads with her pointed chin, a misanthropic sprite.

"Ssshh," I greet her, none too cordially, "you'll wake up the whole building."

"I can't help it if this suitcase weighs a ton."

"I thought your father was going to drop you off after eight."

"Their plane got switched or something. What's for breakfast?"

"I haven't gotten that far. The buzzer woke me up."

"Can we go out? *Please?*"

"I don't think so, not this morning. We'll cook something here. How about French toast?"

"Yuk. You always make it with whole wheat."

"What's wrong with that?"

"I like how Nilda makes it."

I at least know enough to ignore that one. "Come in, put your things in the closet. Did your father send a note?"

"Oh yeah. Here," And she hands me a piece of paper on which is scribbled a hotel address and phone number.

"What's going on in Cleveland, anyway?"

"I dunno. Daddy had work."

"How come Brenda went along?"

"I dunno. Well, see, it's hard to explain. She said she was freaking out or something, so Daddy said he'd take her and give her a little rest. I think that's it, anyway. Leah's been sort of a brat, she's in the Terrible Twos, Brenda says, and she has these obnoxious tantrums."

"So where is Leah staying?" I can't resist pumping, but it makes me feel a bit guilty—not because I elicit any state secrets, but because I intend her innocent replies to fuel my covert resentment of Daniel and his doings.

"At Brenda's mom's. *Please*, can we go out?"

"Ericka, you heard me the first time."

"How *come?*"

"There's plenty of stuff to fix right here in the house. We'll be going out later to do some errands. Now I'm going to get dressed, so why don't you figure out what you want in the meantime. We could have eggs, pancakes...I could make matzoh brie."

"It's soggy, how you make it."

"Then you think of something."

When I emerge from the bathroom she's "watching cartoons," her rigid, mirthless features two feet from the screen.

"Aren't you a little old to watch that stuff? Decide what you want yet?"

As though intent on some riveting sports match, she declines to turn her head. "Lox and a bagel. No, I meant a bialy."

"Sorry, kid. That's not on today's menu. It's a pretty expensive treat, but maybe we'll have it sometime."

"*We* have that every weekend. It's Daddy's favorite. He likes onion bagels, but I usually tell Brenda to get me a bialy."

She can't be fully aware of how such comparisons aggravate me, but telling myself this never seems to diminish their impact. I want to blot out the TV's sullen light; to seize her, shake her, remind her where she comes from. I want to inform her she talks like a very spoiled brat. But I confine myself to announcing rather coldly that I'm mixing up some pancakes, and she's welcome to let me know if she decides she wants any.

As I work, scattered bursts of animated mayhem assault my cringing eardrums; but to make her turn the thing down would invite a further hassle, and on days like this one picks one's skirmishes. In the end, of course, she elects to eat with me, and though I eye with disapproval the provocative volume of butter and Log Cabin syrup with which she annoints her two modest pancakes, I don't say anything. Better to give her credit for basic compliance and the fact that she doesn't mention the real Vermont maple syrup Brenda probably serves.

"You don't seem to be in a very good mood," I venture finally.

She shrugs, masticates pancakes. "Neither do you."

"Maybe we could both try starting over."

"Fine with me." Another belligerent shrug.

"Did something happen to upset you before you got here this morning?"

"How could it? There wasn't time. Brenda just woke me up and kept saying hurry this hurry that help Leah hurry hurry hurry and then we got in the car."

"Something last night, then?"

"Everything's dumb, that's all."

Eventually I get more out of her, but not for an hour or two. By that time we've adjourned our morning struggle session to my usual laundromat which, although it's still early, is a jam-packed mini-inferno appropriate to our sour, scrappy mood: close, steamy, rife with peevish kids and frenzied mothers admonishing them in English and/or Spanish, with blows and imprecations aimed at malfunctioning machines, and bitter competition over access to ones that work. Will the family wardrobe get washed and dried without major incident, without some cheap dye running and ruining an entire load, without mechanical failure before the "spin" cycle? Will the day in which so much is to be accomplished proceed relatively smoothly, or merely as a series of escalating frustrations? Such are the stakes in an urban laundromat.

Ericka somehow lays claim to a broken plastic chair in a far corner, and sits there reading her Judy Blume book. Her expression suggests she's above all this vulgar turmoil, and for forty-five minutes I let well enough alone. Then, at the point where I give up on the feeble dryer and decide to fold my clothes although some are still damp, I risk calling her over.

She helps me fold with sharp, resentful gestures— "These clothes are still soaking"—then suddenly takes up our breakfast conversation as though she had never interrupted it. She *is* mad, she says. Nobody wants her. And she bets *I* would feel horrible if nobody wanted me, too.

I agree it's a dismal fate to be unwanted, but dispute her melodramatic second premise. After some probing I'm able to discover that when Brenda decided to accompany Daniel to Cleveland, she first asked Nilda to sit. Nilda had declined due to family responsibilities, and Ericka overheard part of a subsequent discussion between Brenda and Daniel about whether they could ask Brenda's mother to take both her and Leah. Brenda felt this would be an imposition, so Daniel gave me a call.

"So I come here and you don't want me either!" The tone of grievance whines into her voice like the note of gears downshifting for a hill. "Everybody should just say the truth: they wish I'd disappear. I'll camp overnight in Prospect Park, that's what!"

"Oh, Ericka, don't be silly."

"Well, all you could do was act like I got there too early and everything."

"I'm sorry, kiddo. I was half asleep. It's not your fault,

but it makes problems for me when your father doesn't let me know his plans. He told me one time and dropped you off at another. It's just like when he called me about this weekend — I really wanted you to come, but because he didn't let me know until the last minute, I had to switch a dinner date I'd made with a friend. It doesn't mean I don't want to see you."

Ericka, evidently somewhat mollified by this defense, proceeds to another complaint. "Anyway, why couldn't he have called you first thing! I can't *stand* Brenda's mom."

"Did you let him know you didn't want to stay with her?"

"Uh-uh. See, I wasn't really supposed to hear them talking about it. But I don't think she likes *me* that much, either, so how come she always has to come over and hug me and make me call her Grandma? Some of her perfume even rubs off," She wrinkles her nose, graphic in distaste. "You could choke from how that stuff stinks."

"It doesn't sound too pleasant," I allow. She's watching me to see whether I'm inclined to rebuke or encourage this unprecedented critique. Either seems a mistake, so I shift the subject slightly.

"I think your father and I need to have a talk. I really do want us to spend more time together, so I hope we can set up a different schedule."

"You mean, like have me sleep over more and stuff?"

"I'd like that, if you want."

"How come I stopped sleeping over every week, anyway?"

"Your father wanted you over there more."

"Why?"

"He never did explain very well. Basically he said since it was a hard time for you he felt it would be better for you to be in one place."

"That's a dumb reason."

By now Ericka has dropped her pose of aggrieved hauteur, and with it has dissolved my stance of puritan denial. We parade home with the laundry through warm, almost festive, spring streets; and when she asks if we could do something "fun" this afternoon, my alacrity in agreeing surprises me.

"Could we see—," and she names a current box office hit which, I gather from ubiquitous subway ads and TV commercials, nostalgically pretends to re-create the teenage working-class culture of twenty-five years ago. She already knows two of the songs, she says. Lots of kids in her class went.

"No, kiddo, not that one, I'm afraid. How about something we could do outside? The weather's so nice."

"How come not that one?"

"Because I've seen the ads for it, and for one thing I'm not crazy about movies that exploit women."

"What's *exploit* mean?"

"Treat like a piece of shit."

She giggles at my daring, then reflects, "Oh, you mean, because they, you know, *do it?*"

"They what?"

"You know, *do it,* the boys *do it* with the girls. TeriAnn's mother said she couldn't go because she heard the girls and boys...you know..." she trails off, unnerved. "She said it was too sexy."

"Well, not exactly." I don't know how to put it.   "I mean, just like in a lot of other movies, they try to make you think girls like to spend all their time dressing up and acting silly in order to get boys to pay attention to them."

"Yuk, that's stupid. I wouldn't do that."

"Let's figure out something else you'd enjoy doing."

We end up on the F train to Coney Island. The very name invokes the desired note of magic, the aura of pure, wholly irresponsible pleasure required for a celebration of spring. And Ericka seems satisfied with the idea. I've never taken her on the rides out there, though she's been several times with friends and their families. Rhea and I used to make a pilgrimage once or twice a year to wander beneath the huge neon-lit ferris wheel; to witness the crawl and plunge of the world-famous roller coaster with its shrieking passengers; to inhale the reek of the matchless fast-food stands with their catholic arrays of clams and pizza, knishes and sausage, calzone and corn on the cob; and to draw a definitive sense of participation in summer from proximity to acres of beached flesh, boardwalk multitudes, and the Spanish-speaking families thick on the pier: their encampments of blankets and pillows and babies and coolers, their crab-traps baited with hunks of raw chicken, their pursuit of some northern inkling of island life.

Erick assures me that the rides will be functioning. Apparently it's knowledge common to every child in Brooklyn that Easter weekend, just past, is opening time out there. On the train she teases me by reciting a litany of harrowing rides to which I will be subjected. I listen for a while, then sink into my own thoughts. The train has groped up from its familiar underworld into the strong light of extreme south Brooklyn, and I bask in our jerky progress toward the earth's blue end. It's been months since I've voyaged to anywhere but Manhattan, and on a day like this when the seasonal shift is palpable, even a ride out to Coney Island can feel like significant travel.

But a sudden non sequitur from my companion commands my full attention: "Josie, what does *sexy* mean, really?"

"Well, different things...," I attempt, caught totally unprepared. "Something to do with sex, or that makes people think about it." I'm aware of providing a circular definition; though I know she knows, for instance, where babies come from, that doesn't seem quite the point.

"Am I sexy?"

Amused and alarmed both, I scrutinize her. She's looking a rather young ten years at the moment, hair now an unkempt mop, a residue of lunch lingering around her small red mouth. Not for the first time, it occurs to me how little I know about her and her world of social intrigue and private prurient fantasy. One day, not long ago on Seventh Avenue in the Slope, I found myself walking behind a clutch of schoolgirls, aged perhaps thirteen at the most. They were wearing plaid skirts and knee socks of parochial school pupils, and were engaged in a voluptuous consumption of ice cream cones, giggling in speculation as to what their mothers would do if they ever "found out." It took me several blocks of assiduous eavesdropping for me to ascertain that their tremendous secret consisted not in the fact of having spoiled their dinners with sweets, or having cut sixth period, but rather in having "made out" with boys at somebody's birthday party. I thought, then, of Ericka, with a fatalistic sense of how the gap between us seemed destined to widen with time, Daniel or no Daniel. It seemed to me that all the feminist theorizing, analyzing, anger, and agitating of the past ten years or so should have made more of a difference in the world than I suddenly felt they had, looking at those sweet, sticky-faced, ignorant little girls.

"Josie, am I sexy?" she pursues. "See, I'm almost starting to have... tits." She pokes out her bony rib-cage, half-serious, half-clowning. "Saundra in my class has real big ones."

" 'Sexy' isn't exactly one of my favorite expressions," I begin, trapped now by my initial failure to define the term adequately. Sex education has never been my strong suit, and I'm doubly self-conscious in this setting. We're only a stop or two from the end of the line, and the car has emptied out; our companions now consist of a mother with several kids at the far end, a teenage boy standing by the nearest doors, and a man across the aisle from us reading a Russian paper.

"Why not?" she has to know, of course.

How to say, without seeming a hopeless prude? "It's a word I feel like men use a lot to put women down, to say we should just be acting in ways to please them. They make it sound like it's a compliment, when really it often isn't." But I know I'm still not touching on her real question, whatever it is. "You're very nice-looking, and you're strong and smart," I try to reassure her.

"Brenda said I might get my period soon."

"Yes, I guess you might. It's hard to tell."

"She gave me a box of sanitary napkins to soak up, you know, the blood. She said when she was my age they had this stupid kind with a belt that was really uncomfortable, but now they make them different, so they stick to your panties, sort of. Josie, how did you get to be a lesbian?"

Clearly I'm in for a day of strenuous discourse. It's always been like this with Ericka: what seem like months of superficial chatter, then a sudden spate of profound and knotty questions.

"Let's talk about that later, okay? I want to tell you about it, but I'd feel much better doing it when we're home by ourselves." I feel guilty putting her off, but the car is far too quiet. Beyond the screen of his Cyrillic columns, the newspaper-reader may understand all our English, and as for that tall youth in his spiffy creased jeans, who knows what he is thinking?

At last the train grinds to its final halt, the conductor proclaims our arrival, and we take the concrete ramp that leads down to the vast, spooky station, forlorn in the absence of its hot-weather multitudes. Outside, stores are closed, some gutted: everything in abeyance, waiting to begin. A block or two—the rides, maybe half of them open—then the empty beach, the token strip of water.

In fact, Coney Island toward the end of March is reminiscent of L.A.'s Pacific Ocean Park in December or January. Like that pivotal locale of my adolescence, it is clearly a haven for drifters, unemployed persons, and lovers illicit or impoverished enough to seek the chilly charms of an off-season beach. Only a few young parents loiter by with strollers in the alley ways between the kiddie rides; only a few hopeful dark-skinned boys weigh opportunities to "test their skill" and win green or pink stuffed animals. Seduced by thin sunshine, everyone seems to be shivering in light, inadequate garments; only the peripatetic radios, blaring disco hits of last summer or of next, enter fully into the pretext that we've gotten over winter. But Ericka moves happily to the sound of staticky music, and I buy her a big blue cloud of cotton candy to mark our descent into ultimate decadence.

For a while I get away with merely applauding her bravery on several of the tamer adult rides, but eventually she prevails on me to "try" a lethal-looking arrangement called The Hammer. Business is slow, evidently, for a serious-looking young man in spectacles and long dreadlocks has to put aside a copy of *Pedagogy of the Oppressed* in order to strap us into the cab of a mobile torture chamber that slams us back and forth for an interminable several minutes, while Ericka claws at me and bleats ecstatically for it to *stop*. After, she pops out not visibly worse for wear, and begs to know wasn't I *scared to death*, and couldn't we maybe go on the roller coaster, just one little time?

In fact, I *was* quite sufficiently terrified, though I'm not about to say so. The mere fact that I couldn't recall having heard of any fatal accidents on Coney Island rides in recent years didn't seem to do a thing to reassure me that this rusty-looking contraption with its preoccupied attendant wasn't even more likly to self-destruct with us inside than the average American car, airplane, or nuclear-powered metropolis, unsafe at any speed. (But how is it I've so quickly aged, come so soon to shun a thing just because it terrifies me? There was a time not so long ago when I used to test myself by getting too wired on acid to scream when I rode the roller coaster beside the prismatic ocean; when I knelt half-dressed on the floor of Michael's car and groped clumsily in his lap, scared to death of cops and scared worse of being shown up in my virgin ineptitude, but resolved to master the arts of womanhood, or choke in the attempt.)

Luckily, Ericka's enthusiasm for death-defying amusement seems easily deflected. She agrees to my suggestion that we take one more ride, of my choice this time, and then call it a day. I pick the Wonder Wheel which is, despite its creaks and crotchets, wonderfully soothing after the frightful Hammer. Hung in a bucket, we rise like a shaky sun into the blank air above the densely inscribed boroughs. This time we hold hands calmly, given to sane, detached, visionary pleasures: below us the crawling, self-obsessed human landscape, pocked with industry, patched with commerce.

"Josie."

"What."

"Don't you feel...powerful?"

"How do you mean, powerful?"

"I feel like I feel in an airplane when it's taking off, or when me and Daddy went up to the top of the World Trade Center. Like I could stay up here forever. Like being a king or something."

"A king?" I frown, disapproving the reactionary image; but in fact I know just what she means, of course. Why else do drug users talk about "getting high?" Or, as I generally end up reflecting when I'm hiking in the mountains: how terribly acute of the Evil One to have tempted Jesus Christ at substantial altitudes.

But that's New Testament: not her metaphor. "Well," I allow, "I feel sort of like that too. But unfortunately we're just regular old people, and we've got to live down there."

"I know that," she answers, very soberly, as though I weren't joking, but stating a simple truth, one she wants to demonstrate she's old enough to grasp.

The wheel turns, and we come in for a quick landing. Sated with enjoyments, Ericka seems content to take a fairly direct route back to the train station, and before we know it we're rattling down once more into the old familiar hole.

When we emerge into the light at Seventh Avenue, it's to find the streets enveloped in sudden rain. We sprint back to my apartment, and arrive soaked, giggling, pleased, but thoroughly chilled.

"I can't stop shivering," Ericka objects.

"Dr. Muller prescribes a hot shower, followed as soon as practicable thereafter by a piping hot bowl of soup."

"Yuk, I don't want soup."

"How about the shower?"

"Could we take it together?"

"Well...I guess."

We used to do this often in the old days, when she would kick up a fuss about taking showers on her own because she was small enough to have trouble getting the water properly adjusted. But it's been a long time, and in the interim we've both grown self-conscious. I can sense, in the careful way she keeps her eyes off me, her secret interest in my perfectly average breasts, the impressive achievement of hair in spots where she doesn't yet have it.

"Brenda's really fat now," she volunteers.

"Is she?"

"Yeah," she giggles, "you should see her stomach. Her breasts got big, too."

This, I suppose, is intended to put me on notice that she hasn't forgotten our afternoon conversation, or my promise to discuss certain things later. I soap myself quickly and brace for further adventures.

Early as it is, we both get into pajamas. I pour apple juice and wine; I scramble eggs. Hopeless decadents, we take our plates into my room to eat with the TV set turned on low at the foot of the bed.

Slowly Ericka relaxes against my shoulder, flannel on flannel. I've gone a trifle limp myself with wine taken on top of exhaustion.

"That was a fun day," she says. It is her highest tribute.

"I'm glad you enjoyed it, kiddo. I enjoyed it too."

"Did you ever used to like rides, when you were little?"

"Yes, though when I was 'little' I never went on anything like that thing we were on today. When I was a teenager, I used to go to an amusement park near the ocean in L.A. that had some really scary rides like that."

"You went with your parents, then?"

"No, with friends."

"Like who?"

"A boy I liked, and some other kids."

"What was his name?"

"Michael."

"And what did you do there, just go on rides?"

"No, other things. Wandered around, hung out. Smoked

cigarettes and dope and ate pickles and played transistor radios loud on stations that had Pete Seeger and Bob Dylan and Joan Baez. And we'd act crazy just to freak people out, and this boy, Michael, would play his harmonica."

"My father smokes dope too." But she's clearly impressed. "What else did you used to do?"

"We took acid sometimes."

"What's acid?"

"LSD, a very strong, dangerous drug. I was probably lucky it didn't really mess me up." Belatedly it hits me what a lousy example I'm setting.

But tonight I'm tired of being exemplary. Let Brenda and Daniel handle that department. "Or sometimes we'd take dex or methedrine instead—those are other drugs, also bad for you, that make you want to talk a lot and smoke, and you don't notice so much being tired or cold or hungry. We'd sit out there on the beach in January, wearing just thin sweaters—that was California, of course, but it still could get pretty chilly. And we'd rap about how we were going to be great when we grew up, like Albert Camus or Woodie Guthrie or Nikos Kazantzakis or Norman Mailer."

"Who're all those?"

"Men we...well, men Michael taught me to admire. We smoked Pall Mall non-filters, or hand-rolled Bull Durham tobacco, either of which is terrible for you, of course. It's a wonder I still have any wind left to play the flute with."

"How come you did those things if you knew they weren't good for you?" I have to smile at her air of adult prudence.

"We were unhappy. Miserable, and mad at the world."

"I don't get it. How come?"

"We didn't exactly know how come ourselves. Everything just seemed pointless. We had to grow up, obviously, but we didn't know what we wanted to do or be. There was a terrible war going on, the Vietnam War. We blamed the adults for the mess things were in."

"But you could have had demonstrations or something to try and make it better."

"Well, thanks, kiddo, that's a good suggestion, but we

didn't know that then. Some people did, but we hadn't caught on. I wasn't raised like you were, going to meetings and demonstrations and Washington rallies." It feels like a foreign country I'm trying to describe; how can I really expect her to picture its conventions and assumptions? I myself can hardly recapture, anymore, the sense of just what it was about that time and our position in it that lashed us into such stoned, directionless fury.

Ericka observes casually that she hasn't been to Washington in "ages," and I reply that, no, it's clearly not her father's idea of a scintillating vacation, but maybe she could come down with me for a demo later this spring. The minute that's out, I worry that I've overstepped the limits of permissible sarcasm, but Daniel's daughter appears to have other preoccupations.

"Was Michael your boyfriend?"

"Yes."

"And did you and him—?"

"Did he and I what?" But I think I see where this is leading.

"You know. Like those kids in that movie we didn't go to. Did you...." Her voice trails off against the backdrop of TV noise, and I have to ask her to repeat the question.

"Did you fuck," she gets it out, almost delicately.

"Yes, Ericka," I admit, endeavoring to conceal my inevitable sense of shock at hearing her use for the first time, literally, a word which, being a thoroughly modern child, she's flung around for years as a defiant expletive: a word I'd never heard pronounced, at her age.

"But did you like it, though?"

"Yes. Well, sometimes. In a way." I can't imagine how I'd tell the truth. Would I emphasize authentic, raw desire? Or mechanical ignorance and furtive risk of those days when illegal abortions and homes for unwed mothers provided the only backup if the quality control should fail at the Trojan receptacle tip condom factory? Or the blundering ideology of it all, a half-baked blend of Mailer brutality and good old-fashioned Lawrentian cock worship?

Or my wild, repressed horror at being the *girl* in all this?

"But...How did you get to be a lesbian, then?"

"It's not that simple, kiddo. People aren't always one thing or the other. And I didn't know I had a choice in high school. I'd never met anybody I knew was a lesbian. Girls were just expected to have boyfriends. Besides, I used to think boys had all the interesting ideas, got to do all the fun things. It took me a long time to figure out I'd rather be with women."

"And is that how Mommy got to be a lesbian too?" She bites her grubby knuckles, overcome by a case of the fidgets. I see we're finally getting to the point.

"Basically, yes. We sort of decided together."

"What did my Daddy say?"

"Well, he wasn't too happy at first. But I think everything worked out better for all of us, after a while."

She bows her head, then peers up through tangled hair. On her face, a grimace intended for a grin proclaims she isn't really serious.

"Josie, what do you think *I'm* gonna be?"

I feel the full honor and weight of my responsibilities. I'm the only one in the world she thinks she can ask that question.

THE BIRTHDAY PARTY

It's such an unaccustomed pleasure and relief to leave work at lunchtime on Friday that I mind somewhat less than I ordinarily might the demoralizing trek through the wastes of midtown in search of a gift suitable to be offered up on the common heap at Ericka's birthday party. (In fact, the task is not too strenuous, since this object is to serve a purely ceremonial function; I'm saving the important present, a sweater I've been knitting since December, for presentation on the weekend.) I thought of stopping off on the Lower East Side, but Rhea and I used to go there all the time, and I've been steering clear of it lately. Anyway, it's an extra fare.

So I settle for Fifth Avenue, which prompts in me the usual reaction, a wish to locate some method, however brutal, of wiping the smirk from its slick, overprivileged snout. After a while I wander into a record store and light on something wholesome-looking by Pete Seeger and the Weavers, though who knows what ten-year-olds listen to these days: punk sex, probably, or rock 'n roll. Then there's time for coffee, and a half hour of wandering the far, echoing reaches of the Forty-Second Street Library, my habitual midtown refuge. No point in rushing back to Brooklyn. The kids won't arrive from school till after three-thirty, and in any event there won't be much for me to do once I get there. Like a diplomat summoned to a state occasion, my main obligation is simply to show up.

This wasted interval of leisure, fancy stores, and the library's archaic grandeur, which culminates in a three o'clock D train with a minimum of standees in its wide, clean aisles, at least has the merit of preparing me for an afternoon *chez* the upper middle class. So I reflect, arriving at Daniel and Brenda's clean block. Oh yes, this still exists—

even, improbably, here in New York City—this universe of comfort and convenience which I tend to connect with California and my childhood; which I solipsistically think of as extinct, simply because I no longer inhabit it.

Already on its way up in the world when I first made its acquaintance, the block has since then risen with Park Slope's ascending fortunes to become one of the area's most affluent. When Daniel Fein and Rhea Krevsky were new homeowners here, and rented me a room at the top of their crumbling brownstone, many of the buildings were still split up into rooming houses or dark, tacky little apartments. Now they're almost all occupied by single families, some of whom rent out an upstairs apartment to help with mortgage payments. The renovators of that early vintage, the ones who took credit for "turning the neighborhood around," plumbed, wired, carpentered, stripped, and sanded, and endured the foibles of their indigent Third World neighbors (who would shortly be driven off to look for housing in less desirable locations) amid a spirit of pioneering solidarity. Those remaining tend to look down on more recent arrivals, who have paid a premium for their original detail, scraped floors, and exposed brick. Daniel, no booster, and certainly no handyman, evinces little nostalgia for the good old days but he knows he lucked out, buying when he did. He's been heard to remark that the prices would be prohibitive if he and Brenda were looking now; while they'd be in good shape if they ever cared to sell—though his job and their commitment to the area make that unlikely for the foreseeable future.

Unaware of New York's characteristic contradictions, the naive visitor to this "prime block" (in the realtors' phrase, which always makes me think of beefsteak) would scarcely imagine the decrepitude and squalor which still flourish a few blocks away. Here the street is innocent of litter and even of dogshit; the identical brownstone fronts, once-deplored soulless tract housing of a century ago, march up the incline with all the posh allure of a Brooklyn Union Gas ad. Even nature has thoughtfully been made room for.

Most of the houses enjoy the luxury of small front garden plots behind wrought-iron fences, and everywhere the Block Association's saplings lift their ugly, ambitious branches, the buds standing out on the tracery of twigs near bursting. The day is warm, almost muggy (for New York knows only two authentic seasons, two poles of climatic discomfort, and March weeks which start by resembling January quite often end up like June), yet no children's games impede my progress up the sidewalk. At this hour my own block would be swarming with kids desperate to escape the confining walls of winter, and those whose equally desperate mothers have banished them to the street. Here the young have rooms of their own, and backyards to play in.

Daniel's house is as handsome as its neighbors, immaculately maintained as it's come to be in the years since his remarriage. I study the carved door by way of composing myself, then ring the buzzer hard. A pause, and Brenda materializes, smiling her hostess smile.

"Oh, hello, Josie. Come right on in."

She's wearing a wide, bright print dress that flares cavalierly over her distended middle; she's lugging Leah, hefty at two and a half, professionally on her hip. Her face and arms look a trifle puffy, her eyes faintly circled with fatigue, but her hair swings out from her high cheekbones straight and shiny and obviously recently cut at some really *good* place in the Heights, or maybe Manhattan.

Aside from marrying Daniel, this knack of hers for visual effect was about the only thing she and Rhea had in common.

But Rhea, no matter how striking (some people called her beautiful out loud, and in circles where that was not a popular adjective), almost never appeared particularly respectable; whereas Brenda is the consummate healthy, weary, well-heeled Park Slope matron, in her face the strain and triumph of her calling: chaos of children and marriage crossed, contained, with a scrupulous attention to detail, a loving involvement in perfectable surfaces.

I always think of Brenda as being older than I am.

In fact, we are almost precisely the same age, but Brenda
has put her decades to the obvious use, has successfully
completed her metamorphosis into that creature I have been
known to describe with amused hostility as a "real
grownup." Whereas I... Sometimes lately as I walk home
from my train I stop for a moment to watch the little girls—
sweet, rowdy little girls who block pedestrian traffic with
games of "double dutch" jump rope made boisterous enough
to rival their brothers' intrinsically livelier stickball—and
am seized by sudden confusion as to my true identity, my
proper place in this world. Smiling, I murmur hello and
prudently withdraw, secretly thinking it seems almost
within my power to cross some invisible line and join them,
if I chose. After all, nothing official has happened in my
life to cut me off from them, I'm nobody's keeper, nobody's
wife or mother.

I might add that these minor episodes of vertigo have
nothing at all to do with what's popularly termed being
"good with children." As a teenager, I never liked
babysitting; my brief interval of employment at a daycare
center is one of the least fondly remembered of my work
experiences; and even today, at political conferences and
meetings, I avoid getting stuck doing child care. My
surprising good luck with Ericka never tempted me to
experiment further. It's just that I'm frequently assailed by
this inappropriate sense of identification, and don't know
what to do with it, beyond smiling and muttering inanities
for which I am rewarded by suspicious glances betokening
children's natural mistrust of the motives of this lady who
lacks credentials, who is not related to any of their friends.

On the old block, of course, at least they knew who I
lived with. And some of them mistook me for Ericka's mother.

"I'm so glad you're here, Ericka's been looking for you.
Come on out back. What a relief the weather's cooperated."
Why is it that, no matter how trivial her remarks, Brenda
always succeeds in rubbing me the wrong way? I must have
a chip on my shoulder. Already I'm making mental
comparisons between her tone and that of the aristocratic

mother addressing the cherished retainer, dear old nanny or governess.

She leads me back through the long parlor floor. Inured to the front rooms' casual opulence, I'm unprepared for the kitchen.

An exclamation escapes me. I'd forgotten Ericka told me they were having it remodelled.

"That's right, I guess you haven't seen this, have you? They finished it about a month ago. It took absolutely forever, and it was a real pain in the neck, but it's so convenient now," Brenda responds, taking my surprise for admiration.

They've added a counter, stainless steel, and built-ins. Everything gleams, ordered, immaculate; to look at it you'd never guess that a family with small children lives here. Keeping it up must require a semi-heroic effort on Brenda's part; even given the services of one Nilda Campos—the eternal "Nilda" of Ericka's conversation—who comes in on the days when Brenda works to clean and take care of Leah.

Strange indeed to contrast this with a former reign: Rhea's loom set up on worn carpet laid over the bare, splintery floorboards by the front windows; chaos of leaking ceilings and flaking plaster; the flooding basement; the problems with the furnace. Rhea, with her far different purposes—she envisioned a free school in these spacious rooms—at least had gotten the basics in order by the time she moved out. Brenda inherited solid wiring and plumbing, and on these foundations built her grand effects.

Actually, I've often wondered how she manages all this on Daniel's City University income and her own part-time one. Another of her innovations has been the addition of a deck which provides access to the back garden from the parlor floor. Her lawn chairs are arranged beside a picnic table heaped with brightly wrapped presents. Seven or eight adults— a bearded man who looks rather out of his depth, and some well-dressed women who seem to be quite within theirs—sit watching the children in the garden below. No Daniel, note.

"Josie, this is Linda, June, Donna...Josie is a friend of Ericka's," Brenda explains, disposing with flawless tact of the scandal of my childlessness. No question but what the others are *real* parents. Several of the women even have toddlers hanging on their skirts (there' a very high ratio of skirts to pants in this crowd); sticky faces and fingers menace dry-cleaned laps.

"Have a seat, Josie, and let me get you some wine. I'm trying to make this thing as tolerable as possible for the older generation."

Brenda laughs, intimating she takes in stride the ordeal of arranging an afternoon's entertainment for twenty kids. I accept the glass she offers. To go down into the garden now would be to make myself more conspicuous, when I'm already uncomfortable enough. Sooner or later Ericka will notice me. I prefer to stay put and sip my wine and watch her from above as she flits in and out among crocuses and bare lilac bushes, a manic debutante; her air coiffed and beribboned, she's clad in a silly femmy spaghetti-strap dress, but it doesn't appear to slow her down any.

"That cake is absolutely ravishing, Brenda. Where on earth did you get it?" This question, posed by a worn-looking, sallow-faced woman in a chic maternity smock, fairly represents the general level of conversation. The cake reposes on the picnic table beside the tower of gifts. About a foot and a half in diameter, it sports an elaborate two-tone frosting job and the legend HAPPY BIRTHDAY ERICKA— TEN YEARS OLD picked out in a mosaic of nuts and raisins.

"Thanks, I'm glad you like it. I custom-ordered it from Sweet Surrender—you know, the place that just opened on Seventh Avenue. They're very nice, they'll do whatever you want. Ericka was talking about an ice cream cake from Carvel, but I persuaded her ten is old enough to be a bit more adventurous. I just hope the kids eat it."

"How much was it, if you don't mind my asking?"

"Oh god, don't make me think! Somewhere in the neighborhood of fifty. Still, they use all natural ingredients...really, it's not out of line, when you consider the quality."

A silence while the mothers mull over this precedent. "Thanks for telling us. I think I'll look into it," one woman at last announces firmly. "Todd has a birthday coming up next month, and I'm so sick of those cheap, gooey, icky, cardboard-tasting things!"

Nods of agreement at this, and a tinkle of social laughter which, since there's nothing intrinsically funny in the remark, I interpret to mean relief and gratitude. For Todd's mother is Black, yet has managed to introduce the minimum possible level of disharmony resultant from that fact into these pale proceedings. You can see how they love her for being so poised, so attractive, so subtly made up, so stunning in that simple dress and elaborate, sculptural necklace. A cute, plump-cheeked two-year-old in scarlet rompers, hair minutely corn-rowed, clings shyly to her chair. She outshines even their luster. I guess she has to.

And here I sit, in cropped hair and clunky shoes, lumpish, unable to think of a thing to say. Isn't that how Brenda sees me, as she watches, vivacious with wine, with the triumphant sense of having brought this off to the admiration and envy of her neighbors?

But I look perfectly respectable, I remind myself. Haven't I just come from work? My pants cost twenty-five dollars on sale. I'm even wearing a bra; hoop earrings in my ears prove I'm a girl. What more do they want? Should I pluck my eyebrows, tote breath spray in a purse?

Of course it doesn't help that I'm nobody's mother.

Once upon a time, when Ericka wasn't much older than Leah is now, Rhea used to tell her, "You have two mothers." That was an error, of course. I might be many things; I might wake her in the night and guard her play and comfort hurts and read monosyllabic books and praise her and scold her and make her eat vegetables—but children do not have two mothers. Anyone knows that.

So we got it settled: I was not her mother. But still I was something significant, if nameless. Which is part of why I now feel the way I do about Brenda. "Brenda is my new mother," I've heard Ericka remark, upon one or two occasions when circumstances called for an explanation. I don't hold it against her; she has to say it. But I do hold it against Brenda.

For other reasons, too, this competitive resentment I harbor against my child's stepmother is an interesting phenomenon, quite different from my attitude toward Daniel, and perhaps worth analyzing. What, for instance, occasions the irritation I feel when, strolling Seventh Avenue of a Saturday morning, too late to cross the street I glimpse Brenda coming? Engaged in that arduous labor of consumption upon which the middle class family's existence is predicated, she's wheeling Leah in a fancy stroller. And though I know full well how tedious toddlers can be in public, there's something that particularly irks me in the sight of a child who's perfectly capable of walking lolling there like royalty borne on a litter. I smile; I exchange the requisite brief greeting (Brenda's evidently no more eager for conversation than I am); they proceed down the block. I'm left there holding that mixed bag of emotions— prideful scorn, contemptuous envy—which I suppose the drab in the gutter used to feel, splashed by the wheels of the good wife's shiny carriage. (Rhea was, I might add, even more scathing than I in the matter of Brenda, who was in her view a sort of domestic scab. By way of coping with the endless aggravations which child-related transactions between ex-spouses give rise to in the wake of modern divorce, she and I used to indulge in certain malicious jokes. D & B was one of our shorthand appellations: Daniel and Brenda, but also the Discipline and Bondage of *Village Voice* personals.)

Daniel and I are mere class enemies—assuming you admit a class analogy for the sexual contradiction. It is a more distant, far less intimate enmity than the one that binds me to Brenda.

In short: a pox on famous sisterhood.

Not, mind you, that I'd wish to undermine the fundamental proposition that Brenda suffers oppression as a woman. She's not the "B" in "D & B" for nothing. But I run into problems when I try to put my finger on the precise location of this oppression of hers. Suppose one could X-ray her perfect-looking days. Where would the hairline fracture, the suspicious mass, show up? Where's the flaw in this crystalline structure? Where does it hurt? She believes she's chosen this opulent servitude.

And what would Nilda Campos have to say about it, as she stoops to fold yet another load of Brooklyn laundry, and wonders how her own kids up in the Bronx are doing?

Thanks largely to some of the more peripheral achievements of a women's movement in which she has not participated, Brenda finds herself furnished conveniently with "options." On her checks, I notice, she keeps her "maiden" name. Yet I've no doubt she'll be Mrs. Fein at the hospital, when she goes in to have the baby.

But these reflections are destined to be cut short. Forlorn as I look, I tempt intervention. The woman sitting to my right has determined to make a charitable effort. I can see her leaning forward, revving up for it.

"Isn't this just the most fabulous party? I'm enjoying myself so much! I'm just afraid now TeriAnn, my daughter, will expect something really fancy!"

On second thought, this seems too vehement to be a calculated rescue effort. I take a closer look at my neighbor, who turns out to be a small woman with tiny, almost babyish features framed by a heap of black curls. She rather resembles a miniature poodle—cuteness the effect she's aiming for, I suppose. Her clothes are too frilly for sophistication, and there's an excess of fuchsia-stained cigarette butts in the ashtray she holds in her fuchsia-tipped fingers.

"It looks like an awful lot of work," I hedge.

"Oh, but it's so important to them, their birthday, you know. Especially the girls. At least I know it is to my TeriAnn. Isn't it to yours?"

Rather striking, this assumption that I have "mine," particularly given Brenda's ambiguous introduction of me as Ericka's friend.

I decide to ignore the question. "Is TeriAnn in school with Ericka?"

"Oh no." A rueful shake of the poodle curls. "That's a good school they send her too, though, Lincoln Prep. A very good school. Expensive. I'm afraid we couldn't afford it, even if—but we're Catholic. The kids go to St. Saviour."

"So you live on the block?" Best keep control of the questions.

"Oh no." Once more sorrowful, apologetic. "No, I'm afraid not. It's a lovely block, don't you think? Our block's okay—Second Street, just below Seventh—and we own our own place, but it's nothing like this."

"So how did TeriAnn and Ericka meet?" Thinking some insight into my child's other life might be forthcoming; I can't recall her mentioning this kid.

"Dance class, they were in a dance class together last fall. Just for one term, but they've sort of kept it up. Not that TeriAnn has much talent in the direction of dancing or anything, but I thought it would improve her posture. Actually, I do feel she's becoming somewhat more poised. It's nice now they're old enough to walk to one another's houses, don't you think? Not that I let TeriAnn go *anyplace* by herself after it starts to get dark, though she tells me the other kids do. She's got to that age, you know, where every other word that comes out of their mouth is, 'But Mom, the other kids get to.' Have you noticed that with yours?"

"Which one is TeriAnn?"

The mother points out a thin, braced, bespectacled girl wearing a sashed dress in a synthetic fabric that takes me right back to my own early "party dresses." Sure enough, the child's posture leaves a great deal to be desired.

"And yours?"

"I'm sorry, I should have explained, I guess. I don't have kids. I'm here simply as an adult friend of Ericka's," I manage quite gracefully. It's a gentler awakening than such presumption deserves, but I don't have the heart to be rude. TeriAnn's mother seems so touchingly anxious to feel herself at home, here in Brenda's illustrious circle.

"Oh, I see." She looks uncomfortable, as women do when they perceive that the answer to an innocent question tends to reflect discredit upon the person of whom they've asked it. Gallantly changing the subject: "How about you, do you live on the block?"

"Hardly." I divulge my apartment's modest coordinates.

"How do you like it down there?"

"I like it fine."

"I always wondered—I mean, it looks a little—"

I reiterate firmly that it's worked out well for me.

"But didn't I hear—isn't that the block where they had that awful thing happen a couple weeks ago? A woman got stabbed or something? Of course, it could have been any place, the way things are. And since you don't have kids...it's true sometimes you can get a real nice apartment on those blocks that haven't gotten so fixed up yet. The values can be a lot better. Do you have a nice place?"

"Very nice. Just what I need right now." She's right, of course, though I wince at her assumptions. I could not afford a comparable apartment on a more prosperous block. Objectively viewed, I am one of those transients whose role in the drama of urban manifest destiny is to form an opening wedge for the relentless drive of brownstoners, contractors, and co-opers eager to "take back" the block, the borough, and by extension, the world.

"What sort of work do you do?"

Here we're reprieved from our laborious efforts; Ericka, coming up behind, has flung herself on me. "Josie Josie Josie! Guess who!" Her small, cold hands cupped tightly over my eyes.

"Not hard. Hello, birthday kid. How are you?"

"Hello, Josie, I didn't know you came. I was looking for you. I wondered where you were."

"You were too busy having fun to notice when I came in, I guess."

"I wasn't having fun, I was playing. Like my dress?"

"It looks kind of chilly. Don't you want a sweater or something?"

"No, I'm *hot*. Honest, it's *roasting*. How do you like my party? Isn't my cake *scrumptious*?"

"It does look good. When do we get to eat it?" I'm none too taken with this keyed-up, show-off mood. Hard to tell, though, how genuine her enthusiasm is. She strikes me as protesting a bit too much.

"Hey Brenda, when are we eating my birthday cake?" she tosses rhetorically over a bare, shrugged shoulder. "How come you didn't come down and say hello, Josie? Is something the matter? Aren't you even going to wish me happy birthday?"

"Happy birthday, kiddo. Want me to give you your spanking?"

"*No way*—" and she darts playfully out of reach. "Daddy did that to me already...What's that you're drinking?"

"Wine."

"Uh-oh, you're gonna be drunk. Can I have some?"

"Ericka, aren't you being a little bit silly?"

"Ericka, come here a minute, please." Brenda's tone is firm but pleasant. Casual: the expert manager. As though I were any childless friend of the family, a novice incapable of self-defense, whom her kid's harassing.

I glare, detecting a calculated intervention. Particularly here on her home territory, of course, Brenda wants to avoid a display of Ericka's and my intimacy. Thus the counterpose to which we're pointedly treated: the woman drawing the boisterous daughter to her, murmuring in discreet maternal reproof.

Ericka returns more businesslike, subdued. "I'm sorry, Josie, I have to call the kids. I'm opening my presents now, Brenda says. I'll come back later."

She rounds up the scattered herd down in the garden. Brenda is fetching scissors, a wastebasket. I stay put in my chair, content to watch from a distance the rending and tearing, the ritual violation.

Of course I'm familiar with this climactic moment, endemic to birthday parties: the remorseless frenzy of the defloration; the jaded, indifferent gesture with which each gift is laid aside as the young roué gropes about for fresh stimulus. Elsewhere in the world, in kibbutzes and communes, children are not encouraged in these consumer orgies, and I've known parents who, with that foreign ideal in mind, strove for a wholesome, socialist atmosphere at their own kids' American birthday celebrations. Belonging more or less to the laissez-faire school, Rhea and I used to grit our teeth and supervise the carnage. Gathering up what we could of the wrapping paper for re-use, we told each other Ericka would probably survive, since we ourselves had.

But today the inevitable rapacity of the proceedings is sharply emphasized by the costliness and sheer quantity of the gifts. There are complicated-looking board games, and fancy jumpers; necklaces and bracelets and rings with real little opals; picture books about horses and the ballet; and from Daniel and Brenda a long procession of items, including a digital clock radio and a tennis racket. I'm more and more glad I didn't suggest inviting Jasmine, who lives in a railroad flat and wears hand-me-downs, and always used to show up, on Ericka's birthday, with a meticulously wrapped offering of the dimestore variety.

Meanwhile, the audience grows restless. This event doesn't make it as a spectator sport, though several of the girls dutifully finger each item as Ericka discards it. They frown responsibly at the boys, who are speculating audibly as to the timing of the refreshments.

Moving quickly to quell insurrection, Brenda promises cake and ice cream the second the presents are opened.

My Pete Seeger record elicits the usual tepid thanks, along with the observation that Grandma and Grandpa Krevsky have that record, too. By now the deck around Ericka is ankle-deep in wastepaper and cardboard boxes. Soon she's down to the final item, a small box wrapped in heavy patterned paper.

"I saved this one till last. I think I know—"

"Don't shake it, Ericka," Brenda admonishes.

"Oh look oh look I love it. Just what I asked for. Look

everybody, what my daddy gave me. You saw it already, didn't you Brenda? Josie, look, a real grown-up watch!" And she elbows through the press of kids to show me.

The thing is silver, delicately banded. She particularly wants me to examine the accompanying card, on which sprigs of flowers frame the scrawled message, "For Ericka, with tons and tons of love, Your Father."

"Where is he this afternoon?" I can't resist inquiring.

"He had to work. He'll be a little late. We're supposed to be sure and save him a piece of cake... Hey Brenda, don't forget to save some cake for my father." She's expertly casual—glib is the word, I think—almost like a woman with too much practice covering up for a philandering husband.

"Here. Put it on for me."

Obediently I removed the superseded timepiece with its cartoon-character face, and fasten the clasp on the gift watch. TeriAnn's mother looks on. What does she think?"

"There. Oh, doesn't it go *perfect* with my party dress?"

"It's fine, very nice. Better go back with your friends now, so we can all have cake."

Femmy. I'll wager she senses how I dislike that pose, one which never used to be characteristic. Then why insist, why come to me for approval?

Let her appeal to Brenda for compliments.

Though this is perhaps unfair. She's at that age. It may be she's just trying out available roles which in any event would have tempted her at this point.

We sing "Happy Birthday." Ericka blows out her candles, laughing she won't let us in on her wish. Then Brenda dissects the cake with professional-looking implements, while Todd's mother serves up Häagen-Dazs. The mollified children subside onto chairs and benches. Soon enough, however, several of the less sophisticated begin complaining that they don't like the cake, it has "things" in it.

"Okay, Jason, just eat your ice cream, then."

The children settled, Brenda offers cake around to the grownups. The predictable wail over calories goes up, predictably resolved by calls for "just a sliver"; but in the midst of cutting she's summoned to deal with the arrival of the magician who's been hired to provide the rest of the entertainment. TeriAnn's mother enthusiastically takes over for her.

It seems to be now or never for a quick getaway. Foolishly, I attempt to decline refreshments.

"Come on, live it up. You're not on a diet, are you? *I* should be, but I'm going to have a piece. Who knows when we'll see another cake like this one, right?" Finally I yield to this cheerful, insistent patter, and the conspiratorial wink which seeks to imply the two of us are in something together.

Brenda returns, nibbles cake. The conversation flows in broad, smooth channels. Abandoning the lone adult male guest to the morose consumption of several helpings of sugar, we concentrate on the female mysteries. There soon unfolds a close consideration of the risks and ramifications of amniocentesis, a procedure recently undergone not only by Brenda but by June, the other woman in a maternity smock.

Having rather enjoyed the element of surprise in her previous birth experiences, June finds she regrets knowing the sex this time, though of course it makes names easier. Brenda, on the other hand, is simply glad to know it's a boy because, though Daniel is so marvelous with his daughters and of course would have welcomed another, she does think it's nice for a man to have a son as well.

"You don't know what you're in for!" TeriAnn's mother brashly interjects. "I mean, I'm real glad for you and all, but boys are so much harder than girls to raise. They're so much more active, right from the first, and into everything...." She trails off, rather crestfallen; several of the other mothers are regarding her with considerable severity.

"Boys and girls raised without sex-role stereotyping exhibit fairly similar development, I believe," the father stiffly corrects her.

Brenda, ever tactful, heads the talk in another direction. Soon her guests are eagerly swapping anecdotes about crimes against property.

"We changed all the locks; we thought it was an inside job—I'd had a mother's helper who had a key—and we waited six months to replace Hank's sound system, and wouldn't you know it, two weeks after we finally did, *they* were back!"

"*They* must have something worked out with a fence, because every time we've been robbed I've had some fairly valuable jewelry lying right out in plain sight, and *they* haven't touched it."

"*They* know what they're after, all right."

"I just got done paying—oh, let's say a small fortune—to have bars installed on all the windows where we didn't already have them, parlor as well as ground floor. Madge and I have started referring to the old homestead as 'Fort Jorgensen,'" the father—Mr. Jorgensen, presumably—puts in, evidently relieved that we've finally hit on a topic to which he may contribute with authority. But I notice he's got cake frosting in his beard.

June says she's been considering a dog. "I don't have a Doberman, but Nick says shepherds will do if they're trained properly. I get so nervous sometimes when he's out of town and I'm alone with the kids."

"You've got every reason to be."

"Why not invest in a really good alarm system?"

"You're lucky, Brenda, to have a solid block association. I really believe *they* tend to stay away from blocks where they know people are organized." It's the Black woman, Todd's mother, speaking. Of course she must guess the shade of the blurred faces her listeners (yes, I accuse myself in this) see, hearing this *they, they, they.* But her tone admits nothing.

"I wouldn't bet on it," Brenda laughs sharply. "About six months ago *they* forced the back door—this was before we had the gate put on—one weekend while we were upstate. I think something scared *them* off, so we didn't lose much. But *they* did take some meat from the freezer, and, of all things, Daniel's scuba-diving equipment!"

"I wonder what fence handled that!"

"Well, fortunately, he hadn't used it for years. Still, you stop feeling safe..."

"Yep, it's sad but true. Nobody's immune." Jorgensen looks determined to face the music. "Not in this town, anyway. You start to wonder whether it's even safe to let your kids out to play. Just last week some punks tried to rip off Pete's ten-speed."

Ericka used to play out all the time, with all the other kids on our sleazy old block. She lived to tell it. But I can't say this, of course.

Brenda sighs. "I've lived in the city almost ten years now, and I'm telling you, I've lost patience. I never was crazy about the suburbs, but at least you could send your children to the schools you're supporting with your taxes."

Her comment provokes a plaintive recitation from which I gather that a number of those present have experimented with the local public schools, found them lacking, and now feel personally affronted by the failure of what they consider their good-faith effort.

I've heard enough. It's high time I went. If only I could disappear and find myself safe on the street, not to have to go through the motions of leavetaking, not have to smile at Brenda, not feel their eyes.

But, if it can't be helped—

I lean forward in my chair.

"Ericka went to P.S. 321 through the third grade, and she got along fine," I hear myself remark.

They turn to me with the mild, anxious interest that people on a New York City bus display when a passenger they've judged harmlessly dotty suddenly starts to exhibit threatening behavior. Encouraged, I plunge on.

"She really had some decent teachers. Not that their methods were very advanced or anything, but she liked them, and she learned to read really quickly. She had some friends in her classes. Rhea and I didn't have any problems with the idea of keeping her there."

It's a well-known rule of human interaction that as long

as you assume your authority in a given situation, as long as you act like you know what you're doing while avoiding the fatal mistake of explaining yourself, people are hesitant to challenge you. *Chutzpahdik* isn't exactly my middle name, but sometimes, emboldened by bitterness or wine, I can pull off a scene like this.

They smell trouble now, these bystanders. But it doesn't appear to threaten them directly. Only Brenda flounders, panicked, in her lawn chair; and TeriAnn's mother turns to me with her exasperating candor and squeaks, "Rhea?"

The adrenaline is slowing everything, enabling me to admire my own performance. I turn to Brenda and add, quite pleasantly. "Actually it surprised me that you and Daniel switched her to private school, when she was doing so well."

Goaded, Brenda defends, "Ericka really loves it at Lincoln Prep. And I must say we're very pleased with their approach..."

I permit an awkward silence to ensue.

It's gallant Jorgensen who, displaying a social acumen rare in one of his sex, dashes to the rescue. "Well, I think several of us have had public-school experiences that, you know—I mean, you figure, give it a whirl, what the hell, it sure is a heck of a lot cheaper than the other route, but mostly we've arrived at the same conclusion, unfortunate as that may be. Of course it's not so rough in the lower grades, but ultimately you've got to be realistic. I mean, you care about your kid, you want him to get what he needs.... Now take Madge and me, we found out pretty fast the administration was not interested in being even remotely cooperative, which is sheer suicide if they're sincere at all in saying they want to keep the middle-class kids. Which, let's face it, in the long run is the only way they'll save the city schools, if they *can* be saved, given how things are going."

The women around me look relieved; they seem to feel that this rambling peroration releases them from something. Grateful, small talk commences, a trickle and then a torrent.

A flood-tide of trivia rises, drowns the jagged contours of looming controversy.

Sobering, I begin to feel anxious. Yet what can Brenda *do*; what real power has she?

Well, Ericka.

But that nebulous, broad threat is nothing new. All year it's shadowed every move I make.

I must talk to Daniel. I've put it off too long.

"Whose mommy are *you*?"

The voice, which at first seems to be coming from under my chair, startles. Turning, I confront a blond three-year-old; finger-sucking, portly, androgynous in overalls.

The question is so much the last straw that I'm tempted to come back with, "Which are you, a girl or a boy?" Little kids, I've noticed, generally can't abide confusion on that score. But, not being a monster of cruelty, I compromise and reply, "I'm nobody's mommy. Whose mommy are you?"

"I'm not a *mommy*"—solemnly indignant—"I'm a *boy*."

High time I went, indeed, I perceive. So I get up to go look for Ericka. The little prick tags behind me, chanting, "I'm a *boy*."

"Oh, shut up, Greggie," Ericka commands. I've located her in a corner of the deck where she's whispering with a clutch of sticky girls. Disheveled, wired on sugar, they plot some mischief. "We don't want any spies here!" She orders him off; explains, "Greggie's Melissa's brother. He's kind of a pain."

"I came to say goodbye, and thanks for the party."

"You mean you're not staying for the magic show?"

"I think not. I've got stuff to do at home. But I'll be seeing you tomorrow."

"Gimme a kiss."

"Okay, chocolate face. Here. Have a good time."

I discharge my last duty of the afternoon by thanking Brenda, who interrupts her talk of child-care woes to smile impeccably at me. "Thank *you*, Josie, for taking the time to come." Her tone seeks clearly, publicly to establish the extreme remoteness of my connection to her stepdaughter. But of course I've asked for this, with my insolence. TeriAnn's mother says she'll walk out with me.

"Wasn't that party terrific!" she enthuses, once we're out on the sidewalk. "But I was beginning to get a little headache, maybe from the wine. I'm not used to drinking in the afternoon! Anyway, I've got to pick up my son at the neighbors', and then my husband will be expecting dinner. TeriAnn can walk back alone, now it gets dark later. Did you enjoy yourself?"

"It was fine," I mumble, to encourage her. Somehow I don't mind that she talks too much.

"That cake was fabulous, and TeriAnn's having a ball."

"Oh, the kids seemed to be having a great time."

"But..." she sounds a surprising hesitant note of doubt. After a pause, she resumes, "I've never felt all that comfortable with Brenda. Not that she's not a nice woman. She's very nice. And Ericka's one of TeriAnn's nicest friends. But... I don't know. Maybe I shouldn't be going into all this now. Are you close friends with her?"

"With Brenda? No, not close."

"Oh, from what you were saying about the schools and all, I had the impression you knew each other pretty well. Anyway, it's hard to put my finger on it. I don't know if it's something to do with him being a professor, or... but then, it's a classier block. And she always dresses so well. I mean, I don't guess her clothes are really super-expensive, but she always looks so sort of *sophisticated*, you know? I end up feeling ugly and dumb around her. And then I get nervous and put my foot in my mouth. Did you see how they all looked at me when I said that thing about raising a boy?"

"I know what you mean." I try to assure her. I suddenly want to be worthy of her trust, and am painfully conscious of having indulged myself in secret amusement at her frilly clothes, her sex-role stereotyping.

"I haven't offended you, have I? I mean, about Brenda?"

"No, no. In fact..." I grope for some suitably inexplicit

method of suggesting my own position. "I suppose I was feeling some of what you felt. I mean, here I'd just schlepped in from Manhattan, where I have this not terribly exciting job, and I'm wearing these old pants, and—well, I know what you're getting at."

"Oh, that's good! I hate to sound weird."

"By the way, tell me your name. I keep thinking of you as 'TeriAnn's mother.' "

She laughs, rueful. "Donna, Donna McInerney."

"And I'm Josie Muller—so you'll know, just in case we run into each other somewhere around the Slope."

"I'm sure we will, I sure hope so. It's been *good* meeting you, Josie. Look, I guess I'd better run in here and pick up some meat for dinner."

Her odd, voluble friendliness has kindled a small glow that warms me a minute or two after I've watched her glossy curls bob off to disappear inside the butcher's. Then I'm alone with my worries.

I let things slide after the accident. Belle, Rhea's mother, flew up from Florida, and after the funeral she and Rhea's father, Sam, took Ericka back down there for a brief stay. Then Daniel said he wanted her over at his place. Nothing was ever made very definite. He talked about a period of adjustment and used the word "flexibility" a lot, and I, having no legal rights, clung to that. He said we could work things out better after we'd all had a chance to recuperate; meanwhile, Ericka would be spending regular time with me. I was stunned and afraid. I didn't press anything.

But it's more than the fear, even. To fight might mean to feel more than I want to feel.

I miss Rhea so sharply in these moments, when I can see how I counted on her in any trouble. But none of that matters. I've got to say to Daniel: look, I'm here. I'm Erica's parent, too.

I'll have to plan. But not now. I'm too tired, now.

Nevertheless, I don't want to go home. The traffic-pulse pounds toward evening, the dinner hour. Soon, night, but I'm expected nowhere. I want to walk the streets for a long time; to let motion tumble and sort my thoughts as water sorts and tumbles pebbles in a stream; to stare into the shop windows and lighted, familial houses; to peer into the faces of the others, the hurriers rich and poor, the shoppers, workers, mothers and fathers, the *real* grownups, the people with obligations.

Debbie Lubarr

I am a thirty-eight-year-old Jewish lesbian. I am the mother of a ten-year-old son, Lee. For the last two years, I have been a member of a lesbian mothers' group in Boston. The love and support of this group has allowed me to come out as a lesbian mother, to bring those two pieces of my life together.

LOSING IT

Debbie Lubarr

One day I watch.
You just get up
and
walk out.
Nice and clean.
Someone is waiting for you.

I am left alone
with
hurt
anger
grief
aloneness.
Fine,
I've been here before.

Only this time
I am solely
singly responsible
for the care
of another.
My child.

You're no longer
here to call
when I start
to lose it with him.

So while I'm losing it with him,
a new rage builds up inside.

How dare you say

you care for me
for the lesbian mother me
for my son
for our lives
And just
one day
get up
and
leave
nice and clean.

January 1986

A CYCLE

I look
And suddenly
See the man in you.
Gone is the gentle sloping chest.
Gone is the rounded hill of your tummy.

In their place are broadening shoulders,
A crested chest,
A flat stomach.
Plump thighs and chubby calves
Overnight become
Long slender limbs.

The cycle moves on.
Now
My breasts slope down
To my rounded belly.
My legs once again sturdy.

I feel comfort in my body,
Where you are just beginning
That hard transition
Called puberty.

July 1987

Joyce Jones

I am a forty-two-year-old middle-class woman. I had been married for thirteen years before I met the woman in this story, and we are still together. We live in the country just outside a small midwestern town and we both work with children with special needs.

Outside of work my main interest is organic gardening and we spend the summers canning and freezing enough fruit and vegetables to last all winter. I am working on a Master's Degree in Counseling Psychology and someday would like to be able to help women in crisis.

My sons live with their father while they attend school and live with us on weekends and during the summer.

FRAGMENTS

Joyce Jones

Pulling myself into focus, retrieving and rejecting images along the way, has not been easy. The word "mother" brings to my mind the softness of a blanket, the warmth of a breast and the traditional comforts of husband, hearth and home. But what is a Lesbian? Aggressive, courageous and determined, she strides into my mind with a confident step and direct look. I do not see toddlers clinging to her skirt! Yet, somehow I am both of these women and in the last few years the fragments have started to fall into place. Now at forty-two, I find the picture they form is a pleasing one for me. After many years of wondering who I am, the answer is more clear now than it has ever been, and despite the pain and struggle of the journey, I am at peace.

But where did the journey begin? At age eleven I fell in love with women (all of them at once) at summer camp. By age twelve, I had narrowed it down to just a few and I showered them with impassioned love letters until one girl said, "Girls just don't say those kind of things to other girls!" I was surprised. It hadn't occurred to me that my feelings shouldn't be shared.

At age fourteen, I spent a lovely winter afternoon in the arms of my dearest girlfriend. Later in the day, I flew home on wings of joy, eager for the next time. But Sandy told her mother what had happened and we never spent time alone again. Another fragment of innocence lost.

I was passionately attached to several women in high school, but I had learned enough from Sandy to be wary of touching anyone. I kept my hands off women but, unfortunately, fell in with a young man I cared little for. I got pregnant at age fifteen and endured the humiliation of seeking an abortion in 1960. The episode left me feeling dazed, confused, and totally degraded. My brief experience with Sandy had filled me with astonishing joy. What a contrast to my experience with a man.

Then college—1963. I met Karen on the first day and fell wildly in love within the week. We became inseparable. Every day I ran back to the dorm as soon as classes were over just to be with her. We spent every waking minute together, and more than one night, smoking and talking until dawn. On the verge of becoming lovers, we trembled with longing and fear. But before that happened, one day I returned from class to discover she had quit school, packed her bags and left town. I never saw her again.

Losing Karen left me shattered and I avoided involvement with women entirely for the next several years. Only recently have I put these fragments into focus clearly enough to realize how devastated I actually was. I convinced myself at the time that loving women was a sign of my immaturity and basic confusion. Men became the focus of my life and I dated many, generally alcoholic, ne'er-do-wells.

I met Kathy in graduate school one summer. That same summer I began to date Bob. He put a great deal of pressure on me to marry him but I felt a deep unwillingness to make such a commitment and in August I broke it off. I continued to see Kathy in the fall although our classes were held in different cities. Occasionally, I would be at her house until late and she would invite me to sleep over. One night, after a glass or two of wine, we crawled into bed in very high spirits and it suddenly dawned on me how badly I wanted to make love with her. I imagined she would react with horror and loathing and I could not bear to think of it. When I got home the next day, I told Bob I'd marry him. We were married in the summer of 1970.

Alex was born in 1973 and Corey in 1975. I wanted to be the most traditional mother in the world. I quit my job, became deeply interested in natural chidbirth and breastfeeding, and ended up as a La Leche League leader. The fragments of my past began to fade and I believed I was exactly where I should be, doing just what I should be doing. Yet I was not entirely happy. After Alex was born, I became nervous and frustrated. By the time Corey was born we had moved to the country, nearly fifty miles from friends and family. Bob spent three hours a day commuting to and from work, and I was alone a great deal. Isolated from my former support groups, I became fearful and withdrawn. All the women seemed perfectly content with their role as housewife and mother. It was difficult for me to understand why I felt so miserable. But I was afraid to face the issues. I had felt no attraction for women since Kathy, and was completely convinced that those kinds of attractions were far behind me. My world centered on Corey and Alex and the few classes I took at the University. In effect, I was wearing blinders.

I couldn't refuse to face my own issues forever, and in 1978 I returned to work. Four years later I met Kelley. Once Kelley stepped into my life, the issues began to fall into place almost at once. What had previously been unthinkable was suddenly right. At age thirty-seven, I was at last ready to face myself.

In the midst of dealing with coming out to myself, I was forced to deal with coming out to Corey and Alex. By then they were eight and ten years old and it appeared to them that their world had just turned over. I wanted to be cautious and not tell them too much too soon. However, there was a sense of urgency because Bob was suing for custody and I felt my time might be limited. I knew he would not hesitate to fill their heads with ugly stories. I managed to hang on to them for nearly a year before they went to live with him in a town about forty miles away. Losing them was terrifying for me, but before they left, I had managed to be quite honest about my feelings for Kelley and they had begun to accept and care for her.

For many months I would pick the boys up on Friday and bring them home with me for the weekends. Corey would ask, "Where's Kelley? Is she here? Will we see her?" I couldn't understand his anxiety until a long time later when Alex told me Bob had said over and over that Kelley would be leaving soon and that I would probably have "a new girlfriend every week." Another time I was taking the boys to my mother's house for a visit. We were driving across the state late at night and Alex was asleep in the back seat. Corey curled up beside me and began to cry. "Is it true you hate us now?"

"No Corey. Why would I hate you?" I said.

"Dad said you hate us now because we're boys and you don't like boys anymore."

They have learned to be cautious. "Does Grandma know that you and Kelley are gay together?" Corey used to ask. "Is Jane gay too? What about Jack?" It took some time to get all the relationships straightened out and to feel perfectly comfortable with everyone. I have learned to be cautious, too. As a Lesbian mother with two sons, I find some women do not want to be around young men, and as they have gotten older, it has become important to always ask if they are welcome. But, in general, they have been more warmly welcomed, with more interest shown, and more attention paid to their thoughts and opinions, by our gay friends than by our straight friends. It has been very important, however, not to lose touch with straight friends, and in particular, those straight families with children about Corey and Alex's ages. Some of the parents are aware of Kelley's and my relationship, but most are not. So far, there have been no problems. No hysterical fathers have shown up at our door accusing us of tainting their son's manhood!

Alex is now fourteen and Corey twelve. We still have a lot to talk about. They still can be deeply hurt by their father telling them, yet again, that I gave them up because I preferred my lover to my children. In many ways I am lucky. Kelley, the boys, and I are able to be completely open with each other, because I chose to be honest with them from the beginning. I really had no idea how difficult things would become after I made the decision to make my life with Kelley. Yet, I endured and gained a sense of wholeness and integrity in the process. I am a far more capable and caring mother than I would have been otherwise. My hope is that Corey and Alex have also gained strength from the experience. Perhaps by choosing to accept my Lesbian identity, I have paved the way for them to someday accept their own painful truths and to avoid a life lived in fragments. Surely the greatest gift I can give them is the courage and willingness to face life with honesty.

Karen Anna

I live on the island of Maui in Hawaii, where I work as a counselor/advocate for battered women and their children, do free-lance photography, raise my son, tend my plants, and edit a monthly newsletter for the gay/ bi/lesbian community.

My photographs have appeared in The Blatant Image, Common Lives/Lesbian Lives, On Our Backs, Yoni, Honolulu Magazine, and Best of Photography Annual 1987. My multi-image slide shows are becoming a legend in their own time.

LIFE AS A LESBIAN MOTHER

Karen Anna

In 1973, at the age of thirty, I was in the process of ending a six year marriage and was the mother of a four-year-old daughter, when I unexpectedly (not surprisingly) fell in love with a woman. It seemed as though that event caused all the jig-saw pieces of my life to fall into place. The process of identifying myself as a lesbian took place over the next several years; my one subsequent intimate relationship with a man resulted in the birth of a son in 1976. So I've been a mother for eighteen years and a lesbian mother for about fourteen.

My experiences as a lesbian mother have been as varied as any mother's. For me, being part of a small but closely-knit gay and lesbian community in Hawaii has given me a kind of support that few mothers find in the isolation of mainstream American society today.

Until 1976, most of my information about what was then referred to as the gay lifestyle came from a variety of books and magazines obtained from the library and through the mail. My concurrent investigation of feminism introduced me to the riches of the lesbian/feminist press. In late 1976, the handful of lesbians and gay men I knew decided to form a support group. Within a month of our first public announcements, up to thirty people were attending meetings. We have now grown from the original group of six to a non-profit educational organization providing support, services, and social contact to hundreds of lesbians, gay men and bisexual people in Hawaii.

As one of the few mothers active in this organization, I have sometimes found difficulty in attending events for which child care was not provided, or encountered prejudicial attitudes because I chose to bear and raise heterosexually-conceived children. Much more often, though, I have received support and affirmation as a lesbian mother from my community. Recently a lesbian couple told me that observing my parenting has given them hope that they could successfully raise a child, something both want but had thought they couldn't do as lesbians. I am often acknowledged as a good mom — and when the going gets rough there are some gay and lesbian parents of now-grown children to whom I can turn for advice. I believe my experience and awareness as a lesbian mother enriches this community. My openness about my sexual orientation and the comfortable level of communication I've fostered with my children serves as a role model to other lesbian and gay parents.

When, a few months after my son's birth, I took a part-time job, a gay male friend did child care every week — and usually cooked dinner for us too — for free. He did this not only because he enjoyed my children (they weren't always enjoyable!) but because he feels it's important for gentle, caring gay men to be part of children's lives. (This same man and other gay brothers provided free child care at our annual women's conference for several years.)

When my daughter was dying of brain tumors in 1980, it was two of my lesbian sisters who came to our home, softly singing and talking and comforting both of us through that last, long night. Later, when the shock wore off and the reality of her death hit me full force, it was lesbian sisters who took me into their homes and hearts, giving me the support and safety I needed to work through my grief, remorse, and pain.

Today, the lesbians and gay men in our community are my son's friends as well as mine. They play with him, exchange information and ideas with him, and provide him with role models of nurturing, interesting, kind adults who enjoy a cooperative way of life. He is welcome at and enjoys many of our social events, and I see that his participation brings enjoyment and awareness to the non-parents in our community as well. One night at a party a group of gay men included my son in a dice game they were playing, apologetically telling him it would cost him fifty cents, fairly high stakes for a ten- year -old. However, they hadn't counted on his luck with the roll, by the end of the game, they were all out fifty cents, and he left with a pocketful of change for the weekend!

As my son approaches his teen years, he is becoming more sensitive to the prejudices of others and to peer pressure to comform. Interestingly, he chooses to wear his hair long, despite the fact that it's not the fashion for boys at his school, and despite the teasing he sometimes gets about it. He knows he's okay, and that it's all right to be different from the norm, and he likes the way his long hair looks!

I have always left it up to him to share information about his family with his peers, and he has chosen to tell only a few of his close friends that his mother is a lesbian. Unfortunately, he knows very few other children with lesbian or gay parents (only one his age), so he doesn't have that kind of peer support.

I have been asked over the years how I would feel if my son grew up to be gay, or how I would feel if he were straight. Neither of these possibilities is an issue for me, nor do I expect my own sexual orientation will have an influence on his. (After all, I was raised by heterosexual parents!) I do believe that having an openly lesbian mother who feels good about herself and being raised in such a community gives children such as mine a foundation of acceptance for the wide range of human differences with which we are blessed. In addition, these children will exercise an informed freedom of choice which few children raised in today's repressively heterosexist society enjoy. It's not all roses, both my son and I have been the subject of a few rude remarks due to my lesbianism. But as my son once said, "That's a dumb thing to tease anyone about!"

What's it like, being a lesbian mother? Is it difficult? Is it challenging? Is it fun? YOU BET! I wouldn't miss any of it!

Virginia May

Virginia May is the pseudonym of a thirty-five-year-old fiction writer and teacher who lives outside of Boston with her teenage son.

THANKSGIVING

Virginia May

Sometimes when Roger Grady walked along the street in the wake of his mother and Abby he felt an odd kind of safety and pleasure, as if they were a family of ducks walking across a parking lot in a row to their pond. Sometimes when it happened that Abby and his mother gazed at each other in a certain way or their arms brushed, with people looking, he felt a *thwump* of panic and his chest would go tight, as if he were steeling himself to rise like a force-field and protect all three of them from the danger. He could never say what kind of danger it was; he only knew it was out there.

It was Thanksgiving. The family was coming. At every other holiday he and his mother left Abby waving on the doorstep and set out for Gram's, but this time, now that they had a house, his mother dug her feet in and said if they wanted to see her, they'd have to come. Weeks before at the beginning of fall when the decision was made, it seemed an excellent one, the house filling, the idea of all of them coursing from room to room, his hefty uncles with their strong voices yukking it up at the table, his aunts marching into his room to go through his things and flop on his bed and Gram and Gramp on the sofa, himself between them, wedged tight. When he tried to put Abby in this picture he kept moving her around, finally settling on a spot by the stove, where she would stand quietly in a big canvas apron and keep checking the turkey. There had been two thousand phone calls in the last few days; the details kept mounting. Now you could smell the dread.

Abby finished setting the table and stood back to look at it as Roger went around and laid out the place cards he had made in the shape of pilgrim hats, although the scissors hadn't worked right on the cardboard and they all came out crooked. Abby was wearing a cream colored wool dress. Roger felt a shyness near her until he realized it was because he'd never seen her like this before. He'd seen her legs; of course he'd seen her legs countless times, he knew the shape of her body as well as he knew anything. But, she had stockings on and black shoes with square blocks of heels that made her even taller. She walked strangely on them, as if she thought she might fall over. His mother called out from the living room where she was still pushing a dust cloth over the furniture.

"Don't put the wine near Stevie. And don't let Teresa sit near Gramp, they'll do something." Teresa was twenty. She had colored the ends of one side of her hair bright orange, like Bozo. His mother's voice was high and pinched. Roger didn't have to look at her to know that the lines around her eyes were pinched and troubled. He began to wish he could shrink himself to something small; he could squeeze himself to something that fit in a box, and go away.

"Oh, God," said his mother. "I hear a car."

Abby looked up at Roger with a sigh as if to say, I can't believe we put up with her, and Roger felt his old tug toward her coming back. Abby laid a hand on his shoulder and he was his own size again. "I like your hats," she said.

"You look very nice," he told her.

Then suddenly they all were there. *Once at school Roger's class made a hut of straw and grasses when they were studying African villages. Inside it was cool and dark, and in the fields of his mind there came moving toward him huge and colorful crowds of people in their best clothes, talking and laughing, their eyes crisp and shiny with merriment. All the tribes fit together in the one hut, their bodies pressed closely, and then they would pull the meat off the fire and plunge in their hands and eat. He could hardly imagine anything more wonderful. Whenever someone bickered, drums would play and the sound of the beat would drown out their fighting, and all the mothers let the lines of their bodies go loose, and let their feet tap.*

There were Matt and Kenny and Teresa and Paula and Stevie, his mother's brothers and sisters, and Kenny's wife, Joy, who was pregnant, and had to sit far away from the table and looked tired. When Gram and Gramp said hello to Abby, Gram didn't look at her directly, but Gramp covered it up by getting too loud and throwing an arm out and thumping Abby on the back of her dress the way you'd hit someone if you thought they were choking. Abby called them Mr. Grady and Mrs. Grady. They didn't say "Abby" to her; they didn't call her anything at all. Roger's uncle Matt was fifteen and he belonged to the track team and threw the javelin. When they sat down he rolled up his napkin and speared it across the table toward Roger and knocked over Roger's water glass which hadn't been filled yet, but everyone went, "Oh, Matt, grow up"; and that started it. They hadn't even started their fruit cups. Matt sat back and looked sulky and wished he hadn't left the football game. Aunt Paula who was in her twenties and nervous about everything tried to cut the tension before it rose any higher, but when she leaned forward and went to say to Abby, "So, how are things at your new office, is it hard," it came out wrong and she said,

"So, Abby, how are things at your new office, it's queer, isn't it?" Her face turned red and she said, "Oh!" Joy put her hands on her belly as if the baby in there were in danger. Roger lifted his spoon, a heavy, heavy thing, and skimmed at the sherbet on his fruit. He closed his eyes and thought about what it felt like when he lay on the rug with his head in his mother's lap and watched Star Trek, his mother scratching the back of his neck half-consciously, as if he were her puppy. "Warp speed five, Mr. Sulu," said Captain Kirk, his mouth half-up in a smile. "Take us home." When he looked up again his mother was coming in with the salad bowl and a pitcher of water. His Aunt Teresa jumped up to help. Her earrings jiggled wildly down the sides of her neck: a pair of parrots and two gold hoops.

Gram said, "I wish you'd take those awful things off

before you sit down again, it's Thanksgiving." And Teresa spun around and plopped back in her chair and shook her head so they jiggled louder. Roger felt his chest constrict. His mother went around the table asking everyone if they wanted water, like a waitress in a restaurant. The family sat still, entangled in weary silence.

Then Gramp said as he started to rise, "Guess I'll go carve the bird." Maybe he thought he was home. A hurt look crossed over his face when Roger's mother, holding the pitcher over his head teasingly as if she'd pour it on him, laughed and pushed him down again. "Oh, Dad, it's all done. Abby carved it already."

Uncle Kenny said, "What did she use, an ax?" He was a tease; he'd meant it lightly. Normally he liked Abby, they were both district managers of the same firm and often had lunch together, but it came out like a pointed ill-tempered thing and the air around them turned foul with it. Gramp let out a laugh and forgot about his hurt feelings. Roger's Uncle Stevie looked at Abby and laughed too. She just sat there. The terrible pressure in Roger's chest didn't expand this time; it kept getting closer. His mother set the water on the table and drifted to the kitchen with the kind of slow-moving dreamy abstraction she went into whenever something troubled her and she was pretending it wasn't there. Stevie and Matt started talking about a guy they knew; Gram leaned toward Joy and started talking about the baby. Abby took the salad bowl and passed it to Paula and Roger saw that—it was just a little thing, he was sure no one else noticed—Paula had her napkin in her hand as the bowl came to her, and touched the napkin to the spot where Abby had held it. She didn't even know she did this; it just happened. Roger watched Abby grind the pepper mill over her lettuce. Then she reached forward to put some on his. The tightness inside was the same as getting stuck beneath a heavy piece of furniture, as if the table was on top of him. He was too small to move it himself. Gramp and Uncle Kenny and Teresa were talking about people in their neighborhood, people Abby never heard of. The bad feeling in the air started leaking away. Abby's long strong hands hovered over Roger's food. She turned the mill, saying, "Say when, Ro-Ro," and he felt the clenching inside move up, up, to his throat and mouth and whole head. He was eight and a half years old and she was calling him by his baby name! He hated her! In a flash he felt himself wriggle free of the weight. *On the floor of the hut there wasn't any furniture at all, there were only warm bodies all together in the coolness, thinking the same thoughts, the sound of the drums close by. Sometimes a fourth grader tried to get in the hut and the tribe would seal; they'd smush themselves to the door and wedge the space shut with their huddled bodies.* He saw he still held his spoon. As the tightness passed out of his head he brought down his weight in his hand, whacking the spoon with a clean, cutting swing against the bones of Abby's wrist. He would remember for a long time afterward the way she looked at him. It wasn't with anger and it wasn't a storm-cloud of quick unhappiness and it wasn't even a look of hurt. It was surprise. He caught her off guard. The pepper mill crashed to the table. Abby drew away with that look of raw amazement and he could not seem to stop himself; he pulled back his arm for a throw and flung the spoon at her. He heard a small clicking sound as it struck a button of her dress; then he threw himself out of his seat and charged around the table until he reached Gram. He was too big to fit in her lap but he let himself go limp against her, draping himself in her arms and pressing his face against hers and squeezing himself until he knew he was tiny. When he looked up again there was a hole in the table where Abby had been. There were bowls of vegetables everywhere, and two small pots of gravy, and in the center of the table there was cranberry sauce with bits of oranges, the way he loved it. His mother was crouching beside him.

She said, "What happened, Rodge?" He knew that nothing would come out if he tried to talk, so he didn't. Gram brushed back his hair and gave him a hug.

"You know how it is, at this age," Gram said. Roger's

uncle Matt held up his hand for high fives. Roger smiled.

"I'll go see about Abby," Roger's mother said. But she didn't. She moved some bowls around in her distracted way, and then took Roger by the hand and led him back to his chair and sat down beside him and reached for one of the bowls. "Poor Abby," she said, as if talking to herself. "She gets into moods sometimes. She'll be back in a minute. She'll be fine."

Barbara Zanotti

I live on the north coast of Maine, where I work as a counselor, teacher, and crafts-woman. "Letter to My Children" originally appeared in A Faith Of One's Own, which I edited for Crossing Press.

LETTER TO MY CHILDREN

Barbara Zanotti

My dearest children,

So many times over the past eleven years we touched on the story of our separation; of how it came to be that you live with your father, and I live with and love a woman. So often I have tried to tell the story, but always fumbled with words, stumbling to give language to feelings that are a powerful mix of grief and joy. When I began to put this book together I knew I wanted to write about us and the road we have walked down together. I felt deeply that the geography of our lives could best be explored within a discussion of faith and integrity.

The roots of our situation are found in my own childhood. I lived in an unpredictable world of fear and loneliness. When I discovered God I dug my roots deep in His presence. He became a loving father who knew every hair on my head, a faithful friend whose love I felt in the world around me. In turn, all of my feelings—sensual, emotional, intellectual, physical— were directed toward loving God. Daily Mass, devotional reading, prayer and personal sacrifice, all were a part of loving God and giving thanks for the blessings of His presence and faithfulness to me. As I look back on my childhood, two truths become very apparent: the first is that religious faith helped me survive, and the second that I learned to equate love with pleasing others and sacrificing myself for them. Religion turned me to God and away from myself.

In a Catholic school setting these dispositions were complicated by teachings on sin and holiness which left me feeling guilty, anxious and unworthy. On the one hand, God loved me; on the other, I was a sinner entirely undeserving of love. These were confusing matters for my eight-year-old mind and heart. Today, I still feel traces of the inner tensions of those years in my personal struggle with assertiveness.

But my school years also included warm, gentle moments. I remember with great fondness my feelings of attraction to, and comfort with, the sisters whom I honored. I especially recall pleasant summer afternoons when I walked the hot mile to my piano lesson and passed through the convent garden. I still see the sisters sitting in the clear light, each engaged in needlework, talking with one another. I hear them say hello to me, and feel again the pleasure and awkwardness of those moments. Feelings of peace rise within me as I remember those afternoons. Then, I could only imagine their love for God; now, as a lesbian woman, I can imagine their love for each other.

When I became a teenager at a girls' Catholic high school, I looked forward to reading *The Imitation of Christ* at recess while other girls talked about boys. I wanted to be a nun and to deepen my intimacy with God. The few boys I dated couldn't measure up to God—and besides I was bewildered about sex and disconnected from my sexual feelings. Given your own vital self-awareness, I expect that this is hard for you to understand. But I lived in a very enclosed Catholic mental world guided by institutional authority and established rules.

In August 1958 I entered the Notre Dame Convent with only one desire: to give myself to God. Scattered on my desk now as I write you are pages of a journal I kept for the three years I remained. The entries alternate between love, grief and resignation. The life I had longed for turned out to be full of difficulties for me. We were instructed never to question authority, to seek suffering and rejection, and to conform our lives to the crucified Christ. In those days these attitudes were considered the very essence of holiness. I had known this from childhood, but in the convent I found the practice of obedience a source of great anxiety, and the mandate against friendship simply inexplicable. I remember kneeling in the chapel contemplating the figures of Christ and John at the Last Supper, sensing their love for each other and the blessedness of their intimacy. For almost three years I struggled with loneliness and anxiety, praying for an inner peace that never came. In the end, I sadly took off my habit in a tiny corner room.

In shock and bewilderment I returned to the world. The novice mistress, whose letter I now hold in my hand, wrote that "God has other plans for you. Trust Him." The trauma of leaving generated a kind of mental cataclysm. I sought the help of a psychiatrist who analyzed me as having suppressed sexual needs. "Get married," he said, "and you'll be fine." And so it was that when I met your father, a likable, good-natured man, marriage seemed predestined.

I remember a retreat I made just prior to our marriage. The retreat director spoke of the family as a reflection of the Trinity. He preached that the fulfillment of woman was in wifely submission and motherhood. He urged us to contemplate Mary at the foot of the cross and to find in her suffering the strength to endure our own sorrow. We were told that our bodies were a chalice to receive the seed of man, that our arms were altars on which our children could rest. Fifty young women considering marriage attended that retreat. None of us spoke with one another. None of us questioned the ethic of sacrifice that was offered to us. It was as familiar as communion bread.

I want you to know this because those religious feelings had everything to do with my intention when I married your father. They were the commitments that shaped the first six years of our marrige. With great enthusiasm I developed family religious rituals, meal-time prayers, and various holy day customs. I gave myself completely to serving the needs of your father, and you children as you came along. Maybe David and Stephen can remember my blessing them at night, or being brought to church, or hearing stories about God's love. I was creating a strong Catholic family and fulfilling God's will. and then Susan died.

You asked me to tell you about her so many times, and I did. How she was born with a weak heart that could not sustain her fragile life; how she died ten days after her birth. We've visited her grave together. Do you remember?

Your father said I was never the same after that; he was right. In my inability to grieve for her I confronted my own numbness. No tears. No rage. Nothing. I had a dream shortly after her death in which I died and was condemned to hell— because I was not real. This new and very disturbing awareness was a profound shock, a painful first nudge towards personal honesty and liberation. To resolve this dilemma of self-alienation I began to explore the terrain of my own feelings. Slowly I set aside rules and laws and realized for the first time the deep inadequacy of living according to reason and will.

Seeking interests outside our home I embarked on a program of teaching and study that brought some measure of satisfaction, but also family strains. Your father missed the carefully tended home, the cozy smells of home-cooking, and my reliable presence. As I became politicized by the anti-war movement and the Black struggle for civil rights, our political differences increased the tension. While he celebrated the American way and traditional family values, I began to understand political and economic systems of oppression. I remember the afternoon when I stood in the sun porch, picked up my copy of *Sisterhood is Powerful*, and read the words of women claiming freedom. Terrified, I put the book down. Here were words for my feelings. Here were other women who felt as I did. Your father and I were on a collision course.

On the one hand I felt some exhilaration in searching out the meaning of things on my own terms, but on the other I could see the wrenching consequences of my searching on your life. By this time, Carolyn and Elizabeth were born. I was juggling internal chaos with some modicum of external calm. I tried to shore up family life with folk Masses in our dining room. Father Bill and Sister Kathy became a part of the wider family circle and their presence helped me to hold things together for a while. Inwardly, I felt alone, isolated and terribly fightened, seeing no way to resolve the conflict without enormous suffering. I began to sleep on the couch, finding great comfort in a bed of my own. In prayer I invoked the God of liberation for wisdom and strength, writing in my journal: "The word of God to people is always to remain open, to let go of anything that holds one back from being fully human."

I became depressed, weepy, and listless. Your father and I sought counseling help, a process which helped me to accept my own feelings. I was finally able to admit to myself the deep alienation I had felt in our sexual life, and the absence of intimacy that rendered our marriage lifeless. By this time, family life was filled with arguments between your father and me. You probably remember how awful it was. After a wrenching process, I decided to divorce your father. What the future held was uncertain, yet I was sure that I could not remain his wife. But the decision about your care was the hardest decision of all.

We all stood in the kitchen that fateful winter afternoon. I began to talk about divorce. David and Stephen began to cry. I tried to assure you of my love, but you felt what was really happening: family life was drastically changing and Mom wasn't going to be around. In a flash I remembered all the wonderful times we had shared. How I liked to take Stephen to the kitchen window to watch the sunset. How I delighted in the warmth of David's hand as we trekked through the woods behind the house. How we piled Carolyn into the toddler jumper and enjoyed her playfulness as she swayed back and forth. How we gathered around Elizabeth in her baby seat to sing sweet lullabies. All that was changing for me, too. I could scarcely hold myself together, with all these memories rushing in on me, but I could see no other way. I knew in my heart that I was unable to be a full-time parent. I felt literally uncreated. Without myself I had little to offer you. For his part, your father welcomed the task of everyday parenting.

We all made the painful transition. You to a household with Dad and a housekeeper, me to a tumultuous journey of self-discovery. I felt torn by guilt and shame; some family members rejected me, most old friends ignored me. I knew that their disapproval of me broke the circle of love around you and this grieved me enormously. The early years of our living apart were especially difficult. Sometimes our visits were loving and intimate, other times you felt the freedom to rage against me. In this desperate transition I felt sustained by religious faith. I wrote in my journal, "I experience being held by a Power greater than myself. Only this comforts me through these terrible days. I must have faith and create meaning."

I focused on work and joined with the Catholic left in a variety of political struggles. I tried to make my work seem important to you in the hope of justifying my absence from the household. What you thought and felt was so important to me. Sometimes, looking back, I recall only problems, but there were also many happy times: Carolyn and I swimming in the waves at Singing Beach; Elizabeth's sixth birthday party at the Mobilization office; celebrating with Stephen at the Boston Pops; watching and listening to David play his trombone with the Weymouth town band. What happy moments come to your minds?

During the third year of our living apart I began to be aware of my feelings for women. Very slowly I let my needs for intimacy come to the surface. On the day I said out loud, "I am a lesbian," I felt an enormous sense of liberation, integration, and personal power. I wrote about the process this way, "My ache was for communion of mind, spirit, flesh—a relationship in which I could be myself at last." Peeling back all the old definitions, setting aside all the old authorities, I came to consciousness as a lesbian feminist woman, finding myself outside everything I thought was true, and searching for other women with whom I could create new paths defined by our own words.

I like to think that our relationship improved as I achieved some measure of pleasure and integrity in my own life. Just as I saw you grow up, you witnessed steady changes in me. I remember when you boys asked me if I wanted a tie for Christmas. Aha, they suspect, I thought. I know it was more difficult for you, dear daughters, so your friendship with my lover, your thoughtfulness toward her, and your delightful participation in our life together is a deep gift to me.

Things have turned out so differently than I expected. I wanted to provide you with a rich religious heritage because I knew from my own experience how sustaining faith can be. But when I felt the weight of patriarchy within Christianity, and identified the misogyny that pervades the tradition, the entire system gradually eroded and ultimately the symbols collapsed, unable to mediate meaning. I suffered the loss of God and began to plough a spiritual land I could call my own.

And so, when you ask me if I believe in God, I draw a deep breath. I start to say, "It all depends on what you mean by god," and you, in frustration, shrug your shoulders and say, "Ma, just tell us if you believe in God." And so I say, "No, if what you mean is a supernatural being who rules the world, but yes, if you mean the Essence which unites us with one another, the Holy Communion we create through our love, the Strength we experience in striving to birth a feminist world." When I begin to speak in female imagery you become quickly embarrassed, but I want you to know how my lesbian existence led me to Changing Woman, Spider Grandmother, Old Woman—She who is known by many names; She who is the Source of all. My hope is that you find Her, too.

The security I set out to give you turned out to be a difficult and often painful childhood with a live-away lesbian mother and a landscape of religious questions. Each of you has emerged from this complex cocoon with goodness, courage and a generous openness to life. I thank you deeply for all you bring to me. What I am trying to bequeath to you is still in the making.

My love to you, Mom

Ila Suzanne

My sons are sixteen and twenty-two years of age. We have all changed "castles." They are still comets in my life, zooming in and out. I raised them as a single parent and each in turn went to live with their father at age fourteen.

I co-parented my lover's daughter from the time she was twelve until this past summer when she left for college.

I am a forty-five-year-old, working-class, fat dyke. I spent twenty years teaching preschool children in day care settings and I still find special solace in being with little ones. My first love is for wimmin, then poetry writing. I also make drawings and porcelain goddess figures. I am doing "magic" with wimmin in circles in a way I never dreamed of when I wrote "Castlewomyn."

CASTLEWOMYN

Ila Suzanne

I

Once there was a womyn who lived in a castle with
    her children
The womyn had much magic
She shared her magic with other wimmin
Her magic only worked outside of her castle
Within the castle were cobwebs, dust, disorder and
    confusion
Sometimes another womyn would happen to come
    across the castle
Her new magic would make the castle shine and
    sparkle like a jewel
The inhabitants would remember that it was a castle

Now one spring
When the weeds were blooming in great glorious
    profusion on the castle grounds
The spiders in the rafters were spinning symphonies
The mold in the corners was dancing up the walls
The magic womyn who lived there was shrinking,
    shirking and sobbing
She was thinking of running away
There appeared a quietwomyn
She came with quiet questions
With books, maps, tools and soft smiles
She touched castlewomyn with her words
She was careful, cautious, catlike
She caressed castlewomyn with kneading/needing
    embraces

The quietwomyn brought her own magic to the castle
Cobwebs disappeared
Windows let in light
Mirrors reflected beauty
The grounds around the castle celebrated with
    quietwomyn's magic
Until there was such peace and order and tranquility
That castlewomyn and her children celebrated
    quietwomyn's magic daily

Castlewomyn used her words, drawings, and magic more
    than ever before
Castlewomyn kept falling in love with quietwomyn
Castlewomyn worried that quietwomyn would disappear
Searching for another place to use her magic
When everything was perfect inside and outside the
    castle
Sometimes castlewomyn felt alright about that
    leavetaking
Sometimes she thought to conjure more chaos
To keep quietwomyn there forever
Mostly she loved and accepted the presence of the
    quietwomyn

II

Now the castlewomyn had sons
The sons were magic too
Bright as stars
Wild as dragons
Full of love
The sons were curious, growing moving noisy forces
Given to bursts like meteors
And softnesses like kisses and goodnights

The sons moved in and out of the castle
Making messes
Tilting things
Sometimes putting things in order
Castlewomyn loved them deeply

They loved castlewomyn

There came a time for the sons to visit other
    castles
The sons and castlewomyn were afraid of apartness
In their hearts they knew they were everbound
Even in different castles

So the sons gathered their belongings
And started their first journeys out of the castle
Knowing it would be many seasons
    before/if they returned

There were tears in castlewomyn's eyes/heart
She embraced her sons
She gave them a share of her magic
She gave them amulets and ribbons
She gave them bits of food and candles
She gave them spells to remember on dark nights
She gave them tokens and part of her own treasures
She smiled and waved them gone

She turned back to her castle
With thoughts/dreams/hopes/fears
Past/present/future jingling in her head
Not music
Just rhythms
Beginnings and endings
She looked to quietwomyn for holding
She looked to all the wimmin in her magic circle
For holding and sharing
She wrapped herself in a cloak
    woven of many wimmin's magic
And opened her castledoors wide to let in the light of the
    moon

Cathy Cockrell

I have been a friend and lover to several lesbian mothers. A Baby Boomer from a white middle class family, I am a board member of <u>Nicaraguan Perspectives</u> magazine and write for a gay weekly, the <u>San Francisco Sentinel</u>. "The Tree Farm" is part of <u>A Simple Fact</u>, my second short-story collection published by Hanging Loose Press.

THE TREE FARM

Cathy Cockrell

All the way from Philadelphia to the tree farm mother and daughter fought. All the way Quinn sat surprised and watchful in the front passenger seat, feeling as though she herself might be drained when it was over.

It was Sheila who had decided they should leave the city by early afternoon. She pulled up at 30th Street Station right at twelve, as planned, motioned Quinn with a beckoning flick of a finger into the car.

"Hi stranger," she said, giving a warm bear hug across Quinn's bag, on the seat between them, then held out her cheek till Quinn pecked it. "Now to get the girls." Sheila knew the streets so well they reached the school in no time.

Two teenagers were standing on the curb in front of the building as they pulled up. One wore a large woven bag slung from one shoulder of her Levi jacket, a scowl on her face. Quinn recognized Sunsh—short for Sunshine— immediately, recalling the once small-for-her-age seven-year-old who'd raced around the tree farm in Oshkosh overalls. The other girl was tall and pretty, with a straight brown braid hanging down between her shoulder blades. Sheila waved. They climbed in. Sunsh slammed the door hard behind her.

"Hello kid," Quinn ventured affectionately, as Sheila opened her door, dragged the bag off the seat, and stowed it in the trunk. Quinn regretted immediately the word kid. Sunsh must be fourteen by now, a real teenager, and the bang had been to announce her bad mood.

"Hi," Sunsh answered, barely audible, as her mother got back in the car.

"Ain't talkin' while the flavor lasts!" Sheila chimed in

promptly, trying to be jovial. "You'll thank me, Sunsh," Sheila continued, apparently taking up some quarrel where they left off. "We'll miss the worst of the traffic."

Sunsh seemed unappeased. And no sooner had they reached the freeway than a guy in a Corvette passed on the right at breakneck speed and cut sharply into their lane, oblivious to a motorcycle cruising along right in front of them. When he saw the bike he braked suddenly, and hard. The Toyota nearly climbed his back.

"Mom!" Sunsh said—alarmed, accusing, infecting the car with tension.

"I see him!" Sheila snapped back, rattled. "When you get your license I'll let you drive, OK? Right now it's my turn." But the close call had scared Quinn too. She felt angry and instinctively, irrationally blamed Sunsh. "I bet there was some cute guy in class who Sunsh didn't want to leave. Am I right, Linda?" Sheila probed, peering back through the mirror. Linda loyally refrained from answering. "And by the way, Sunsh, what ever happened to that lovely boy, Timothy?"

"Last week a girl accidentally broke 'that lovely boy's' pot," Sunsh sneered, "and he threatened to 'slap her tits together.'"

"Good God, you're kidding! .... Anyway," Sheila persisted, after a small pause to recover, "I bet you've got your eye on *someone* there."

"Oh Mom!" Sunsh protested. "We were firing today!"

"Sunshine, I didn't *make* you miss pottery. Didn't I say you girls could take a bus out tonight if you wanted? Or you could have stayed home, for that matter. It was *your choice!*"

Sheila, the anarchist, trying to incorporate the principles of individual responsibility into her childrearing—how typical, and unchanged. At this thought Quinn felt both comfort and alarm. The same quartz crystal still hung from the same black cord around Sheila's neck. She still drove barefoot, sneakers cast off between the two front seats, as she had in the old days. And now she'd worked it out to go back to the tree farm as summer caretaker, while the owners were away. This trip was to bring up the first carload of stuff; in a few weeks they'd bring the rest, and stay on.

"Some choice!" Sunsh said. "You know I hate buses. *Hate*," she repeated for emphasis. "They make me nauseous....And it's called ceramics, not pottery." The complaint about getting nauseous bothered Quinn. She thought of teenagers as fickle and self-involved; they faintly repelled her. "You could have waited two hours. What's the big rush? What's it to you?"

Quinn considered that the rush might have been about herself. She remembered Sheila's prediction that they'd have a wonderful Memorial Day weekend together. "For auld lang syne," she had enticed Quinn over the phone.

It had been Memorial Day, 1973 that Quinn had gone to visit Allison, a friend from high school, and the other women on the tree farm. The first evening of the visit, after saying they needed more womanpower on the place, and again the next day, showing Quinn the stand of evergreens being grown for Christmas trees, Sheila had said: "So you're staying." Half option, half instruction: it had been compelling. Ever since, when people asked her about that time in her life, Quinn told them she had moved to the tree farm within a week because she knew suddenly she needed to live lightly on the earth with women. But it seemed to her now that what had cinched it was a tone of voice.

A vast petrochemical plant loomed up outside the car window at the side of the highway. Its tanks were huge and rounded like puffballs; its silver and white pipes cut complex shapes against the sky. At one time Quinn could have mired herself in depression almost at will by looking at this landscape of pollution-making monuments. She wondered if she were growing or just morally eroding. At one time, too, she told herself, she'd lived on women's land, considered herself part of the cutting edge. Now she felt like a tame, harmless adventurer-gone-home. Quinn felt so normal that it frightened her.

The chemical plant disappeared behind them and Quinn heard Sheila saying that getting stuck in traffic gave her headaches. "Like two bull goats," she told Sunsh, with a wry smile Quinn caught from the side. Sheila took her hands from the wheel to butt the knuckles together in the center of her forehead, like the headache sufferer in the old T.V. commercial. "Would you have wanted that?"

And Sunsh plunged on, in dead earnest: "You always tell me that I give you a headache. So what's the difference?"

"You've got a point there," Sheila laughed generously. Sheila could give, let go, slip out of anger into laughter and back again with ease. It was something Quinn had always admired about her. One of the *many* things, Quinn amended, flinching at the thought. For a year and a half, or a year (it was hard to define the end; it had faded away slowly, painfully, not ended with a bang) they had been lovers. Even now Quinn could recall the pride she'd felt about her special relationship to Sheila, along with specific moments of humiliation she had endured because of it. Even now she could still recall the sting of a particularly direct, fierce, and exasperated demand Sheila made one morning six years ago: with a hand on one hip so that her blue bathrobe hung unevenly below her knees, Sheila had said:

"You're not the first one ever to put me on a pedestal, Quinn. But I liked you. I figured you grow out of it." Quinn felt devastated; Sheila had looked solitary and almost desperate as she paused, then asked, as if betrayed: "How was I to know you wouldn't?"

The intonation matched disturbingly the one in Sheila's voice now as she asked Sunsh with annoyance: "Can't you be a little more grown up about it?"

"Why should I?" Sunsh said angrily. "Besides, I didn't want to stay home!"

It would be comforting to side unequivocally with one of them, Quinn thought. No doubt Linda was sure of where she stood, sided squarely with Sunsh.

"Your mother's a trip," Linda might tell her pal, once they were alone. And maybe Sunsh, to counter any trace of admiration in Linda's comment, would point out how much of a pain her mother was, how dumb and predictable her lesbian feminist enthusiasms.

"Capital L, capital F," she'd stress.

A slim, winding, road through the woods brought them the final stretch to the tree farm. Quinn recognized its turns, the side roads joining the main one, the pond that bred bullfrogs and mosquitoes.

"There's Edna Frazer's," Sheila said, for Quinn's benefit, as their former neighbor's prim frame house came into view. Sheila seemed to think that five years away, a new life in New York City, had eroded all Quinn's memories of the tree farm, though she herself had been away for four. It seemed she had never really understood how Quinn thought, what things faded first for her, what stuck. The road plunged down under the canopy of leaves that shaded it for the last hundred yards before the house.

One time, on their way home from a weekend outing, Quinn's parents had stopped to visit her at the tree farm. Her father had waited at the top of this road; her mother had come down on foot and appeared in the clearing without warning.

"I left your father in the car," she'd said pointedly, as if hoping for an invitation for him, as she climbed to the porch of the main house in her sturdy deck shoes, her crisp checkered shorts. "He wasn't sure he'd be welcome."

An awkward moment followed. People looked in Sheila's direction to see if she'd volunteer an invitation to him. She didn't; no one did.

Someone, probably Redwing, instead invited Quinn's mother with strained hospitality to stay to dinner. She agreed to "just a bite" and helped set the table on the screened-in porch. They started the meal with their customary moment of silence—heads bowed and hands joined in a circle. Quinn was seated between her mother and Sheila. Sheila's hands were hard from hoeing and weeding and pushing wheel barrows. Her mother's were small and smooth, the way Quinn remembered them from childhood—making tight worried gestures, or idle on her apron, or pressed together in church like an obedient child's; "Our Father, who art in heaven, hallowed be thy name..."

The silent prayer on the porch ended; they let go of each other's hands. It stayed horribly quiet for one prolonged moment except for the sound of mosquitos through the screen, of women mumbling requests for tamari or couscous.

Afterwards, Quinn walked her mother up the hill to the car, said hello to her father. Her mother got in, then leaned out the window and pointed at Quinn's feet, dropping her voice suddenly to a low, private whisper as if there were someone else there besides family.

"Please don't throw those out ever," she requested. "I want to have them. As a memento. Of this terrible period."

Quinn looked down at her dusty toes, the sandals with the tire tread soles that Sheila had made and had said she could keep.

"So long, Quinn," her mother said then, as if, having found a symbol to contain her pain, she could now bear to leave. Quinn watched, astonished and crestfallen, as the family Dodge lumbered away.

She still kept those sandals, buried in a corner of her apartment.

The Toyota shuddered, then gasped to a complete halt as Sheila pulled the car up in front of the house, turned off the ignition, pronounced happily: "Free at last!" The back doors popped open instantaneously; the girls jumped out like prisoners released.

"Let me get the gas on," Sheila said as she slipped out of the driver's seat and bounded toward the house, her red-brown trousers, lavender bandana, and tiny pouch on a long string leaving the impression of color and discord in her wake. Linda and Sunsh grabbed their bags and followed, disappeared up the stairway just inside the door. As she unpacked the car, Quinn could hear one of the girls opening an upstairs window, Sunsh giggling inside.

Quinn searched the car's interior—among driftwood pieces, gay community leaflets, seaweed candies wrapped in edible rice papers, and "This Insults Women" stickers—for anything she'd missed. An orange day-glow frisbee protruded from under the seat. She tugged at it and the frisbee came free; a prehistoric-looking jawbreaker rolled out from somewhere underneath the seat. Quinn picked the jawbreaker off the mat and flung it full force into the bushes, laughing. What would Sheila be like at eighty? she wondered. And was struck, as she carried in an armload, by the knowledge that what she wanted this weekend was Sheila to herself.

Once the "girloids," as Sheila called them, had gotten settled in the bedroom upstairs they came down to say they were going for a walk.

"While there's still light," said Sunsh.

"Be back before dark then," Sheila instructed.

Sunsh threw back a scowl as she shut the screen door, as if to say: "Yeah, yeah, we're not kids anymore, or idiots!"

Quinn admired Sheila for not saying the obvious to Sunsh, but noticed Sheila's need to say it out loud once the girls had disappeared up the drive: "They'd be twiddling their thumbs in the dark instead if we'd waited all day to leave Philly." Quinn giggled, but she found herself giggling alone, for Sheila abruptly turned reflective, almost sad: "Look what a nasty old crab I've become." She cast a glance at Quinn, looking self-conscious. Suddenly she bounded toward the door, threw it open and yelled up the drive, where the girls had been: "Watch out, girl, or I'll slap your tits together!"

Sheila collapsed against the doorway, laughing tensely, as Quinn stood staring at her. In this same house, on this tree farm, in the old days, they had spoken, behaved differently, almost decorously. And because of Sheila. It had always seemed that Sheila approved of, even expected, the right-minded tone that had been achieved and sustained on the tree farm. Intrigued and confused now, Quinn searched Sheila's face for whatever it was that seemed aggressive, even hostile, in this outburst of irreverence. But Sheila would not stand still for this examination; she was on a roll.

"C'mon," she said, "this old crab needs daylight too," and grabbed Quinn by the elbow and swept her along. "Let's take a look."

They walked through an open yard next to the house, where their big garden had once been. Now the space was occupied by a car body and a woodpile covered by a tarp. The path starting on the far side of the yard cut through some tall grass and past the apple tree that would drop bushels of fruit all over the ground later in the summer.

Twenty yards past the cabin, Sheila and Quinn came to the stand of commercially-cultivated evergreens. All the trees were straight and well-formed; they grew in regular rows to an even height and stood apart from the wild profusion of honeysuckle and hardwoods that covered the nearby ground and the surrounding countryside. Quinn played the game of narrowing her eyes 'til the edge between the cultivated rows and the woods blurred, and it become one continuous, unbroken landcape. When she opened her eyes, it changed back. She noticed nearby, off to themselves, two trees perhaps three feet high, different from the others.

"What are these?" she asked, fingering their stiff, narrow, pointy-tipped leaves.

"Yew. Sunsh planted those before we left here. Someone in town told her the wood is especially nice for carving. Maybe she can use them now after all." Quinn imagined the elegant wood spoons, boxes, chess figures Sunsh would make in Industrial Arts class. "Can you imagine planting something so slow-growing as a tree—at that age? Remember how you were at eight?" Sheila asked, with what sounded like motherly pride.

And Quinn remembered something she'd once known about Sunsh—how uniquely determined, almost relentless she could be. Once someone had shown her how to curl dandelion stems in water and Sunsh went out and picked virtually every dandelion within a quarter mile radius. Later she'd appeared for lunch, head covered by a pile of wet, pale green curls like an eccentric belle.

"Those classes of hers must really be important to her," Quinn said to Sheila in a commiserating tone of voice.

"It's not just that," Sheila answered, and Quinn felt herself deflating in a way she remembered from the old days, whenever Sheila had spoken to her gruffly. "It's a lot of things she's mad at me about." Sunsh resented the years in a commune instead of a nuclear family, growing up without her father. Sheila had left that difficult marriage when Sunsh was still a baby, and soon afterwards became, as she put it, "an Amazon—one of the Amazon nation."

"Have you and Sunsh talked about it?" Quinn asked, carefully putting more question than suggestion into her tone.

"No, we haven't talked. But we should. We're going to," Sheila said unequivocally. And Quinn, to her own surprise, felt left out instead of pleased that Sheila had come around. They used to quarrel over Quinn's desire to discuss things, Sheila's insistence that talking didn't help. Plus, here at last was Sheila sounding committed to someone, the way she'd never been with Quinn. On the way back to the clearing, Quinn asked where the owners had gone for the summer, what their plans were for the farm; but Sheila didn't answer, perhaps hadn't even heard the question.

Inside the house Sheila moved about furrowing her brow and talking out loud—not to Quinn, but to herself—about a pie she wanted to make for the girls, even though Quinn remembered Sheila as a rather lackadaisical cook.

Miffed, and hungry for nature, Quinn went outside. In the dirt beside the porch she saw a bent up trowel; she pulled it out and began digging around the flowers. It was relaxing to yank out crabby little weeds with stubborn roots and shake them free of dirt.

After a few minutes Sheila came trotting out with a multi-colored string hammock, probably Mexican from one of her trips to the women's land in the southwest where

Allison now lived. She found the two hooks—one screwed into the house and one tied to a nearby tree—and hung the thing.

"You want the hammock?" Sheila asked, suddenly attentive, as if to make up for her earlier lapse of attention. There was a look in Sheila's eyes—needy and vulnerable, almost. "You can rock and dream about that new girlfriend of yours," she joked.

"I'm content," Quinn said firmly as she faced Sheila, a clump of weeds dangling from one hand. "Don't you want it?"

"I've got to go into town. I promised Sunsh they could have chicken pot pies for dinner, and I forgot to buy them. She loves those things," Sheila said, and curled her lip with resignation, as if she had hoped Sunsh would opt for wheat berries and steamed vegetables. "Actually," Sheila said, drawing the word out as she glanced at Quinn, "would you come with me?"

There was the thought of cashiers and concrete and sidewalks, when she'd longed for a retreat from all that. There was being in the car again. There was the thought that the hammock had been a pretext to ask this favor. And there was the hopeful look in Sheila's face, that Quinn wanted to deny; she had hardly ever denied Sheila. Quinn was aware of a wincing pleasure as she shook her head no, saw Sheila's hopefulness collapse.

Even as Quinn finished speaking she heard Sheila add hurriedly: "It's all right though if you prefer to stay," then watched her retreat around the corner of the house, strands of long dark brown hair flying away from her head. Sheila had her motherly responsibilities to fulfill, Quinn thought, disquieted. She heard the car engine turn over, the gravel pop under the tires as the Toyota pulled out.

The wicked pleasure that she had been feeling slipped away from her; the trowel felt heavy and ridiculous in her hand and the scraggly flower bed seemed a sad substitute for their glorious old garden. Quinn left the trowel on the ground, stood and looked hard at the yard. The woodpile was bathed in late afternoon light. So was the path. She found herself retracing her steps through the grass and out past the apple tree. She paused in front of the cabin, then mounted its two plank steps, lifted the latch.

The door opened and Quinn stopped still. In place of the original, small panes in the wall opposite there was a large plate glass window. It filled the room with light and a view of the strange, silent rows of evergreens outside. The fist that formed in her chest took her by surprise. She had imagined only the comforting sight of familiar objects: the butcher block, wood stove, chair, rug, mattress.

Quinn saw herself again on the mattress by the window, holding onto Sheila. Sheila's fingers ran along Quinn's beasts, and side, and thigh, then slipped inside her, pushed deep, as Quinn rode them. A breeze, and the sound of crickets, came in the open window from the woods. She used to make sounds but had always been too shy and tongue-tied to form words; if Sheila said something, even something as simple as Quinn's name spoken tenderly, Quinn would shudder.

Sheila had always slept soundly after they made love, and Quinn had almost always been restless and unable to sleep. She would get up, watch Sheila, so thin between the sheets; her fingers seemed tiny, clutching the cloth. Sheila must not be woken, Quinn would think protectively. And would tiptoe across the carpet, lift Sheila's robe gingerly from the hook on the back of the door. It was the first thing Sheila put on in the morning, the last she took off at night. When she wore it open, without a sash, you could see Sheila's breasts, one heavier than the other. Or else she'd gather the blue-green cloth in her fingers to hold it closed. Its color was dazzling, almost irridescent, its cut simple and elegant. One day in a burst of enthusiasm (she was the collective's oldest and most impassioned member, and its leader, though they never spoke of leaders) Sheila had stencilled interlocking women's symbols on its back with lavender fabric paint.

"My dyke robe," Sheila called it; Quinn had thought of it as Sheila's fish robe, too. At the hem, below the dyke symbols, was a border design of fish with wide-eyed expressions of permanent surprise, circling her loyally in a single direction. Quinn thought of the fish as intelligent creatures; she assigned them emotions. She imagined their pleasure as Sheila put the robe on and as she wore it; then, when she took it off for the night and hung it on the hook, their sense of abandonment.

Quinn had know the exact number of steps it took to cross the carpet to the door, the number down from the porch to the ground. Clutching the front of the robe, she became a smaller, younger replica of Sheila. She knew the direction the outhouse door swung, took care to gather the robe up to keep its hem from catching on splinters or falling down the hole as she squatted.

Returning from the outhouse, Quinn used to shut the cabin door quietly behind her, hang up the robe and scoot quickly across the room and under the covers. Once, instead, she stood awhile near the mattress and watched Sheila turn in her sleep. She saw she might have to fight to reclaim her side of the bed; she took off the robe, laid it over Sheila, climbed back in.

The sun had dropped just behind the tops of the trees as Quinn returned to the house, hearing the sounds of voices that floated out from the windows. Maybe they were arguing again. Then she heard laughter, and Sunsh's distinct above the others'. She pulled open the screen door and followed the sounds to the kitchen. Linda was seated at the kitchen table arranging a set of toothpicks in a row. A pot of water was beginning to heat over the stove's blue flame. Sunsh and Sheila were stabbing with forks at a single pot pie that rested on the edge of the stove, like two giant children squabbling over a dessert.

"Quinn, she's stealing my Swanson's" Sheila protested theatrically, giggling, then said: "Go ahead and hog it all. We've got better things to eat."

"Where were you when we got home, anyway?" Sunsh demanded.

"Town. You know who I saw? Gretchen. She said the

Fairfield kid will be here all summer."

"Ick," Sunsh said quickly. "I bet he's a hulk by now." She explained to Linda: "They're the ones who live down the next drive. He's a creepola."

"More than a creepola," Sheila said. "Gretchen calls him 'a handsome charmer with a streak of evil.' She says to avoid him if we can. He better not come onto this property," she said threateningly. Sheila actually looked worried. "Anyway, what about you girloids?"

"What?"

"Where'd *you* go?"

"To the pond awhile," Linda said. "But mostly on the bridge."

"The overpass," Sunsh said.

"We were waving at cars."

"Yeah, a lot of them waved back and honked," Linda explained enthusiastically.

"That's nice. So you had a good time."

"Yeah," Linda agreed.

Sheila asked them, in a vaguely strained, scout leaderish tone untypical of her: "If you could have a banner and hang it from the overpass, what would you say on it?"

Sunsh and Linda looked blankly at each other.

"Hi!" Sunsh exclaimed.

"Love ya!" said Linda.

"Oh, you must really be in a good mood toward the world!" Sheila told them, clucking. Linda took the kettle off the flame, poured the water into two mugs with Snoopy pictured on their sides, dunked the tea bag first in one, then the other, wound the string around the spoon and wet bag, and squeezed.

"What about No Nukes: Weapons, Power, or Families?" Sheila asked with enthusiasm.

"That's you!" Sunsh retored venomously, and like that said it all. She made a lets-get-out-of-here gesture to Linda and left the room, holding her steaming mug in front of her as Linda followed two steps behind. Sheila looked dejected; she called out after them into the hallway: "Sunsh, you want to visit Edna Frazer this weekend?"

"She's a drag," Sunsh answered back.

Sheila started to say something, then stopped herself. "Well, *we're* going," she said instead, meaning herself and Quinn.

"Anyone who's female, even is she's a real bore, she thinks is God!" they heard Sunsh tell Linda at the bottom of the stairway. And Quinn, aware of Sunsh's conspiratorial tone, thought that if Sheila for any reason decided they should leave Philly before Sunsh finished high school, Sunsh would never forgive her. Quinn wondered whether Sunsh, like her mother, might thrive on social contact yet always come out hungry. She pictured Sunsh clinging, fiercely as a little animal in a tree, to her world of school hallways, hamburger joints and friends.

Crouching on the cabin floor, Sheila produced from out of her pouch a picture postcard of a woman on a flying horse, a fluted clam shell, a small silver labyris, and a vial of volcanic ash that might have been mistaken at first glance for cocaine.

"Fire, air, earth, water," she said, crouching, as she arranged the objects thoughtfully on a straw mat on the floor. Quinn took the book of matches with the cover reading "Dykes Ignite," that Sheila held out to her, and lit two small candles, one on either side of their altar. The candles' glow enlarged the intimate circle of light cast by the fire, in front of which they'd stretched their sleeping bags.

It would be fun, Sheila had decided, to stay in the cabin one more time. "It's like clubhouses when you were a kid," Sheila said, charming in her playfulness. "Feels cozy, doesn't it, Quinn?" Quinn thought of Sunsh, in the upper room of the main house, and wondered if Sunsh resented her.

Sheila intended to use the cabin as a work space through the summer, to design and silkscreen feminist and anti-nuclear posters—when not looking after Sunsh and Linda. The girls were going to look for jobs in the area, but they'd probably get part-time ones; they'd be around a lot with time on their hands.

Sheila rooted through her knapsack, pulled out a book, then her familiar blue robe looking only slightly more frayed than before, then an unopened pack of Juicy Fruit, then the thing she was hunting for: a cassette tape of Edna Frazer talking about the area, her long life, what she thought of "all you girls" living down at the tree farm. The tape never failed to bring back memories of their days at the farm. Quinn had heart it last in March, the weekend Sheila visited New York. They did a lot of other things too: went to some photo galleries and to an off-Broadway matinee and to a reading at a woman's bookstore. A few women at the reading had come up to greet Quinn; one had asked after Camilla.

Quinn remembered an odd moment of silence on the subway home that seemed about more than just the noisiness of the ride. It was the two of them digesting something new: Sheila had always been not only older than Quinn by nine years, but a mother, a militant and a star. Now Sheila needed Quinn to guide her around New York. Now Sheila was on the sidelines and Quinn had someone new—her first real love since she'd left the tree farm.

There was some relative of envy afoot now, too, as Sheila, cross-legged on her sleeping bag, said: "So you think you've met Miss Right."

"Yes," Quinn agreed, wondering if her lingering feelings for Sheila amounted to a betrayal of Camilla. And then she added: "I guess you could call her that."

"A married woman and you're not going to hold me?" Sheila asked—coy, teasing, and quoting words ("aren't you going to hold me?") that Quinn had used once when Sheila started seeing someone else besides her.

"I'll hold you," Quinn said, a little defensively, then added, to lighten things: "But I won't hem your slips." Sheila smiled thinly. "What about you? What's going on? I guess there's the friction with Sunsh?"

"There's that. Or maybe it's that kid next door. Sheila had had hopes of running around the tree farm again this summer topless, like an Amazon. "It's going to be a hard summer in some ways," Sheila said, and looked off.

Quinn reached out instinctively to put her arms around Sheila, and pulled near. Sheila's body felt tense and almost unnaturally still, as if it held back a great flood of tears. Quinn longed for their release as if they were her own.

Over Sheila's shoulder, out the window, the dark sky and darker evergreens laid jigsaw shapes against each other. Before long the moon would rise, just there, and Sheila's body would relax. She would fall asleep, and Quinn would arrange the robe once more over Sheila's shoulders, wondering what person she herself might become if—when—what had charged this devotional act was gone.

Maria Starr*

A thirty-one-year-old biological co-parent of a fourteen-year-old son, cat, kitten, dog (and 3,700 fleas) I have been in a monogamous lesbian relationship for six years. Raised in a middle-class career-military family, I now live with my lover, son and pets in New England. As a social worker, I do psychotherapy, and community education/organization with adults. My interests include camping, hiking, reading, music, socializing with friends and exploring a budding spiritual self.

*Maria Starr is a pseudonym chosen to respect my son's privacy.

BOYCHILD

Maria Starr

To mother as a lesbian is to choose to be different.
To mother a son as a lesbian is to be different from the
       world and my child—while trying to balance it all.
To mother a healthy son is an act of hope, and blind faith
       that somehow he'll make a difference,
       somehow he'll be different
       from the average man.
To do all this is to raise someone who experiences isolation
       while tilting at windmills.
To mother a son is to hold my breath
       as I dance the picket fence, wobbling,
       hoping,
       that my beliefs and balance are possible,
       that my dance takes us both
       to higher levels—
       somehow.
For in a tunnel without guides,
On oceans with few beacons,
We can only guess and sail on.

     This is an exploration of my journey through mother-
hood, and the particular joys and trials of raising a healthy
young man, in the face of many who press for old, entrenched
ways. Beyond mere motherhood, this is a journey of identity
and hope. It is this search, this opening up the raw and
diverse parts of who I am, that mothering my son has
required of me.
     A friend once told me that we get the children we need
to grow. For me this has been true, from my earliest
yearnings at seventeen for a girl baby, to my present stage

of letting go, as my son enters the more separate manly spheres of his high school friends. Throughout, his existence has involved my concern for his growth and identity, but also a continual wrestling and growth of my own. He has touched my life in ways that a girl could not. In these fourteen years, my relationship with him encompasses many of my own roles as a mother, a woman, bisexual, lesbian, co-parent, feminist and visionary.

All parents must grapple with our beliefs, in raising children. We are almost all, by definition, visionaries in our efforts to sculpt the adults of tomorrow. Yet, as lesbians, this process becomes more conscious, as much of our alternative lifestyle is a new path of our own choosing. Although our preference may not be choice, how we incorporate that identity into our parenting, is most certainly one. So, in creating and sustaining my alternative family, those typical parental visions and self-explorations become magnified to mythic proportions.

As a typical feminist mother of an adolescent male my hopes are not grandiose. I merely want to alter the face of "man"-kind by introducing one of a new strain of men. I want my son to be an androgynous, sensitive, assertive, feminist man. Of course, in the process, I want to protect him from the pain of isolation, ridicule and feeling different, while helping him achieve his own agendas as well. All in all, a piece of cake.

My career as a mother began at seventeen, when I discovered I had given birth to a Joshua instead of a Stephanie. At that time, I was newly married and did not relate to my role as a mother, any exclusive sexual preference, or a career. I was, quite barely, a woman. I was, simply, young. Escaping from a consuming incestuous relationship and a strongly male-dominated military family, I ran to whatever would allow me to keep my child: a seven year marriage.

Looking back on my romantic notions about my baby, I recognize much of what I now hear in the lesbian baby boom's yearnings for girl babies. I wanted a carbon copy of myself to mould, be my companion, nurture and strengthen in ways that, as a girl child, I had not been. Fortunately, she was a he, and the challenge became one of translating all of that to someone who, from the beginning, was different from me, and who in fact, was a member of a sex which had consistently diminished my existence.

Through age six, this was not difficult, as I offered him the usual feminist-alternative toys, activities and non-sexist models. He was a joyous, sensitive child who delighted in the dramatic, and was unusually adept at responding to people's moods. He went everywhere with me those first years. He even went through college with me, listening to my books and papers as I read to him. His dad was not traditional in dividing labor, so Joshua had a positive male role model for non-sexist behavior in some respects. As our marriage neared its end, however, this changed, as did their relationship.

I discovered my major focus was not my identity as a mother, although that was an ever present fact. I continued to grow, as a teenager should, through school, jobs and into a career. Although I was loving and cared for him, putting him at the center of my time and world was disastrous. We both fared better with the supports of day care. This was never a wrenching decision, in part, I believe, because of his sex. As many have noted (Gilligan, Chodorow, Burch) it seemed easier for us to be close and yet separate because the difference, that sense of separation or "other," was already there. This separateness allowed me less anxiety as I grew up myself.

As he moves into adolescence and away from me, into more male spheres, I am again forced to deal with our differences and the limitations of my role. I am forced to deal with control and separation, knowing that he must grow into a space in the world which I will never occupy or fully understand.

Mothering a son has forced me to grapple with who I am in relation to men. Though I have had unpleasant experiences with men, because of Joshua, I could never simply write them out of my life. Because of my belief and hope that there exist sensitive, humane men, and the belief that Joshua needed a male role model, I continued to search for such a male partner despite my attraction to women. In finding such partners, I was able to learn what I would have formerly referred to as the culture of the enemy. This made clear to me that my bisexual and lesbian selves came from wanting something different, rather than as a reaction to anger or fear of men. In acknowledging my lesbianism, while simultaneously having to understand and even love a growing man, I found I was less angry than before. Given the man-hating lesbian stereotype this is ironic, indeed.

Seeing beyond stereotypes, I have come to know the fears, strengths, differences and similarities in male and female behaviors. This has helped me see ways in which the behaviors of people from my past are reflected in my current relationships.

In parenting Joshua, this is crucial. For example, if I draw upon my father's controlling and forceful rigidity to get things done myself, I can duplicate the same destructive patterns in female form. Yet, before I could see those as my father's behaviors, I labeled them male. Not only did this prevent me from dealing with them in myself, but I over-exerted to extinguish them in my son. At the same time, this built a poor sense of identity for him as a man. Additionally, I temporarily lost some of the positive sides of those behaviors (i.e., confidence, assertion, ability to make decisions). Being aware of this impact on my son opened many painfully important realizations.

In essence, being mindful of my son's male-ness, and seeing him grow and hurt and play as girls do, prevents me from trashing his sex for the sexist behavior which I must daily endure in the world. It is still easy and, at times, relieving to curse men when their macho behaviors frustrates me. But I've had to be watchful around Joshua to reject the behavior, not the sex. Doing that would simply reinforce for him that he's no good. Without alternative ways to feel good he can only fall back on traditional expressions which our culture pressures him to exhibit. In that sense

I undo my own vision.

Joshua's life has exposed me to male culture from a different vantage point. In watching school and peers influonce him, I have seen the power of sex role stereotypes. Ranging from pressure to fight to pressure to have sex, male bravado is alive and well. Yet, he's survived so far. When he does sexist things I have to bite my tongue and seek other outlets. Just when I question whether I've failed and begin to yearn for a female society, he says or does something profound that shows he knows the difference, and is searching for ways to stay congruent while juggling values of two cultures.

As much as I value female culture, I have had to learn the positives in typical male behaviors that women often lack (including assertiveness, appropriate aggression, confidence, even bravado and comfort with power). I do not like the ways in which stereotypical male behavior devalues women, and I see these in Joshua at times. I also see these in men with whom I work. (Seeing with Joshua's eyes occasionally helps me tolerate and more gently guide male students and activists into positive channels, drawing on their resources). This has meant becoming comfortable and secure in myself as a woman, so that their behavior is just behavior—annoying, but endurable. Its dimension changes from a protruding focus of all my energies, to a knotted thread in the fabric of my life.

All of this is most poignant as I merge my motherhood with my lesbianism. I live continuously on at least five levels: the world of heterosexual culture; the world of our family (my lover, my son, myself, and, of course, our pets); the world of my son and me; the lesbian community; and the world of my desires and dreams.

First, the external, heterosexual culture says things like like "Lust and lesbianism don't mix with motherhood—it's a sin" (Mom, circa 1986). Or, "But boys need male role models— you're denying him that." Other gems include: "You're not a *real* family—boys need a mother, a father"; "She's his aunt? (my lover) Not a blood relative, is she?

We couldn't possibly admit her to...the emergency room, teacher conferences, etc." and "He'll grow up like you—bad influences" (He'll be a lesbian?)

There is little support for lesbian motherhood in general, but add concern for that precious resource, a boy, and the resistance grows. To each objection, I initially felt there had to be some sort of internalized response to justify our existence as a family. As I have become more comfortable with my own identity and right to exist, this constant defense has lessened. It becomes easier to acknowledge the difficulties in context with the strengths, and the trials any child faces. Every child must deal with something which can encourage growth or can debilitate. I found the more I dwelt upon how hard it must be, the harder it became. It became defined as a problem rather than an alternate way of being that required creative responses. The more apologetic or even "therapisty" I became, the more it consumed Joshua, and was also used by him to excuse other life issues. I learned the limitations of a white middle class female "processing" approach and the value of simply moving on with empathy, but confidence. This has helped Joshua do the same.

In response to some of these homophobic concerns, I can share part of our process and current resolutions (which are always fluid). Beginning when Joshua was nine or ten, many people expressed a major concern for positive male role models and the lack thereof in my household.

I am blessed with a lover who grew up with three brothers, has a very close relationship with Joshua, and engages him in many physical activities. This helped to further break down stereotypes. She is soft and feminine, and yet often aggressive, rough and tumble—all rolled into one androgynous woman. He didn't miss out on having someone other than myself to understand male concerns (from fights to baseball tryouts to wet dreams). In an attempt to describe her active but nameless role in his life, we gave her a nickname. We occasionally refer to her as "Waddy" (woman daddy). But clearly she is not a man with whom he can identify as he grows older.

For a time, I actively searched for men to be in his life. He had a "big brother" for two years who was a friend of mine. He also associated with men who were partners of female friends. Though these were sporadic, he often talked of the varied models he saw and what he thought it meant to be a man or a woman.

Concern about role models and possible isolation has meant that, at times, we actively pursued relationships as a family with a non-exclusively female community. This poses difficulties since the number of feminist men we know and enjoy being around is limited, as is our social time.

However, over the years we created a conscious balance so that Joshua is not always the only man. For him to be the only man or the "little man in our lives," is both isolating and a burden. It is a responsibility he would gladly assume and often atttempts to act out in protective, "manly" ways. But it is a burden unbefitting a child or a growing young man.

I need also note that the family is not the only place children have male role models. In fact, the age at which I started to worry was ironically, when he began to take his cues from outside our family. Even for those with a male and female parent, a boy's contact with his dad may be limited and he has to rely on others. For Joshua, there is his dad, who has good qualities he can model, as well as qualities Joshua chooses to reject. He also has peers, teachers, fathers of friends, etc. So the concern with positive male role models, though important to consider, is an overreaction that focuses on what is missing, rather than what is there. This is similar to seeing a happy, single-parent family as broken when, in fact, there may be far more strength and resources than when it was "together," "fixed," or "whole."

A last criticism I want to respond to is the concern about sexual preference which I expand to concerns of sexuality and intimacy. It is clear to me that, short of a sex-change operation, my son will never be a lesbian. However, many have concerns about whether he will be homosexual. This concern comes from adults and from his peers. From adults this comes as blatant homophobia or a more general concern that he will have a more difficult life (liberal homophobia). I don't know what my son's sexual preference will be, though I suspect he will be at least ideologically bisexual. That is, in growing up to see a wide variety of people with lifestyles of many shapes and colors, he has developed a tolerance and understanding that is almost second nature. Seeing us loving each other and him, he has a greater chance than heterosexually-raised children to accept the range of sexuality and expression of love within each of us. This gives him more options, more dilemmas, and also potentially less isolation by roles and labels, no matter what his choice. I see this as similar to a child who grows up with many cultures and races of people and then blurs the standard racist distinctions.

Although he may, at some point, need to reject our difference, or follow the crowd, the roots of tolerance are there. No matter what his sexual preference, his chances of becoming a bigot are reduced and his life options increased—not a bad outcome for a mother to wish for. In many ways, he is bi-cultural. He knows and is comfortable with both lesbian and heterosexual culture. Given his age and common adolescent issues, it is the heterosexual, male culture with which he is experimenting and struggling.

Among his peers, our lesbianism is more of an issue. We have an agreement about respecting his privacy and allowing him to decide who he will tell. This means that my lover and I are affectionate in our home, but not in our neighborhood. It also means we have to think twice before coming out publicly. Unfortunately, at times, this means a restriction that goes against our personal desires (e.g., using a pseudonym for this article to respect his privacy). But there are always compromises and trade-offs in respecting those with whom we share our lives. Children are no less deserving of our respect than adults. Our lives are long, and this is a time-limited agreement that we respect, but negotiate. The positive outcome is that he also respects our privacy and rights in many contexts.

He chooses at this point to keep a low profile with his friends, though he is clearly proud of his family, as evidenced by his desire to have his friends know us. He also delights in dropping subtle hints to teachers who he thinks are also gay, or defiantly introducing my lover as his aunt, insisting, "Of course, she's family."

For many this secrecy may seem dishonest, or a double identity. However, I don't have to live my son's life and can only guess at its difficulties. I have heard "queer" used as the most common derogatory remark since his kindergarten days. It seems for boys this is even more common as a way of keeping kids in line. When women break stereotypes it is now more accepted. Young girls are more likely to be called bitch instead of queer, and female closeness is more tolerated. Boys who are sensitive, non-violent or in any way different are labelled faggots. In adolescence it becomes an even greater part of male bonding and distancing to figure out who are the studs and who the homos. And in American culture gay men, particularly since the hysteria around AIDS, are more violently rejected.

To this picture, add a child of gay parents who knows on some level that people worry about his/her parents' normalcy and the child's sexual preference. My son, like many others, chooses to keep quiet what might label him in the eyes of others before he has a chance to establish himself. He speaks out only where it is safe to do so and his heterosexual option is respected (*i.e.*, with liberals, lesbians, kids of gays, and his last girlfriend).

In having lesbian parents who are comfortable with intimacy, communication and sexuality, he has more options than many kids to get accurate sexual information. As he grew up, I always promoted his pride in his body and acceptance of others. Entering adolescence, he turns less to me for this as suddenly I am "the mother." Other kids speak of turning to men for information, frequently finding embarrassment or male bravado. Joshua turns to his friends and hears many stories. Unlike many of his friends, he can check things out with his "aunt" or ask for written information. Given the many changes in his teenage body, having this discussed within our family is an unexpected plus.

Lastly, the lesbian community is the world which gives us the greatest joys and harshest judgements in mothering a son. Generally it is a place where we are accepted as a family and as individuals in a way that exists nowhere else. We surround ourselves with positive, supportive friends that make hard times bearable and good times a joy.

Unfortunately, we have not always gotten such support from the larger community. At one time I associated with people who didn't like to be around kids, period. Funny how people tolerate bias against kids in ways we would never tolerate if it were directed so blatantly in other directions. I quickly chose not to mingle with that crowd out of need for protection and validation. As the community has moved into a baby boom this anti-child attitude is no longer politically correct and has gone underground.

Of more visible impact is the struggle and outrage I have with separatism about male children in general and my son in particular. If I had not had a son, I might be a different person and it could be me arguing for womyn-only space. As a lesbian who chooses to live my life primarily with women, I truly understand women-only space and respect that need. As a lesbian and a mother of a son, I see little community support, role models or credence given to our needs. We encounter diaper checks and segregation at women's festivals and a general disdain or disapproval among many lesbians. This segregation intensifies as our sons reach adolescence. All through their childhood, it is frequently an either/or choice—our sons or our full lesbian community.

There are few events I choose to attend with my son. The major criteria is that events affirm not only women, but respect (if not affirm) him as a growing male. I have boycotted some festivals due to their male child policies which limit participation in festival activities. Part of this I do in protection of my son's self image, in reaction to a community of women rejecting him. But beyond that, this flies in the face of the vision that has guided my mothering. My son loves the festivals, treasuring his memories and singing the lyrics all year. If male children are excluded from celebrations of women's culture, how will they ever learn to be any different than men whose behavior we abhor? It is through participating in open celebrations such as Sisterfire, that Joshua has learned most about diversity and has found a profound support that ends his isolation. It truly teaches him to enjoy and appreciate the wonders of women's culture that no amount of lecturing could begin to touch.

The boy who is limited, scowled at as an intruder, or suspiciously treated as other, learns isolation, rejection and anger. As a man, he either apologizes continually for his existence, or acts out those rejections on others, most likely, on women. This closes doors for all of us, and must be struggled with further if we are to grow. It punishes not only the child, but also the mother who may not have alternative childcare, or who wishes for positive role models for her son. It is just another face that reinforces sexism's assumptions and labels, only it hurts more coming from a community so close to our hearts. Ultimately, we all lose, as the community divides and the old order continues.

In summary, mothering my son has fostered many struggles and much growth. It is a task filled with isolation and with visions for creating a new man.

I share these details of our family life with hopes of provoking thoughts for other mothers, and out of a caring for our very diverse, large community. With the emergence of the lesbian baby boom, we must deal with children, ourselves, and how we form linkages in our community. Perhaps we will also deal with how our own needs and other "garbage" can be unloaded on our children, and how that may vary according to their sex.

With artificial insemination, the chance of having a boy baby seems to increase. So, as lesbians, we all have to deal with how to have little men in our midst and still sustain and honor who we are as women and lesbians. We know the impact that devaluing female babies has had on us. We will have to consider, as we plan our children, how a boy child is affected by hearing so many of us wish longingly for girls and wrinkle our noses at the possibility of having a boy. Do we want to simply create a mirror image of the flawed picture we already have?

I have found the struggle worth it. In the words of the song, "You can't always get what you want—but if you try sometime, you still might find, you get what you need." Perhaps this is the gift of our sons to our lesbian community.

Baba Copper

I am a sixty-eight-year-old woman who is a writer, biological mother to four children, lesbian mother to a lesbian daughter. My Over the Hill: Reflections on Ageism Between Women will be published by The Crossing Press in Spring, 1988. I am currently working on a book, tentatively called Tales of a Lesbian Grandmother, of which the material in this anthology is a part.

MOTHERS AND DAUGHTERS OF INVENTION

Baba Copper

One of the privileges of age is being able to look back at one's choices with eyes re/formed by the evidence which life inevitably provides. This I now feel compelled to do with that large, indigestible part of my life called motherhood. I, along with my immediate foremothers, have a feminist herstory which can and must be searched for patterns — a personal account to contribute to the re/membering needed by new mothers, especially lesbian mothers of daughters.

Re/membering means more than retrieving memories. The inserted dash is a radical signal, invented by Mary Daly, to warn the reader that the word has grown womanist legs and arms — members long supressed or unnoticed — which newly allow it to leap or wrestle. Nor is the old meaning lost. *"Make an effort to remember, or failing that, invent,"* is probably the most quoted advice of the present wave of feminism. It is Monique Wittig's admonition to the women of her imagination, *les guerilleres*, who must *be* warriors despite their lack of any female tradition of women as complete, as free as they must be. Lesbians, Wittig says, must invent our identities as we go. Re/membering creates the psychic roots we need to walk new paths; invented images help to diminish the unfamiliarity of the landscapes in which we find ourselves. Memory, and the stories we tell each other — illuminated by feminist insights — can transform.

As much as any other institution I know, motherhood needs feminist tranformation. As mothers of daughters, women enter the future through the gate of our girl children. Whether we recognize it or not, we are engaged in the woman-to-woman biosocial work which is, quite simply, the transmission of culture. Mothers convey to a highly receptive recruit, *herself a potential socializer*, what it is to be human. The mother/daughter continuum is the spinal cord of the man-made juggernaut we call civilization. The cultural indoctrination women carry out is expected to teach children to anticipate the world as we have found it, to transmit culture *as found* to our daughters. We must succeed at such a deep, unconscious level that they too will be equipped to continue the process. Primary among motherly duties is the genderization of humanity—teaching our culture's definitions of behavior deemed appropriate to females and males.

I am the mother of a lesbian daughter—from my frame of reference, a maternal success story. Over the years, my consciousness has gone through a lot of ninety degree turns, some of which came as a result of the Second Wave in the North American liberation of women. Within feminism I have found validation for the rebellion I had banked to the back of my internal furnace, smoldering there to last through the long night of motherhood. As I changed my life to match my consciousness, I was forced to scrutinize many of the choices I had made as a mother raising daughters within the "enlightened" beliefs of my day—a progressive tradition begun by my maternal grandmother and sustained by my mother and me. I raised three daughters; my mother, two; my grandmother, two. The daughter-rearing practices of our three generations reflected the mainstream feminist thinking of our respective times.

Yet, looking back on this continuum, I now see a high potential for bonding between women dampened by the motherhood we practiced. How did my experience as a lesbian change my mothering? Knowing what I now know, believing what I now believe, how would I have mothered my daughters differently?

I would have begun by projecting a job description which outlined the significance and goals of raising daughters in new woman-identified terms. Men have defined child-rearing as a chore—one of the many aspects of necessity which can be safely relegated to inferiors. Liberalized patriarchy, as currently practiced by the middle-class in industrialized nations, allows daughters equal access to the mothering and education expected for sons, and wants fathers to have equal access to the mother role. As my lesbianism has radicalized my feminism, I have come to realize that equalizing a system based on a misogynist design while pretending that it can be made gender-neutral is not an improvement. Mothering is a lifetime job, lots of work, and at times unbearable, but mothering daughters is also THE most complex, challenging and potentially liberating of all human processes.

Although there are many patterns of mothering shared across cultural differences, it is unlikely that there are any instinctual components left in human mothering. At least three-quarters of what we do as mothers we learned at a non-verbal level from our childhood experience of being mothered. In our heads and hearts is a great muddle of emotion and theory: ethnic and religious prescriptions, admonitions from experts, reactive reversals of the mothering we received, pressures from peers and relatives, generalized cultural expectations of our class and nation. When the girl baby arrives, mothers become entangled in the daily practice of mothering. Few look critically at the cultural information we transmit to our daughters. This inconsistent body of unexamined expectations and ideals rides on the back of a very ancient and abused beast of burden—women under patriarchy. We may think of ourselves as teaching our daughters how to get along in a man's world, just as our mothers tried to do. In reality, what we teach is the partially invisible work-horse of femininity—subordination, alienation and woman-hating—that is taught and learned from one generation of mothers to the next.

My herstory carries strong lessons. My mother was a "liberated" woman as a result of the First Wave at the turn of the century—a professional woman married to a professional man, struggling to express her creativity as well as make a living for her family. She taught theater arts in her own successful school; I have a clipping from a 1915 *Los Angeles Times* praising her production of *The Merchant of Venice* with an all-woman cast. Her personal performance pieces were costumed dramatic monologues, researched and written by her, depicting scenes from the lives of famous women like Christine de Pisan, Anne Boleyn or Madame Recamier. She did not let the mothering of her two daughters seriously interfere with her career. Her husband, my father, was a dim presence who walked away from his responsibilities during the Great Depression, when I was ten.

Sounds very woman-oriented, doesn't she? However it is only in retrospect and with misgivings that I acknowledge that my mother did indeed assimilate a portion of the feminism of her day. She was busy taking advantage of some of their ideas, as well as the new freedoms won by militant feminists. Yet I can remember her expressed contempt for suffragettes and bloomer girls. It was from her that I learned to give my loyalties and attention to men, even if they were "all after just one thing."

She was totally silent about the oppression of women by men. The lessons of creativity and resourcefulness which she taught by example were in contradiction to the admonitions with which she colored my imagination— stories of the guile and sexualized manipulation necessary for a woman to succeed. Above all else, she verbally idealized motherhood and wifehood. The "dear little family" with a strong male at its head which my mother so enthusiastically advocated was not a situation she had witnessed in her own childhood. Her father had died when she was three, leaving her mother with four children to raise. My grandmother did not remarry—despite the urgings of her extended family of birth and several opportunities. Her feminism reflected the main-stream progressive thinking from 1880 to the turn of the century: a strong belief in the temperance movement and higher education for women. Both her daughters graduated from college into professional careers, while she maintained herself for a lifetime through entrepreneurial ventures—rentals, farming, chickens.

It may be that the reason both my grandmother and my mother were silent to me about planning a life direction other than marriage lay in their class pretensions. Although they came from landed frontier people, they were also rural women struggling to be urbanized. They believed that a woman needed intelligence, talents, and skills to be assured a "good marriage." The working life they lived had, for them, class implications. The life of the protected, at-home wife was the myth they dreamed, despite the chosen independence of their lives.

The feminist motivation which was evident in the *actions* of my mother and grandmother was never articulated, never explained to me. We were all single mothers, all financially independent. My grandmother clung to economic autonomy to avoid the powerlessness she had known as a wife; my mother used her education to sustain herself and her children with a career; economic independence and lesbianism sustained me; my lesbian daughter has been self-supporting since her late teens in a non-traditional job as a unionized camera-woman, and now, with even more education, in a high-tech career in computers. That is four generations—a hundred years gone by—with matrifocal households, feminist awareness, bright women with college educations, women who worked hard, women privileged through class and race, women who escaped crushing povety, women relatively unscathed by the economic upheavals and wars of their times. Yet until I started articulating my own transformation of identity to my youngest daughter, the only woman-talk I and my extraordinarily liberated foremothers shared was traditional women-talk.

I cannot remember a time when I did not look forward to having a child of my own. I went to college fully understanding that my purpose there was to catch a husband, who would then provide for me and the dozen children of my imagination. By the finish of World War II I was well launched into this scenario, although after one birth my goal had dropped from twelve to two. By the beginning of the sixties I was an at-home wife with four children and an upwardly mobile husband. My mother was so well pleased with my circumstances — viewed as *her* success — that I would not have dared to voice my discontent to her. I was ripe, ready for some of those ninety degree turns the Second Wave would provide for my consciousness.

It was during the personal and public turmoil of the sixties that I stopped mothering my three teen-aged childen and one toddler as I had been mothered. Bit by bit I shifted my loyalties, my attention, my energies (including my sexual energy) from men to women. The tensions created by a radicalized feminism stretched the seams of my wifehood beyond mending. My civil rights and anti-war activism shattered what was left of my middle-class complacency. By leaving my marriage, by asserting my creative independence, by coming out, I changed *what I as a mother was saying to my daughters*.

This mid-stream maternal shift has costs as well as benefits. My woman-identified radicalism came too little, too late for my two oldest daughters, who have never forgiven me for escaping sacrificial motherhood. But my youngest daughter, the child who witnessed my turnabout, the one who was there to listen to all my doubts and discoveries and confusion and insights along the way, she is the daughter well-mothered. More than that, she and I have extended our commitment to women to include a strong bonding between us. Transforming a mother-child relationship into an honest, mutually supportive bond between equals involves hard work on both sides, work which we continue to do.

My dual experience as "enlightened" mother of conventional married daughters and radical mother of a lesbian daughter has endowed me with strong concerns about the conscious and unconscious processes through which mothers perpetuate female oppession. Although any kind of woman-identified mothering of daughters helps, the patterns in this hundred year herstory indicate that

312 / Baba Copper

mainstream feminist goals do not reach the root of the problem.

The following modern definition of successful motherhood is basically unchallenged by mainstream feminism: A mother is responsible for raising heterosexuals who are also docile citizens, self-regulated workers who want what the machines produce and are willing to devote a lifetime to pay for it. The system turns perfectly on its computerized loop— skills must fit the needs of the machines which structure the needs of those who tend them. As much as a third of one's life must be spent absorbing the idealogies and techniques expected in a high-tech society. Middle-class women have been encouraged to believe that their daughters will be allowed an ever-increasing part of the spoils of technical imperialism in return for doing the double job of home and work. In addition, mothers must teach daughters to sustain their primary biosocial function: reproduction and childrearing. This must be accomplished within the context of loyalty to, collaboration with, and sexual servicing of ordinary men—sons of these same mothers—men who also are caught in the technological loop.

North American mothers have escaped many of the inhuman paths of daughter-betrayal other mothers of the world still walk, not because we are more enlightened, but because we are part of a wealthy culture. We do not arrange the sale of our daughters into marriage or prostitution; we do not mutilate their bodies; we no longer need to teach them female inferiority, however much we and our daughters still carry the ghostly imprint of these past and present horrors. But even feminism collaborates in normalizing false solutions to the challenge of daughter socialization. The Second Wave has focused women's hopes on personal growth and economic independence through equally-paid work outside the home. The work-place grudgingly has expanded to accommodate this new woman, at two-thirds pay. We simply cannot pretend that female subordination is rapidly waning as long as mothers increasingly suffer from the terrible stress of the double duty of childrearing and wage labor, often alone and in poverty.

Why have feminists not recognized that adequate mothering cannot take place in isolation from other women—that socializing the socializers is too important to leave up to one stressed woman? The majority of modern mothers raise their daughters without the help of another experienced mother, except as they get advice from teachers or other professionals outside the home. As working mothers find their loyalties divided between the rock of self-fulfillment and the hard place of mothering, they suppress their feelings of inadequacy or ignorance, perpetuating the patriarchal myth that these circumstances are somehow natural and self-chosen.Worst of all, "enlightened" women hide the gender-specific nature of their struggles from the little girls who are their daughters.

For me, success as a high-tech worker/breeder is not a satisfactory goal for the socialization of daughters. Can the mothering carried out by lesbians avoid some of the pitfalls of the "enlightened" traditions which I both witnessed and practiced? When my mothering was animated by lesbian-feminism, under circumstances of *de facto* separation from male/female genderized interactions, both I and my daughter were strengthened. The cultural leap was greater than those steps of emancipation encouraged by the single motherhood of my male-defined foremothers. Can lesbians heal the sad traditions of mother/daughter betrayal by raising daughters whose deepest trust and bonding are with women? Surely there are other ways in which the powerful intergenerational connection of mother/daughter—this assembly line of culture—can be used to speed up the process of change for women. How do we guarantee that each generation of women expects a great deal more for herself, tolerates much less subordination to men *or* machines, and consciously hones what she teaches her daughter toward biophilic goals for both women and the earth?

One way to begin to answer these questions is for feminist mothers to analyze the *effects* of their childrearing practices, instead of leaving this to the "experts," and to turn the results over to the next generation of new mothers. Their analysis must be free of heterosexist bias, especially all assumptions about the relation of males to the basic matrifocal continuum—mothers and their daughters. Re/ forming motherhood must be done without male input for the time being. While it is true that lesbian motherhood cannot be equated automatically with good daughter-rearing or separatism or even feminism, *lesbian mothers are the only category of women sufficiently alienated from patriarchal traditions to sustain radical modifications in the socialization of daughters.*

Another way to answer these questions is to give more attention to the visions or theories of feminist writers. Only women have given the subject of daughter-rearing any thought when inventing other worlds, especially in speculative fiction or utopias. One feminist science fiction writer, Joanna Russ, has pointed out that men do not imagine worlds without women. True, adventure-environments uncluttered by women are attractive to the male imagination, just like the realms of public power or war or locker rooms. However, speculative fiction depicting all-male worlds is strangely lacking, even in gay male literature. Men do not yearn for the imaginary possibilities— the full responsibility—latent in a world without mothers. On the other hand, both lesbian and heterosexual women writers and readers have been drawn to stories and visions of nothing-but-mothers-and-daughters since the turn of the century. Some of their speculative fiction depicts cultures with no men, in which descriptions of the socialization of daughters is a major preoccupation.

Charlotte Perkins Gilman, born in 1860, was one of the great socialist/feminist theorists of her day. She was a single mother who had been raised by a single mother. The myth of woman's place as wife/mother was more rigid then than now. When Gilman relinquished her seven-year old daughter to the care of her ex-husband who had married a close friend of hers, she was publicly vilified for being an unnatural mother. In many ways, *Herland*, her feminist utopia, was a rebuttal to that charge. The story was serialized in the newspaper she published during the same years that my mother was starting her family. They were both Californians—my mother, a performer, and Gilman, a lecturer—on the West Coast Women's Associations circuit. Yet I had never heard of Gilman or her ideas until fifty years later, when a republished *Herland* joined other works on the shelves of women's bookstores under the classification of science fiction.

Gilman's all-woman world, isolated from the rest of humanity by an earthquake, has evolved for millenia without enemy—a kind of cultural Galapagos. In it, child-rearing "has come to be a culture so profoundly studied, practiced with such subtlety and skill, that the more we love our children the less we are willing to trust that process to unskilled hands— even our own." The women of Herland raise their daughters in a self-conscious ethic "based on full perception of evolution, not the opposition of good and evil." Daughters are neither schooled nor punished. Rather, misdeeds are interpreted to them as errors or misplays, as in a game. Learning comes to the girls through every sense, "taught continuously but unconsciously—never knowing they are being educated." They are closely watched for individual tendencies in ideas, feelings or products which might indicate adult directions for their working lives. Herland is literally a cultural environment shaped around daughters, their felicity being the raison d'etre of the country. Nothing—no technology, no tradition, no value—is sustained if it is harmful to the well-being of children.

Gilman relies upon a geological disaster to avoid the issue real mothers have to face: how to raise daughters to respond to male predation. In *The Female Man*, Russ uses parallel realities existing side by side in time in order to both avoid and encounter the subject. In one parallel reality, the warrior women are busy ridding their world of men, one by one. In Whileaway, the only utopia of her several realities, the male-free circumstances are explained by a sex-selective plague in its past. The Fems and Riding Women of *Motherlines* by Charnas are nomadic survivors and their daughters are escapees from a male controlled City dystopia unaware of their existence, a dystopia on the brink of self-destruction. Gearhart's Hill Women of *The Wanderground* are still engaged in active struggle to free women from city-based male control, although they live and bring up their children in their own male-free territories. All of these works describe cultural designs for raising daughters without gender indoctrination.

The children of these stories (all female as the result of various parthenogenic techniques) are brought up by multiple mothers or in extended self-selected families of racial and age diversity. They are all without gender-specific models of behavior. The experience of the biological mother before, during and up to five years after parturition, is one of privilege within the society. The ordinary expectations of her work-contribution are diminished: in Whileaway she spends this time exploring the arts in a place near to her infant, although without primary responsibility for her care; in Herland she stays away from traveling duties in order to nurse her child for two years; among the Riding Women, all sharemothers nurse the baby. In all four books, the child belongs to the community, but at the same time the biological mother gains status, kin, or leisure through pregnancy and the act of giving birth. Women who do not want to birth are not penalized, but they do not escape mothering. All women raise the young, although the degree of involvement of specific women fit their inclinations, as well as their time of life. Since reproduction is never involuntary for the female as it is in two-sexed worlds, the numbers of births are determined by community consensus, reflecting eco-system responsibility as well as individual desires.

When possible in these utopian communities, pregnant women cluster for mutual support and their infants are tended in bunches, so that early in life all children are conditioned to group cooperation. In Whileaway, children are separated from their mothers at age five to be schooled.

All four cultures put great emphasis on physical agility, on wilderness survival skills, and personal integrity or self-sufficiency. One of the ways that girls acquire these strengths is through freedom to roam in unsupervised groups, or even in solitary self-testing, before their menses. The occasional loss of a child is accepted as the price of learning courage and independence.

The four books all deal to some degree with the contradictions inherent in childrearing between necessary technical training and the autonomous discovery of world/self. Girls are expected to develop relationships and intimacy through their own explorations of sexuality and interests, within a supportive and loving total environment. In Whileaway, there are strong cross-generational sex taboos, while the Riding Women of *Motherlines* encourage adolescents to bed down with one of their sharemothers. Herland women have totally sublimated their sexual drive, which Gilman brands by implication as a conflict-provoking male preoccupation, unnecessary in a one-sex world where reproduction does not depend upon courtship or rape. The cultures imagined by these writers exhibit varied technologies limited by ethical choices. In Gearhart's world, for example, psychic power becomes the primary source of communication, defense, and energy. All the books show industrious cultures where work is both duty and pleasure. All have lots of ritualized gatherings and celebrations, with children integrated into the rituals and the work of the community. None of the cultures are urbanized beyond the level of scattered towns or oases; all practice some kind of agriculture with the total population involved in the yearly cycles of food production. Only Whileaway has advanced technology, such as computers.

The invented landscapes of Gilman, Russ, Charnas and Gearhart are each one different, designed to serve the literary purposes of very diverse women. However, as science fiction writers, all four exhibit a peculiarly female subjectivity. In their need to make their cultures—and the women who evolve those cultures—credible, they intuitively reach for details of childrearing practices and glimpses of the experiences of girls growing up. (When men writers create alien creatures, they never show the mothering which might explain them.) By the literary trick of eradicating gender opposition, these feminist authors allow themselves the luxury of exploring who women are, what women working together are capable of doing, and the kind of social institutions women want. The consensus which bonds the women they invent is a deep valuing of the continuity of purpose possible between generations.

Back in the real world where lesbians are trying to forge community as well as raise children, in cities only slightly less dystopian than the cities of Charnas and Gearhart, some of the barriers to solidarity between us are grounded in our early socialization. Collectives are difficult for women trained to individualized hierarchy. A monogamous lesbian couple mothering a child is subject to many of the same failings as the heterosexual nuclear families blamed by those same co-mothers for so much of their unhappiness. Negative chains of behavior do stretch from one generation to the next. If substance abuse or battering or eating disorders can be laid at the door of parental habits, then it is likely that the disease of female self-hatred is transmitted in the same way. Bonding between women is not being taught to daughters. Mothers are unconsciously teaching loyalty to patriarchy to the next generation of mothers, just as our mothers taught us.

In the *Wanderground*, there were the Remember Rooms, where daughters heard the pain and struggles of their elders— the particulars of women's oppression over time. Suppressed, woman memories fester; spoken, woman memories heal. Earlier I posed the question, "What would I do differently now?" I find a partial answer in the contrast between my mothering of my older daughters and my youngest. The re/ membering of my responsibilities to my Self, hard won through reversals of deep conditioning, was a personal change I talked about as it happened. In all my relationships, I began to ask for a return of the nurturance

I gave—a very radical step for a mother. Once I understood that many of my problems matched those of other women, I verbalized the astonishing details of this to my youngest. She was there to hear me, while the older two searched for answers at college, from curriculums which contained no Women's Studies.

None of us honor woman-ideas enough. Analyzing everyday life with a feminist perspective, not being afraid to generalize about men and their responsibility for the state of things, debunking the myths that naturalize women's unnatural circumstances—such ideas are part of a womanly tradition which it is our duty to transmit from generation to generation of daughters. We tend to shy away from or trivialize woman-visions or woman-centered social criticism. Yet women are often the first converts to utopian communities, the truly devout of the religious, the shitworkers of political reforms, the most persistent nay-sayers to pollution and nuclear madness. A mother of daughters cannot afford to be a closet rebel against patriarchy. She cannot follow her individual path toward genderized liberation, making the hard choices which that path may demand, without being willing to name those motivations and choices clearly to her daughter. In this way, she will teach her daughter to honor woman-ideas, starting with her own.

Many heterosexual mothers avoid this kind of exposure with their daughters because of a real fear of endangering their relationships with husbands and sons. For single heterosexual women, there is the threat of being seen as one of us. But lesbian mothers are free of these restraints. Naming our goals, arguing amongst ourselves, creating vivid images of womanly potential in words and song and drama and dance— this we owe our daughters. They will be less likely to repeat our mistakes if we formulate our goals more clearly and tell them what our mistakes have been. Daughters watch mothers closely even as they mutiny; words and images of rebellion are the daughter's heritage. Let our first language be the language of resistance; our second, that of adjustment or success.

As I take the visions of feminist writers seriously, I find other clues to mothering underdone, or undone by us. The kind of groupmothering depicted in these works is made possible by a cultural and political consensus almost unimaginable at the present juncture of consciousness. The women of these imaginary utopias share mothering with birthmothers regardless of individual differences. The mothers are of different tribes or family groupings; they do not get along personally; they are a mix of sexual partners and singles; they have other demanding duties; some do not even want to mother. Yet all accept their part in this basic cultural function. It will take a lot of political work for the lesbian community to encompass this vision of mothering even as a goal, much less as a practice.

However, in our own way, we are working at it. I know lesbians who have joined groups to explore whether or not they wanted to mother. I was part of a small group who pledged to share mothering of a daughter we hoped to create parthenogenically through energy exchange exercises. I know lesbians who formed a group to support each other through artificial insemination and pregnancy. There are lesbian mother groups which exchange child care, lesbians in living collectives who help mother the children of the household to relieve the birthmother, lesbian collectives who have actually shared the mothering of the children. By sending out a call into the community, I have found many lesbian mother/lesbian daughter pairs, some of whom are extraordinarily close as adults. All these can be said to be *de facto* explorations of feminist utopian images.

What has not been formed, to the best of my knowledge, is an all-woman association where mothers and sharemothers live, work, learn, and create together—a kind of live-in university and think-tank where daughter-rearing is an integral part of the working/teaching/learning process. Women have not yet isolated and studied what it is, exactly, that children teach to their socializers, and how much that learning process contributes to the differences between women and men. We must name and dignify the cultural *function* of the process of mothering, and identify the social costs that have resulted from male ignorance and avoidance of it.

What we now most need are teaching/learning institutions where we can combine work for the outside world with higher education for women and the feminist exploration of daughter-rearing. Institutions where such important research could take place, free of the dead hands of male experts in early life education, are no longer out of reach. Computer technology is allowing for the invention of new, economically viable, decentralized work-places, based away from the source of their income. By combining the high-tech skills which many lesbians are now perfecting with the new cultural forms of living/working, as well as educational facilities which included group mothering, it should be possible to start to restructure society in a long term way—generation to generation.

While I believe that only women can transform patriarchy, my herstory proves to me that it is not enough for each generation to take personal steps toward that transformation. Nor can feminist writers and activists carry the full responsibility for digging us out from under our genderized expectations. Women *must* name their personal steps in womanist terms as we take them, articulate them to each other, make them into instant traditions of womanhood, wrap them in compelling images, and most important of all, give these words and images to our daughters over and over again.

Bibliography

Charnas, Suzy McKee. *Motherlines.* New York: Berkeley, 1978

Daly, Mary. *Gyn/Ecology, The Metaethics of Radical Feminism.* Boston: Beacon Press, 1978

Gearhart, Sally Miller. *The Wanderground, Stories of the Hill Women.* Watertown, MA: Persephone Press, 1978

Gilman, Charlotte Perkins Stetson. *Herland.* New York: Pantheon, 1979

Russ, Joanna. *The Female Man.* New York: Bantam, 1975

Wittig, Monique. *Les Guerilleres.* New York: Avon, 1973

The Crossing Press Feminist Series includes the following titles:

Abeng, A Novel by Michelle Cliff

Clenched Fists, Burning Crosses, A Novel by Chris South

Crystal Visions, Nin Meditations for Personal and Planetary Peace by Diane Mariechild

A Faith of One's Own: Explorations by Catholic Lesbians, edited by Barbara Zanotti

Feminist Spirituality and the Feminine Divine, An Annotated Bibliography by Anne Carson

Folly, A Novel by Maureen Brady

Hear The Silence: Stories by Women of Myth, Magic and Renewal, edited by Irene Zahava

Learning Our Way: Essays in Feminist Education, edited by Charlotte Bunch and Sandra Pollack

Lesbian Etiquette, Humorous Essays by Gail Sausser

Lesbian Images, Literary Commentary by Jane Rule

Magic Mommas, Trembling Sisters, Puritans & Perverts, Feminist Essays by Joanna Russ

Mother Wit: A Feminist Guide to Psychic Development By Diane Mariechild

Movement, A Novel by Valerie Miner

Natural Birth, Poetry by Toi Derricotte

Nice Jewish Girls: A Lesbian Anthology, edited by Evelyn Torton Beck

The Notebooks of Leni Clare and Other Short Stories by Sandy Boucher

The Politics of Reality: Essays in Feminist Theory by Marilyn Frye

The Question She Put to Herself, Stories by Maureen Brady

On Strike Against God, A Lesbian Love Story by Joanna Russ

The Queen of Wands, Poetry by Judy Grahn

Poems of Rita Mae Brown

Red Beans & Rice, Recipes for Lesbian Health and Wisdom by Bode Noonan

Sinking, Stealing, A Novel by Jan Clausen

Sister Outsider, Essays and Speeches by Audre Lorde

We Are Everywhere, Writings by and about Lesbian Parents, edited by Harriet Alpert

Winter's Edge, A Novel by Valerie Miner

Women Brave in the Face of Danger, Photographs of Latin and North American Women by Margaret Randall

The Work of A Common Woman, Poetry by Judy Grahn

Zami: A New Spelling of My Name, Biomythography by Audre Lorde